IMPROVING YOUR HOME FOR PLEASURE AND PROFIT

IMPROVING YOUR HOME FOR PLEASURE AND PROFIT

by Betty Wason and
the Editors of U.S.News & World Report Books

Joseph Newman — Directing Editor

U.S.NEWS & WORLD REPORT BOOKS

A division of U.S.News & World Report, Inc.
WASHINGTON, D.C.

Contents

Illustrations

Acknowledgments

Betty Wason and the Editors of *U.S.News & World Report Books* are particularly grateful to the following individuals, commercial firms, trade associations, and governmental agencies for their valuable assistance in supplying material for this book:

Architect Don Hawkins of Washington, D.C., who specializes in remodeling old houses; contractor George Pettie of Arlington, Virginia; Morton Mann, president of the Home Improvement Company of America, a contracting firm in Kansas City, Missouri; and Robert Feder, director of the Community Services Department of the Kansas City Office of Consumer Affairs.

Alcoa, Andersen Corporation, Duron Paint Manufacturing Company, Farberware, Formica Corporation, Genova Corporation, B. F. Goodrich Company, Hechinger Company, Johns-Manville, Majestic Company, Masonite Corporation, and the Mastic Corporation.

Air-Conditioning and Refrigeration Institute, American Plywood Association, American Wood Council, California Redwood Association, National Paint and Coatings Association, National Swimming Pool Institute, Red Cedar Shingle and Handsplit Shake Bureau, and Southern Pine Industries.

The Farmers Home Administration of the U.S. Department of Agriculture, the Federal Housing Administration of the U.S. Department of Housing and Urban Development, and the Internal Revenue Service.

Roslyn Grant edited the manuscript and coordinated the editorial work on the book, assisted by Barbara Clark.

CHAPTER 1

Remodeling Can Pay Double Dividends

Home improvement is taking a great leap forward these days, a trend bound to increase because of the rapidly rising cost of new construction. Many families who had contemplated looking for a new home have decided it is wiser economy to fix up what they have. Others who must move are shopping around for older houses to remodel because, even after extensive alterations, they can get more for their money in an older house than in a new one.

In new home construction, a big trend is the basic no-frills house: the price tag may be as much as $5,000 less than comparable fully finished houses, but the new owners are expected to do their own painting, carpeting, and other finishing touches.

Remodeling offers a double bonus. The changes you make not only add to the intrinsic worth of your home, but you reap the benefits of the improvements while living within its walls. Besides, remodeling satisfies the creative drive. Each change helps the house to become more distinctly yours, reflecting your personality and that of other members of your household, making yours a "custom house" in a very real sense.

It has been estimated that 42 percent of American families undertook some phase of home improvement last year, ranging from living room redecoration to face-lifting the entire exterior. Apartment dwellers, too, have joined the trend. Not only those living in cooperatives or condominiums, who own title to their apartments, but even tenants, recognizing that rental units are in decreasing supply, are making their own improvements in the form of such features as wall fabric or paneling that can be removed later, easily disassembled storage units, or "built-ins" that actually are freestanding.

There are important considerations to be made before undertaking any type of home improvement, and the bigger the project, the more carefully it should be thought out and planned in advance.

Even if only a simple do-it-yourself change is contemplated, aspects to be carefully weighed are choice of color, durability of materials, and how the change will fit in with the overall style and personality of your home.

The more extensive and expensive the renovation, the more important it is to weigh the cost in terms of increased value for your property. Basic to your decision must be the question of how are you going to pay for it—in cash, with a loan, or by refinancing? And can your budget bear the strain?

Sometimes repairs must be made, such as replacing leaking gutters or an inadequate and wasteful heating system or warped windows through which the winter winds whistle. Then the question may be can you afford not to go ahead with the renovation?

The importance of planning

Few families can afford to do everything they wish to do at once, but that is all the more reason to work out a complete plan, for now and the future. More often than not, one project is closely related to others that will follow and by making advance plans you may be able to avoid duplication or costly changes later.

It is your home, and your opportunity to do with it as you

please. Study the shelter magazines and the home and real estate sections of newspapers, join house tours to see how other people have improved their homes. Visit model showrooms and pick up all the pamphlets offered in the housewares and building supply departments of stores. Keep a file of the items and techniques you like.

As your ideas jell, make rough sketches of how you might change this or that room, add an extension, or create extra storage space. You need not be an artist: make rough lines at first, then with a ruler draw straight front and side elevations. The easiest way to calculate is to use one-quarter inch as equal to one foot.

When you have narrowed your choice to just what you want and need, begin comparison shopping for materials, with notebook and pencil always handy, to keep notations of the cost of items that attract you.

You can also find help in books and pamphlets that specialize in specific areas of home improvement; for example, some deal exclusively with basement remodeling, others with patios or pools, some with how to do your own wiring or appliance repairs, and so on. A listing of helpful supplementary publications of this kind will be found at the back of this book. You may find in such publications layouts and blueprints that closely match your own aspirations or provide solutions to your problems.

A further reason for advance planning is that many renovations must receive prior official approval from a building, electric, or plumbing inspector, or all three. Check with your county building inspections office to learn about local codes and regulations before beginning any extensive project. Do-it-yourself inside carpentry is usually not subject to inspection, but when the exterior of the house is affected, you may need a building permit. Permits are also required for plumbing and electrical installations or changes, inside or out. If you bypass such inspection and it later becomes known, you could be penalized by having to pay a heavy fine, or you might be required to open the walls and redo the work in a different manner.

Zoning laws, too, must be checked, especially if you contemplate renting out space, such as a basement apartment. In some localities, zoning laws even apply to exterior architectural styles, and codes govern how far from the property line each structure must be.

Inspecting the house

The bigger the project, the more detailed the plan should be. If you are among the many thousands of families who plan to buy an old house with the intention of renovating it, you should go over the entire house from basement to attic (in that order), carefully inspecting every nook, cranny, water pipe, window, and door frame. Or, better, hire a professional home inspector to do this for you. There are now a number of such firms in our larger cities that examine such basics as the foundation, construction details, plumbing, roofing, and so on, to look for weaknesses that the home buyer would probably not spot. This same type of service is also available to home-owners contemplating major renovations. The fee charged is usually minimal when weighed against the money that may be saved by having such an inspection made.

Besides pointing out what repairs are essential, such an inspector will draw up a realistic estimate of costs, and when this is for a house to be purchased, such costs should be figured as part of the purchase price. Without such knowledge, you might invest heavily in a house that looks impressive, only to find after moving in that you are faced with such unexpected expenses as complete rewiring, or replacing beams eaten away by termites, or excavating around the foundation to correct a bad drainage problem.

It is also possible to find an architect willing to perform a similar service at an hourly fee for his time (usually about $25 an hour). Whether or not you want him to proceed later with designing alterations and/or supervising construction can be decided when or if you feel you need his further help. When dealing with architects you should bear in mind that their ideas are often more imaginative than practical, and the execution of their plans may far exceed the costs anticipated in your budget.

The architect may or may not also select and supervise the contractor. If he does, the architect usually gets 13 to 15 percent of the total construction costs (not the value of the land or house) as his fee. His contract should also specify that the total cost cannot go over 15 percent of the projected budget. As work proceeds, if he finds that this will be impossible, he should consult with you about making changes to keep costs down. Otherwise, what began as a $12,000 renovation may finally cost $24,000.

Whether or not you hire an architect to go over the house and give you his suggestions as to how to carry out the renovation, it is wise to get opinions from contractors. Let them look at the house, examine your rough plans, suggest what they would do, and give you an estimate of costs. Then you can examine and compare several proposals and cost estimates, which will give you a more realistic idea in advance as to how much it will cost and will help you to determine how you would like the work done.

When a major renovation is planned, blueprints are usually required to present to the county building inspector for approval, and these must be made either by an architect, a draftsman in an architect's office, or a drafting firm. For smaller jobs, the homeowner or a contractor can prepare acceptable front and side elevations drawn to scale, provided these include all necessary details regarding construction and materials to be used.

Old houses are attracting buyers these days to an unprecedented degree. For some families, it is a question of location. For example, because of the ever-rising cost of gas and auto maintenance, many families have decided to abandon suburbia for city life, or at least to move to locations closer to public transportation. Often this means they are forced to shop around for older houses. Others prefer older houses because they are roomier and usually boast more solid construction. Even when such extensive changes must be made that the inside is virtually gutted, the fact that the roof, walls, basement, and foundation already exist lessens the overall per-square-foot cost of the house. And some houses can be found that contain such increasingly rare features as working fireplaces, solid oak floors, plaster walls, or a slate roof.

Price in itself is a reason many families are buying an old rather than a new house. Some young couples simply cannot afford to buy a house of their own otherwise, and families with a larger number of children often cannot find a newer house that has sufficient space within their price range. If they can live in the house while fixing it up piecemeal, and

The Components of a House

1. Gable stud
2. Collar beam
3. Ceiling joist
4. Ridge board
5. Insulation
6. Chimney cap
7. Chimney flues
8. Chimney
9. Chimney flashing
10. Rafters
11. Ridge
12. Roof boards
13. Stud
14. Eave gutter
15. Roofing
16. Blind or shutter
17. Bevel siding
18. Downspout gooseneck
19. Downspout strap
20. Downspout leader
21. Double plate
22. Entrance canopy
23. Garage cornice
24. Fascia
25. Door jamb
26. Garage door
27. Downspout shoe
28. Sidewalk
29. Entrance post
30. Entrance platform
31. Stair riser
32. Stair stringer
33. Girder post
34. Chair rail
35. Cleanout door
36. Furring strips
37. Cornice stud
38. Girder
39. Gravel fill
40. Concrete floor
41. Foundation footing
42. Paper strip
43. Drain tile
44. Diagonal subfloor
45. Foundation wall
46. Sill plate
47. Backfill
48. Termite shield
49. Window well wall
50. Grade line
51. Basement sash
52. Window well
53. Corner brace
54. Corner stud
55. Window frame
56. Window light
57. Wall studs
58. Header
59. Window cripple
60. Wall sheathing
61. Building paper
62. Pilaster
63. Rough header
64. Window stud
65. Cornice molding
66. Fascia board
67. Window casing
68. Lath
69. Insulation
70. Wainscoting
71. Baseboard
72. Building paper
73. Finish floor
74. Ash dump
75. Door trim-casing
76. Fireplace hearth
77. Floor joists
78. Stair riser
79. Fire brick
80. Newel cap
81. Stair tread
82. Finish stringer
83. Stair rail
84. Balusters
85. Plaster arch
86. Mantel
87. Floor joists
88. Bridging
89. Lookout
90. Attic space
91. Metal lath
92. Window sash
93. Chimney breast
94. Newel

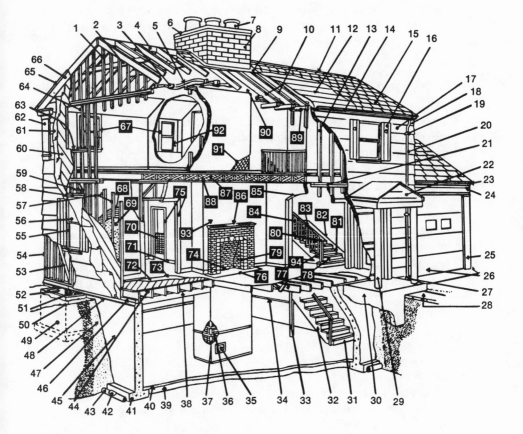

doing much of the work themselves, real savings are possible.

Many young couples are buying dilapidated houses in the inner cities to renovate and, as a result, some slum areas have become chic neighborhoods. Sometimes houses owned by HUD (Housing and Urban Development), as the result of foreclosures, can be purchased for a token $1, with a guarantee by the buyers that they will renovate the houses according to specified standards within five years.

Basics versus cosmetics

The fun of remodeling always lies primarily in what those in the building industry refer to as "cosmetics," that is, the appearance, the beautification of your home, inside and out. No one begrudges spending as much as $2,000 on a new roofed patio or a spruced-up kitchen or bath, but having to "bury" the same amount of money in a new heating system or correcting a drainage problem is another side of the coin.

Yet it is the basics that must be considered first. A homeowner should make periodic checks throughout the house, on the lookout for water spots or other indications of leaks, heat loss through warped windows or doors, bare spots on roof shingles—a warning signal that the roof may need attention —broken downspouts that may lead to basement water problems if not repaired, and signs of termite or other insect damage.

Small repairs cost less than big ones and when caught in time may prevent the development of major problems. This is what is known as "preventive maintenance." In the following chapter, a step-by-step checklist for such inspection will be given, along with suggestions as to what should be done to correct or repair structural weakness or defects when spotted, and how to improve insulation to cut down fuel costs.

Before embarking on any "cosmetic" renovation, a close inspection of walls, ceilings, floors, and pipes should always be made and essential repairs taken care of first, though sometimes the two can be combined.

For example, if it is obviously necessary to have a new roof, consider changing to a different exterior color scheme. If the house is white with a reddish brown roof, you could reroof it in black or very dark gray, paint the shutters black or add prepainted black aluminum shutters, and repaint the front door yellow. Or perhaps the siding is barn red and the roof, trim, and shutters are white. You could replace the roof with shingles of light green, paint the shutters to match the roof, leave the trim white and keep a white front door, but trim the door panels in the same light green in a three-dimensional effect. In this way you give your house a face-lifting which makes the roofing expense easier to bear.

Besides the financial good sense of making basic repairs first, often such repairs must be made to avoid having to do the "beautification" all over again. If you repaint a wall that was badly blistered without investigating why it was blistered, the new paint will soon look as bad as the old one.

Then there was the experience of the Miller family in Boston, Massachusetts. They decided that their ever-running toilet had to be replaced. At a discount plumbing supply house, they saw a "special" on a matching vanity and toilet, which they purchased. Mrs. Miller also persuaded her husband to buy a glass door tub enclosure that was proclaimed to be easy for a do-it-yourselfer to install. But later Mr. Miller fretted that they had gone way over their budget, so he hired a neighbor's son, an apprentice plumber, to install the new fixtures in his spare time. Mr. Miller assisted the youngster and urged him to connect the fixtures to the old pipe fittings because the family could not afford new piping.

After the new fixtures were in, the bathroom looked fine— except for the floor. New bathroom fixtures almost never seem to fit into the holes left by the old ones. The vanity base covered the holes around the new washbasin, but there was an ugly gap in the tile around the toilet. So Mr. Miller decided to install new sheet vinyl himself, over the old flooring, a job which proved more exasperating than he had anticipated.

Less than a year later, leaks from the bathtub enclosure wrecked the kitchen ceiling. The new vinyl flooring had to be pulled up and new copper pipes laid throughout the bathroom and down to the basement. In addition, a new ceiling had to be installed in the kitchen.

This illustrates several hazards to be avoided. Instead of impulsively buying fixtures at a discount house, it would have been better for the Millers to have worked out a complete plan for renovating the bathroom, even if it meant keeping the defective toilet for a while longer. If the toilet was so old that

BEFORE: This city house appears to be ready for the wrecking crew. See facing page for the transformation effected by new siding and roofing and new windows installed in the old framing.

AFTER: In addition to new siding, roofing, and windows, the only major change is replacement of the front porch by a covered entranceway. Solid vinyl materials were used, inside and out, in this renovation.

it was beyond repair, it was likely that the old galvanized piping was not in much better shape. Had he shopped around longer, Mr. Miller might well have found fixtures at a better price elsewhere, or at least of better quality for the same price. Discount houses offer temptingly low prices but you get what you pay for, and saving a few dollars is poor economy when purchasing permanent fixtures.

Also, where plumbing is concerned, it always pays to have professional workmanship. The apprentice plumber may have thought he was doing his neighbor a good turn, but his lack of experience could have resulted in even more costly mistakes.

Do-it-yourself versus contracting

Since labor accounts for the biggest portion of remodeling costs, many homeowners naturally want to save by doing as much of the work as they can themselves. The abundance of products that are advertised as "easy to install" reflects the ballooning demand.

Many renovation jobs can be done just as well by a careful, patient amateur as by a professional. Some homeowners find that it is possible to complete such work without undue strain in the course of weekends, evenings, and vacations. But the do-it-yourselfer about to undertake a major renovation should ask himself these questions:

1. Will I have sufficient time to give to the work? What if it takes six months, a year, or even longer, to complete the project?

2. Am I skilled enough to do a professional-looking job?

3. Will my marriage stand up under the stress? Many projects that sound easy turn out to be grim trials of endurance.

Very often the solution is to strike a compromise. The owner, with help from older children, neighbors, or spouse, does as much of the work as possible, then hires a general contractor, or one or two subcontractors, to do the rest.

A great deal of money can be saved by shopping around for supplies—finding fixtures in junk yards and at auction sales, or purchasing slightly damaged or scratched "seconds" from dealers. Intricately carved moldings, Victorian marble mantels, interesting light fixtures, or even slate or fieldstone for walls and/or patios often may be found in out-of-the-way places, at estate sales, in old houses being torn down to make way for high-rises, or at small lumber yards or garden supply houses.

But these things must be acquired before any plans are submitted to a contractor. Any changes that are made after the work has begun will cost twice as much. A standard contract often stipulates an allowance for "change orders" in the final payment, which is another way of saying that it is going to cost you more than the contract stated.

How to select a contractor

The construction business is, unfortunately, riddled with fly-by-night "contractors" who are either incompetent or unreliable, or both. All a carpenter has to do to become a contractor is to give himself this title and list his "firm name" in the yellow pages. Some have not even been trained in construction work, but believe themselves capable of hiring and supervising subcontractors because of experience in some related field such as kitchen planning or selling building supplies.

As many as three of every four contractors go out of business after a relatively short time; some have estimated the ratio to be even higher. By declaring bankruptcy a firm can evade its contract responsibilities, then resume business under a different name, and the bilked homeowner has no legal recourse.

For this reason, the homeowner cannot be too careful in selecting a contractor. Generally, the best way is to hire someone who has done satisfactory work for people you know personally. But make sure he has or can handle the type of work you have in mind. He may be able to do excellent work in one field but prove to be incompetent in others.

One family's experience

Consider the experience of the Hall family, who decided to have a picture window installed in their kitchen, because the house was located on a hilltop commanding a magnificent view of the valley. Such a window would not only open up the view but make the kitchen sunnier and give it more "breathing space."

Neighbors recommended a man who had done very satisfactory work for them, making a library with built-in shelves and cabinets out of a little-used parlor. The Halls asked this man if he could put in a picture window and he assured them that he could.

Without any investigation of the house, he set about cutting out the space for the window—only to reveal, right in the center, a drain pipe coming down from the bathroom above. For three weeks the family lived with a tarpaulin over the exposed cutout while frantic consultations were held. At last a plumber was located who figured out a way to reroute the pipe so that the window could be installed.

The problem in this case was that the "contractor" was nothing more than a carpenter and, while skilled enough to do a particular type of inside work, was not competent to handle exterior carpentry involving the house structure. As a subcontractor under supervision, he may have been fine; as a general contractor, he simply did not qualify.

How else then can one go about locating the right contractor for the job?

One way is to make inquiries at a building supply firm. They will have many contractors among their customers and may know of someone who specializes in the very type of renovation you have in mind. Also, they are not likely to recommend individuals who do not pay their bills on time, in itself an indication of lack of reliability.

Late in 1973, a movement was begun in Kansas City, Missouri, which may start a nationwide trend. There a group of quality contractors formed an association with the main functions of raising the professional standards in the business, especially of contractors undertaking home-improvement work, and of establishing a continuing consumer education program.

This group, associated with the National Home Improvement Council that has branches in thirty-three cities, announced an annual HOMEE award competition, with prizes offered to those local contractors who were able to solve remodeling problems most effectively and imaginatively and with the highest standards of workmanship. Backed by the Community Services Department of the Kansas State Office of Consumer Affairs, a permanent and continuing function of the organization is to serve as a clearinghouse for complaints.

Beware of pitfalls

What about the firms that advertise widely, proclaiming, "Free estimates; all work guaranteed; get our prices and compare"?

There are two disadvantages in dealing with such a firm. First, the jobs that they are prepared to do are routine, following a set pattern, and it is fine if such plans happen to conform to your tastes and your needs. But if you want an imaginative and tasteful custom job, you may be disappointed. Secondly, the man who comes to inspect your house and draws up the contract is a salesman, not the contractor who will be supervising the job.

You will usually note somewhere in the advertisements one or more clauses admitting that the sum advertised for the remodeling job could run higher; similar escape clauses may appear in fine print in the contract, so it is necessary to read it very carefully.

Also, the contractor who supervises the job wants to finish as quickly as possible and may be rather unsympathetic. It is important for the homeowner and the supervising contractor to have a rapport, for antagonisms can arise in the course of the work that are basically due to personality differences or a lack of mutual respect. Also, because remodeling is always custom work, it is even more important to have skilled craftsmen than for new construction jobs where a crew of men, each assigned to one specific job, carries out orders.

The same disadvantages can be cited for the contractors supplied by the home improvement divisions of the big chain stores. However, if you would be purchasing most of the supplies from the store anyway, and like what you have seen or remodeling jobs they have completed, this could be a good solution. At least you would have the comfort of knowing that the store stands behind the work, and if it were not satisfactory, adjustments would be made.

No matter how well recommended a contractor may be, you should always check his references, both those from his former customers and his credit references, and if possible look over jobs he has completed and talk to those for whom he did the work. If he has been in business many years under the same firm name, that in itself is a good sign. On the other hand, a young contractor just getting started may be willing to take less profit in order to build a reputation, and if he can offer good references, you may get an especially conscientious job performance from him.

Your local Better Business Bureau may have information about contractors on your list, but usually only complaints; they can warn you against dealing with certain firms, but do not make recommendations.

Getting bids

It is always advisable to get two or three bids for any renovation, but in general be rather suspicious of bids that are unrealistically low, especially so if the contractor asks to be paid half of the amount on signing the contract. Sometimes a contractor in need of cash to meet his payroll or to write off some long-standing bills may submit a very low bid just to get the job. Then, when he sees that he cannot possibly make a profit, he may let your work slide while he goes after other game. Some have been known to disappear altogether. They would rather abandon the job than finish it, since the remaining payments to be collected will not cover their costs.

A very high bid on the other hand could mean that the contractor is so busy he is not much interested in getting the job. Bids vary enormously, sometimes by several thousand dollars, for exactly the same job with the same specifications.

To determine which are realistic bids, you can work out your own rough estimates by adding up prices for all the materials required (including nails, cement, plywood, and insulation) and the labor costs. The contractor, who has done this before making his bid, probably added 50 percent or more to the materials-labor estimate, hoping to come out with 33 percent gross profit, and finally 10 percent net profit. The differential is for the unforeseen—problems that rear their ugly heads when walls are torn down or ceilings exposed or inescapable changes must be made. He also has to figure in his overhead, insurance, workmen's compensation, Social Security, and, in today's inflationary situation, increases in prices along the way.

Nevertheless, a competent contractor, who knows what can and cannot be done structurally, and whose work will add obvious value to your home, is well worth his profit margin. And he has to make a profit to stay in business.

Before signing up, make sure that the contractor has insurance coverage and workmen's compensation and that he is licensed. In some areas, contractors are also required to post bonds. Ask your county building inspections office about such regulations.

Being your own contractor

To save the 33 to 50 percent profit differential that the general contractor adds to his estimate, many homeowners decide to be their own contractor, to hire the plumber, electrician, mason, or other skilled workmen, and to do their own buying of materials. Some even do their own wiring and plumbing installations.

How this would work out for you depends largely on the size of the job, how much time you and your spouse can give to the project, and whether your tempers can take it.

If, for example, it is a question of refinishing the basement so that it will serve as a combined playroom and hobby room, and the plumber needs to be called in only to install the piping for a downstairs lavatory near existing drains, and the electrician only to do the wiring for new wall outlets and perhaps to add a circuit breaker, the headaches may be minimal. But if it is something like adding a new wing to the house, or gutting most of the first floor to rearrange rooms, the exasperations can become monumental.

The various jobs have to be scheduled so that each phase is completed before the next begins. If the plumber fails to show up to install pipes or ducts on a certain day, the flooring man cannot do his job when he arrives. The wiring cannot be installed until the studs are in; the dry walls cannot be erected and taped until after the wiring is finished and inspected. If any workman along the line arrives to find he cannot begin his job, he may leave to get involved in another project that may prevent him from coming back for another ten days—and you and any subsequent workmen are left holding the bag.

Workmen's compensation and liability insurance become the homeowner's responsibility when he does the hiring. He may have to pay Social Security as well. And remember that no workman should ever be hired on an hourly basis, only by the job at an agreed-upon overall fee. This applies to moonlighters as well.

But even if you hire a general contractor who is supposed to coordinate such details, this does not mean the homeowner is relieved of responsibility. Very likely your contractor is supervising half a dozen or more projects at the same time. If he falls behind schedule, or if one of his subcontractors has done an obviously careless job, or you see the wrong materials being used, you may have a hard time locating him. It could mean setting your alarm for six in the morning to be sure you get him on the phone before he leaves home.

However it may be handled, both husband and wife must be reconciled to being deeply involved and must learn to put up with delays and disappointments. This does not mean standing behind a workman watching over his shoulder as he pounds nails. This could be so annoying to the workman that he would walk off the job. But it does mean checking up on the progress of the work and making sure that the materials being used are those specified in the contract. Never accuse a contractor of cheating unless you are positive he is. But it does not hurt to let him know tactfully that you are aware of what he is doing.

Budgeting and resale considerations

From the very beginning, as you accumulate clippings and pamphlets and plan what you want to do to your home, you should continuously think of your budget.

The things you can pay for in cash are always an asset if you have selected them with the realities of resale in mind. You probably intend to remain in your present home for a long time, or you would not be making renovations. But no one ever knows what may happen in the future, and in as short a time as two or three years, moving may become inevitable.

For this reason, each "cosmetic" addition should be tailored to considerations of the tastes of potential future buyers. A house sale could fall through because of such a minor detail as too-bright green ceramic tile in the bathroom, or because of mauve bath fixtures. If your taste runs to flamboyant or off-beat colors, at least confine these to easily replaceable materials or finishes, such as paint and wallpaper, and stick to neutral or universally popular pastels for the permanent fixtures.

When you get into heavier costs, and must take out a loan,

it is extremely important that you be able to meet the extra payments without anguish. The types of loans available for home improvement will be considered in the final chapter of this book. If you can absorb the payments, and the renovations being made do add considerably to your equity in the property, you will be ahead of the game, for real estate values keep rising and your home is probably your biggest investment.

Certain renovations will pay for themselves. Better insulation or storm windows, for example, will probably save enough on fuel costs to warrant the expenditure, even if the saving is spread out over several years. Sometimes the remodeling can pay for itself in income: a basement apartment that can be rented out, for example, or a den turned into a home office. The latter not only will save having to pay rent for office space elsewhere but this portion of the house, listed under "business expense," may be a tax-deductible item.

If putting a dormer in the attic results in more bedroom space, the homeowner can justify this expense as costing far less than moving into a larger house, besides increasing equity, making yours a four-bedroom rather than a three-bedroom house, for example.

All these are considerations that should go down on paper as you weigh the extra cost against the realities of income.

Keep careful records

Somewhere in your home you should have a file in which to keep records. This will save you money in a number of ways.

First, there is the question of your annual income tax returns. You can deduct real estate taxes and the interest on your mortgage, and if you keep on file an amortization schedule (available from the bank or other institution through which the mortgage was obtained), you will know exactly how much interest can be deducted each year. This also serves as a record of mounting equity in your property.

Next, you should file bills, receipts, and canceled checks covering every improvement you make, with dates, names, contracts, and total costs. "Capital improvements," which include additions to the house, decks, patios, a finished recreation room, or a remodeled kitchen—any permanent installation—are a part of the equity in your home and what you have spent for such improvements can be deducted from capital gains when you sell the house.

Repairs do not count as "capital improvements," but records of these are also important for several reasons. For one thing, if a piece of equipment must be repaired more than once, the repairman can be shown exactly what was done previously, and this may save him time in locating the present trouble.

Another important consideration is that when the house is up for sale, your receipts offer evidence of what has been done in the way of basic maintenance. Also, if you have the brand names, styles, and serial numbers of such equipment as the furnace, air conditioner, and kitchen appliances, and the names of the firms through whom the appliances or fixtures were purchased, it could be important when ordering parts.

If a part of your house is rented out, all expenses related to the rental are deductible on federal income tax Form 4831. These expenses can include maintenance, heat, water, repairs, and depreciation—but all prorated for only that portion of your house that is rented out. Depreciation is deductible not only for the house itself but for each appliance or fixture in use by tenants of the apartment. To arrive at the depreciation figure, divide the original purchase price of the house, fixture, or appliance by its estimated life. Houses are usually depreciated for twenty-five to forty years; kitchen appliances, for eight to fifteen years.

Besides keeping receipts of all expenditures related to home improvement and maintenance, the careful homeowner will make an inventory of all insured household and personal belongings in case of fire or theft, malicious mischief, or storm damage. This inventory should be kept in a safe-deposit box or a locked fireproof file or safe.

Records of this sort may also be of use in applying for a home-improvement loan or refinancing. If the holder of your mortgage, or another lending institution, can be shown what improvements have already been made on the property, thus increasing equity, getting the home-improvement loan should be that much easier.

CHAPTER 2

Preventive Maintenance:
Insulation
and
Moisture Control

The hidden assets in your home, such as insulation, foundation structure, and moisture control, are basics which must be checked periodically and kept in good repair to protect your investment, just as you go to your doctor for periodic check-ups to protect your health.

Not only should these basics be kept in good repair as a matter of economy, all are features that have a direct bearing on equity and resale.

By checking and improving insulation and plugging all the energy leaks you can find, you probably will be able to save enough on fuel and utility bills to make such changes pay for themselves.

Attic, exterior walls, floors, and foundation all need to be checked to see what insulation already exists and whether more should be added.

The first and easiest place to check is the attic—that is, if it is unfinished. Many old houses had no insulation at all when built, and if yours has, or had upon purchase, no attic insulation, you can be sure there is none in the walls.

Insulating the attic

Adding insulation to the attic is easy. If there is none between floor joists, you should put down blanket or batt-type fiber glass insulation six inches thick (this is now considered a minimum), preferably with foil or other vapor barrier on the down side. If insulation is already installed, check the thickness; if it is only three inches thick, add loose rock wool or micafil to make up the difference, making sure that every crevice is filled. Insulation for the attic floor is considered more important than for the roof (ceiling), but to ensure a cooler attic, you may want to apply batt-type insulation between the room beams as well, with the foil against the attic side. Such batts are very easy to apply with a staple gun.

As important as applied insulation is an attic fan-ventilator. On a hot day, the temperature inside an unfinished unvented attic could rise to 150 degrees Fahrenheit. Some insulation engineers claim that if the attic temperature can be kept at a level no more than five to ten degrees higher than that out of doors, the entire house will be cooler. If you already have central airconditioning, such a fan can greatly reduce your summer airconditioning bill. If you do not have central airconditioning, the fan might make one unnecessary. Even in an already finished attic, a ventilator fan and louvers can be installed in the ceiling or a wall.

Insulating exterior walls

Insulation in exterior walls should be three and a half inches thick. If your house has no exterior wall insulation, there are ways of overcoming this problem. One is to have loose fill blown into the walls. This can be done by a careful do-it-yourselfer, renting the necessary tools and equipment, but in most cases it is advisable to have the job done by professionals. Keep in mind, however, that loose fill gradually settles and in time more will have to be blown in to protect upper floors sufficiently. If you already have loose fill in the walls but it was put in a good many years ago, perhaps you should add more.

If there is good reason to add new exterior siding to the

Effect of Insulation

Wall and ceiling insulation maintains an even temperature throughout a room even when the outside temperature is at zero.

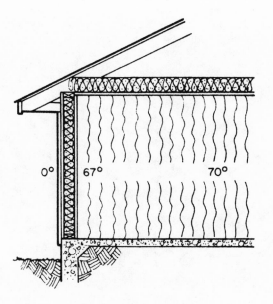

Rigid Insulation

In addition to increasing the thickness of batt-type insulation to achieve better results, some builders are now using rigid polystyrene foam in conjunction with blanket insulation.

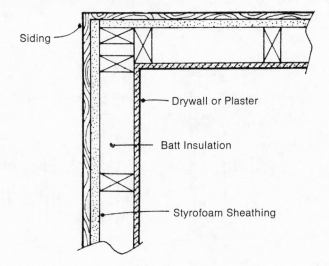

Ceiling Insulation

An airway should be left open between the eave vents and the open area above the insulation. When blown and poured loose fill insulation is used, baffling of the vent opening must be provided.

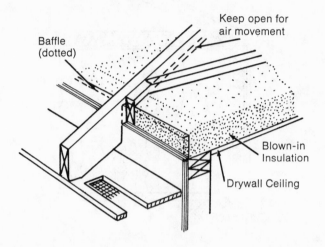

Baffle (dotted)

Keep open for air movement

Blown-in Insulation

Drywall Ceiling

Wall Insulation

Blanket-type insulation should touch sheathing or siding. The insulation should not be cut to go around electrical boxes, pipes, and ducts, but should be pushed in behind these obstructions. Spaces between rough framing and door and window heads, jambs, and sills should be stuffed with pieces of insulation and covered with a vapor barrier.

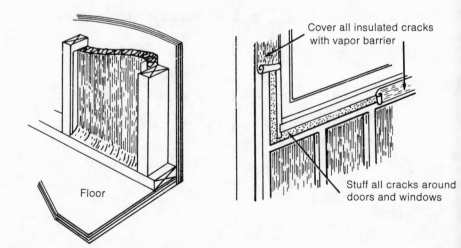

Floor

Cover all insulated cracks with vapor barrier

Stuff all cracks around doors and windows

Perimeter Insulation

Large amounts of heat can be lost or gained through uninsulated floors and foundations. Perimeter insulation of slabs is installed either vertically (left), horizontally (right), or both.

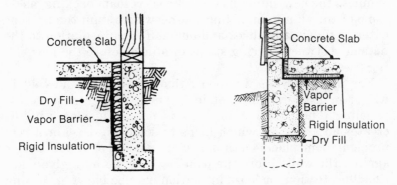

Crawl-Space Insulation

When insulating the foundation walls of unvented crawl spaces, a polyethylene film vapor barrier should cover the ground and be taped against the foundation wall. One edge of the insulation should then be placed on the top of the foundation wall and the remaining portion draped over and against the wall, as shown at left below. Floors over vented crawl spaces and unheated basements can be insulated by placing batt-type insulation between the joists, with the vapor barrier toward the warm-in-winter side (below right). This insulation can be held in place by nailing chicken wire underneath.

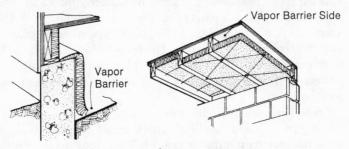

Basement Wall Insulation

One method of insulating walls of heated basements is to attach furring strips to the masonry and place blanket insulation between the strips.

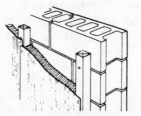

house, insulation can be added before the new siding is put up
—unless the new siding has its own styrofoam backing, as do
some of the aluminum sidings. Otherwise, retain the present
exterior finish, add three-and-one-half-inch insulation to the
outside, between furring strips or studs, before the new siding goes over it.

For interior walls, in rooms that are drafty and cold in
winter or exceptionally hot in summer, it may help to add
paneling. The paneling in itself is not an insulator but it
creates an air space which helps to some degree. For a real
problem room, placing a thin insulation board or vapor barrier
against the wall before the paneling goes up may give additional protection, or loose insulation may be blown in behind
the plaster or plasterboard through holes at the top.

Insulating the foundation area

Next to be checked for insulation are the floors and foundation. Whether you have a basement, a combination of a basement and crawl space, or only crawl space beneath your house,
it is important to make sure that these foundation areas are
well insulated against both heat loss and gain.

Even if it means moving on hands and knees through a
crawl space (usually eighteen inches high), you should note
what type of insulation, if any, has been applied to joists and
foundation walls. Two types are recommended for the floor
above a crawl space. One is the batt type of fiber glass with a
vapor barrier (such as foil), the latter placed against the floor
overhead and stapled or held in place with chicken wire. Or,
panels of rigid insulating board can be nailed or stapled to the
joists.

Over the walls of the crawl space, rigid insulation such as
polystyrene foam one inch thick could be installed, making
sure there are no gaps or cracks. This does not mean that the
crawl space should be airless. On the contrary, vents in the
foundation wall (a one-foot vent for every 150 square feet of
floor space) are important to avoid a buildup of moisture from
the earth.

Batt-type insulation is also recommended for floors above
an unheated basement. The masonry walls of such a basement
can best be insulated by attaching furring strips to the masonry and applying two-inch-thick blanket insulation. Before

doing this, make sure that the masonry walls have at least one coat of waterproofing sealer to protect the surface against moisture. If the insulation has its own vapor barrier, place this against the masonry. If the insulation does not have such a covering, a polyethylene film or foil-backed gypsum board should be applied over it. This in turn will be covered with dry wall or paneling.

While you are checking these various areas of the house, keep an eye open for any "energy leaks." Cracks or gaps may be spotted in the basement between walls and overhead flooring. The best way to search out such cracks is to turn out all lights and look for rays of daylight. Some such cracks may be filled in simply with caulking or weatherstripping; others may need covering with furring or molding strips. When inspecting the attic, bear in mind that many of the "gaps" are actually soffit vents and must not be closed.

Other places to inspect for gaps are the flashings around vents, exhaust fans, room airconditioners, skylights, and chimneys. If the flashing has come loose, it should be nailed or screwed firmly in place and caulked or filled in around the edges with roof cement.

Windows and doors

More energy leaks are to be found around windows and exterior doors than anywhere else. Weatherstripping and caulking will eliminate the most conspicuous drafts, and these are easy do-it-yourself chores.

The glass in windows and patio doors has extremely poor thermal resistance and when not properly insulated permits enormous heat loss or gain. For this reason, extensive use of glass for that delightful indoor-outdoor look is now seen as an energy problem. The greater the area of glass used in construction, the larger the energy loss in direct proportion.

The direct rays of sunlight are a million times more powerful than diffused light, and when the sun's rays can be effectively shut out, interior temperatures remain lower by natural means. When, on the contrary, windows are left unshaded in the summer and the airconditioner is in operation, the unit is forced to carry too heavy a load.

If you do not already have storm windows and doors, it would be worthwhile to add them. Even in southern climates, storm windows are now recommended for use in hot weather to reduce the strain on airconditioners. Combination storm-screen windows on tracks are often favored because they permit the windows to be easily opened in pleasant weather. Insulating glass (thermopane, or double glass with an air space between) does an even better job, and if you are having new windows installed, adding a new wing, or enclosing a porch, these are well worth the initially higher cost, especially for patio doors and window walls.

A product that can be easily added to existing windows and other glass areas by a do-it-yourselfer is called "insulation shading." This is plastic sheeting with accordion-like pleats of thin metallic coating, so constructed that the direct glare and heat of the sun is shut out entirely, while allowing indirect light to enter. Even when the glass is covered entirely with the material, rooms are not darkened nor is the view beyond the windows impaired.

Insulation shading is described by its inventor, retired naval captain S.N. Ferris Luboshez, as combining in one product the best features of venetian blinds, thermopane, and a roof overhang. The metallic-coated "pleats" are so designed that in summer, when the sun is high in the sky and the rays come down almost vertically, no direct sunlight enters, but in winter, when the sun crosses the heavens at a lower arc, the sunshine can enter to add its warmth to rooms. This principle also applies to a roof overhang above a window wall.

An important feature of insulation shading is its versatility. It can be cut with shears into any size or shape, applied directly to the glass for year-round insulation, placed in easily constructed metal frames to be installed on tracks like screens, or made into pull-shades.

Venetian blinds, when the slats are turned to deflect sunlight, offer some shading. Awnings over window areas also keep out direct sunlight. The best types of awnings are those that can be raised or lowered as needed, allowing sunlight in to warm rooms in cold weather. Some aluminum awnings have slats that can be opened or closed, like venetian blinds.

Vinyl-coated fiber glass shades offer another inexpensive window treatment, and these are available in widths up to six feet. The most effective type is semitransparent so that, while glare and heat are deflected, one can still see out through the

Insulation Shading

Insulation for large areas of glass should exclude the sun's rays in summer and permit sunlight to enter in winter. The drawing shows the different angles at which the sun's rays enter a house in summer and winter. Insulation shading has a reflective coating only on the part of the pleating struck by the summer rays.

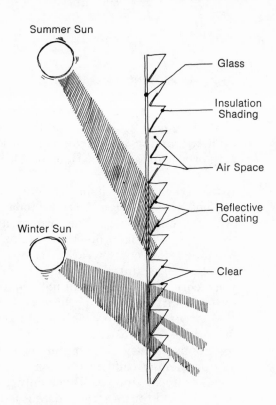

windows. This is always important psychologically. Although draperies help to keep out sunlight if closed during the day—as they help to keep out drafts on winter nights—when rooms are heavily shaded during the day, the effect is funereal.

If you plan a new addition using a large number of windows, make sure the roof overhang is designed both to provide shade in summer and to allow sunlight to enter during the winter. This could entail the services of an architect, for the design must be made in accordance with the changing arc of the sun in each season.

In an older house, it is not only important that windows and doors be properly insulated (double glass, storm sashes, weatherstripping, etc.) but also that they be checked for fit and any damage to the frames. Frequently, in double-hung windows, the putty or glazing around the grilles, the thin strips of wood to which glass panes are attached, has dried and shrunk, pulling away from the glass. This allows moisture to enter the cracks so formed and sometimes a fungus growth begins, which leads to dry rot in the wood. The rotted part should be removed and the hole filled with putty, then painted over.

Sash cords on old windows may need replacing. If a window

does not move up and down easily, a faulty sash cord is probably the cause. Or it could be that as the house settled, the window framing was thrown out of line enough to interfere with proper fit, a more serious problem and harder to correct.

Wood versus metal window frames

Wood windows manufactured today have many advantages over the older types. The frames are made of chemically treated wood for protection against decay, termites, and warping; they come weatherstripped from the factory, and many are prepainted and have vinyl coating bonded to the wood core so that they will not require further maintenance for ten to fifteen years, perhaps longer.

Many of the better contractors regard wood windows as preferable to metal (steel or aluminum) despite their higher cost, because they offer better insulation and rarely present any problem of condensation on the glass, as is often true of metal-framed windows. Since only a few new windows must be purchased for most remodeling jobs, the overall difference in cost is not that great, and the advantages of wood windows more than outweigh that difference. The labor of installation is the biggest cost, and that is the same regardless of what type of window is put in.

Condensation—a moisture buildup on the glass—is caused when there is a leakage of warm air to the space between sash and storm windows or when there is extreme variation in temperature and humidity between the inner and outer areas of insulating (double pane) glass. Wood, with its self-insulating properties, deters this. The problem occurs most frequently with steel-framed windows, and only a little less often with aluminum. Extreme condensation is bad for walls, window frames, sills, and drapes.

Because of the cost factor and their maintenance-free attraction (that is, no need of painting), metal-framed windows continue to be popular, and if they are your choice, be sure to get the best quality. For better insulation, choose windows that have an outer aluminum frame separated from the inner aluminum by a vinyl break and that have glazing of flexible vinyl. This type prevents cold air from being conducted inside and thus forming condensation on the glass.

Older casement windows are more likely to have metal than

wood frames and tend to "spring," so that they cannot be closed tightly. Casements are frequently found in houses built during the 1930s and 1940s, when they were in high fashion. New hardware and fittings may correct the problem of bad fit. The only storm windows available for these older casements are the "piggyback" type, fitted on the outside, a nuisance to put up and take down each fall and spring. But to replace old casement windows could cost as much as $100 each, including labor and the probability that new frames would be needed, while storm windows may cost only $20 to $30 each.

Both wood and metal windows are available in easy-to-clean styles. Some pivot so that the outside can be swung inside; others tilt so that the outside of the pane can be reached easily; and in still others, the entire frame can be removed from the sash, then popped back in again when cleaned.

The choice of shape or size is wide-ranging and purely a question of decor. New casement windows in vertical combinations are especially attractive. Also, it is now possible to use windows of different shapes and sizes in combination.

Windows with self-storing screens or screen-storm combinations not only save time, but when a sudden spell of warm weather arrives in early spring or late fall, it is a great advantage to be able to push the storm sash up and pull down the screen to admit fresh air.

Jalousie windows are not really windows at all but a high-priced screen, and a room fitted with them is all but impossible to heat during northern winters. If the house already has such windows on a porch or sun room, it is possible to put "piggyback" storm windows on the outside, but probably sooner or later you will want to replace the jalousie windows in order to use the room comfortably in winter.

Examine exterior doors to make sure they are solid core, not hollow core. The latter are satisfactory for interior doors but do not have sufficient protection for outside use. Also check the fit of each door. If a door does not close tightly, a large energy leak results. If weatherstripping cannot correct the problem, carpentry may be necessary, to install a new frame or rehang the door, or both.

Wood-framed patio doors cost $150 to $200 more than those with metal frames.

Checking for moisture damage

One of the things that prospective home buyers are, or should be, concerned about is potential water damage. The house-hunter is always advised to go into the basement first, and if he finds a noticeably musty odor and telltale marks of moisture damage or water seepage, that house had better be crossed off his list—unless the cause of the excess moisture can be determined and a way can be found to repair the damage and eliminate the cause. The cost of such repair, of course, should be deducted from the selling price, and if you are the seller, that means a loss to you.

Even if you have never had any problem with flooding or excess moisture in your basement, it is wise to look for signs of moisture problems all around the house and if you spot any, correct the cause before things get worse.

Mildew is one sign: if it exists, you have an excess moisture problem. You can wash off mildew from walls or other scrubbable surfaces with a solution of ammonia in water and repaint with mildew-resistant paint, or cover walls with vinyl alkyd scrubbable paper. But the best thing is to remove the cause.

Dry rot of wood, whether in joints, studs, window frames, or porch steps, is another indication of excess dampness, as is blistering or peeling paint, indoors or out, rust, warping, and uneven floor tiles. All these are warning signals.

Basement moisture problem

A basement moisture problem may be easier to solve than you think. If the problem does not arise from water flowing toward the house, try to correct it by covering the masonry foundation and the concrete slab floor with waterproof sealer. This is an easy do-it-yourself chore.

There are several kinds of waterproof materials. One of the most effective and least expensive is a waterproofing compound, thoroseal, to be mixed with water to the consistency of a thick batter, using two pounds of dry powder for every ten square feet to be covered. Brush on as thickly as possible, let dry overnight, then add a thinner coat. If you continue to have oozing moisture in walls or floors, add a third coat. When floors and walls seem dry (give it plenty of time), a final coat may be of masonry paint, unless you plan to panel the walls.

A more costly sealer would be one of the epoxy waterproofing compounds mixed with masonry paint, available in a selection of as many as ten colors. These are fast-drying and go on like any paint, but because of cost are usually limited to smaller projects or wall areas.

A waterproofing sealant plus a dehumidifier in the basement is often enough to solve a minor dampness problem. If the dehumidifier empties into a drain, or is connected to the drain for a washing machine or dryer, you need not worry about having to empty the pan. The mechanism goes on and off year-round according to the moisture level in the air.

Sometimes when these easy solutions seem at first to be the answer, after a long rainy spell or a heavy runoff of snow, you may discover the problem is still with you.

If the masonry wall has already been covered with insulating material and paneling and you notice signs of moisture in the paneling (warping or dark spots), you had better take the paneling down, give the masonry a coat or two of waterproofing, and check for any cracks or leaks. Look especially around the perimeter of the floor. If you find any cracks or damp areas, remove old particles of mortar, clean the area thoroughly, and add cement bond. When this is dry, paint with waterproofing sealer. If it does not get dry, and the moisture comes up around it, you know the trouble is more serious. But if after a week or so, everything seems under control, you might install a waterproofing cove where the walls meet the floor.

In a properly constructed foundation, before the concrete is poured, a four-inch bed of gravel should be laid, and over the gravel a vapor barrier such as polyethylene. If this technique was observed when the house was built, the floor should be dry. When it is not, one must assume that either gravel or vapor barrier, or both, were omitted, or that surface or underground drainage is inadequate.

Ventilation in the basement area also is important. Windows should be opened occasionally, but if the windows are fixed and cannot be opened, installation of a ventilating fan or exhaust may be advisable, especially in the laundry area.

Be sure window wells are kept free of leaves and trash, and inspect window frames to see if any water has been coming in, around or under them. If so, caulk them.

How to Protect Your Home From Moisture

Outside

Repair flashing around chimney and brickwork to prevent water from entering house.

Keep roofing in good repair.

Rusty or clogged gutters and downspouts may allow water to damage house. Keep them clean and painted.

Caulk window frames and install flashing at top to prevent rain from entering.

Where concrete porch meets siding, use caulking compound to keep water out.

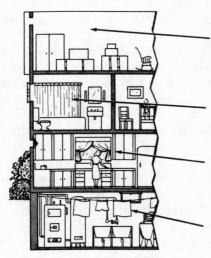

Inside

To keep vapor from condensing on cold surfaces, ventilate attic well.

After bathing, allow moisture to escape through door or window or by exhaust fan. Eliminate plumbing leaks.

Install exhaust fan in kitchen to reduce humidity.

Improve ventilation and humidity control to eliminate dampness in basement.

Gutters and downspouts

Next have a look at gutters and downspouts. If any gutters are badly rusted or broken, water could be streaming into the siding every time it rains. This is particularly damaging for brick or wood, both of which are porous, but also for metal which gradually will rust and warp because of dampness. There was a period when, on contemporary homes, gutters were omitted as being unnecessary, but time has proved this to be a fallacy. If your home does not have gutters, they should be added.

If the gutters and downspouts on your house are of galvanized steel, they may need replacing, for these rarely last longer than ten years and, when badly rusted, repair is a waste of time. However, new gutters of galvanized steel have a baked-on two-step acrylic finish guaranteed by the manufacturer for ten years. This finish makes galvanized steel as maintenance-free as aluminum because no painting is required.

Aluminum gutters are still preferred because they have a "free-floating" hanging system that allows for expansion and contraction as the weather changes and they are now available in seamless lengths, in some cases making joints unnecessary except at the downspouts. Where they must be joined, an improved method has been developed which permits fewer leaks.

To keep gutters clear of leaves, aluminum guards or fine-meshed copper wire should be placed over them. The guards are now manufactured in the same widths as the gutters, which makes them easy to install by do-it-yourselfers. Plastic guards for downspouts help to keep them from clogging up.

Copper gutters are considered the finest because they are not subject to rust and will last a lifetime, but they cost two to four times as much as aluminum and may need strengthening and realigning periodically.

The way to check gutters for realignment is to stand back from the house and make sure that they run at a slight downward angle towards the downspouts. If there are downspouts at either end, the gutters must come to a slight peak in the middle. Streak marks on the gutters indicate that the water overflows in periods of heavy rain, which means they need realignment, or cleaning out, or both.

At the foot of each downspout, there should be splash blocks or drainage tiles to carry the water away from the house, and the ground should slope at the rate of one inch per foot for a distance of six to eight feet. The natural settling of earth over a period of years may have changed the original grading to such an extent that more fill should be brought in to correct it. Stepping stones of tiles or flat rock placed down the slope will help to make the water go in the direction you wish. Or you might attach a "roll-out drain" to the downspout: the weight of the water causes this to unroll to a distance of eight feet, and when it is dry, it rolls up again.

Checking the drainage

If these various measures do not correct your water problem, it could be that the below-grade drainage pipe has become clogged or the tiles have broken. The only way to determine this is to excavate, and you may have to go down as far as six feet. The type of soil around the house can be a factor in poor drainage. If it is heavy in clay, there is little natural absorption, and water, seeking its own level, will go into your basement if that is its easiest route. For a problem as serious as this, you need the help of a waterproofing expert. It is even possible that an underground spring is the culprit.

While the earth is dug up next to the foundation, it is advisable to have the exterior wall gone over with parget (cement) and tar. Some contractors also now apply a rigid vapor barrier against the foundation wall before the earth is replaced. A cove at the point where floor and walls join is as important on the outside as it is inside the house.

You should be aware that there are more fast-talking operators in the waterproofing field than in almost any other phase of construction. For this reason make sure before you get involved with work as complicated and costly as this that it is really necessary and that the man you hire has a reputation for skill and reliability.

Even when medicine this strong has been resorted to, some basements still get seepage. Then the only solution may be to install a sump pit and a pump—one that works automatically —in the wettest corner of the basement. Many houses also require a drain system that ties into the sump pump catch basin.

If your house has a crawl space, even if only under a porch, it is important to check this and make sure it is well ventilated. If there is a moisture problem because of the lay of the land or some other inescapable factor, a vapor barrier should be laid over the earth. Coated-roll roofing or felt or polyethylene can be easily put down and secured with concrete blocks around the edges.

Many of the insulation checkpoints previously mentioned also affect the amount of moisture in your house. A well-vented attic, for example, will also be a drier attic, and by checking all flashings over vents, exhausts, and chimneys, you are eliminating potential or actual water leaks as well as energy leaks. This also applies to caulking and weatherstripping windows and doors, especially the overhead frames.

The three areas above ground most subject to moisture damage are bathrooms, kitchen, and laundry, because of the use of hot water in all three. To avoid a buildup of excess moisture, ventilate these areas frequently, in all seasons, by means of opened windows or exhaust fans, or both.

Be sure to check the flashing around dormer windows, soffits, and fascias under the roof overhang and the roof itself. Vents in the soffit are important to permit escape of moisture-laden air. If damp spots appear on the walls or ceiling of a finished attic, it can only mean that water is coming in somehow from the roof or walls.

Check the roof

The condition of your roof should be checked periodically for its overall condition and possible leaks. If bad spots are repaired, shingles replaced if necessary, and small leaks stopped up, reroofing may be delayed indefinitely.

If your house is roofed with asphalt shingles, the most common type used, danger signals to look for are (1) bare spots where the asphalt granules have washed away and (2) "fish-mouthing"—shingles split and curled or puffed up on the ends. The average life of an asphalt shingle roof is only about fifteen years. If there is only one layer of shingles on the roof, a second layer may be placed over it, but if the roof already has two layers, both should be removed, for the weight of three layers would weaken the roof structure.

Before crude oil prices zoomed, asphalt shingles were used

for nearly all residential roofing because they were one of the least expensive materials (one-third the cost of slate), yet attractive and reasonably durable. However, being a crude-oil product, they are now far more costly, prices having increased anywhere from 25 to 117 percent, depending on the area of the country.

If your house has a slate roof, be thankful, for if kept in good condition, it will never have to be replaced. Such a roof should be rechecked every two or three years. When inspecting it, examine the ridges, which may need retarring, and keep an eye out for broken or split shingles. These may be replaced individually with much less expensive fiber glass, designed to resemble slate shingles so closely that any difference is not apparent when viewed from the ground.

Cedar shakes, comparable to slate in cost and durability, are back in fashion, but scarce and outrageously expensive. If not already fireproofed by the manufacturer, the wooden shingles should be dipped or sprayed with a fire-retardant chemical. They have the good self-insulating properties of all wood products and look very handsome. These shingles, too, can be individually replaced.

Shingles made to resemble cedar shakes are available in asphalt, vinyl-coated aluminum, and solid vinyl. These cost somewhat less than the real thing, and are very satisfactory.

Halfway between asphalt shingles and cedar or slate in cost are asbestos shingles, which will last up to forty years, if not walked on. But they are brittle, and in repairing an asbestos roof, this should be kept in mind.

Metal roofs are quite common in some rural areas and if repainted regularly (every three years) to prevent rust, will last twenty years or longer. Before repainting, any rust spots should be removed (naval jelly will do the job) and cracks or broken seams patched with roofing cement. Instead of paint, the roof can be sprayed or brushed with colored aluminum roof coating which reflects the sun's rays and therefore keeps the interior cooler. However, before the coating is applied, the roof must be clean, dry, and free from cracks or loose material, and any patched areas must be completely dry, well-brushed, and smooth. Also, avoid applying the coating if rain is forecast; coatings require from twelve to forty-eight hours to dry completely, and if rained on before dry, may blister. If on the other hand the coating dries too quickly in hot weather, it will not bond well.

Roof coatings may also be applied over felt or concrete roofs —over almost anything but asphalt shingles. They are particularly useful as protection for flat roofs and decks. Many of these are covered with metal but more with what is called slag roofing: five layers of coated tar paper and a final coat of gravel. If properly laid, such a roof can last twenty to twenty-five years and if during that time it springs a leak, is easily patched with roofing cement. But make sure any flat roof or deck has been sloped in such a way that water runs off after rains, for an accumulation of water can shorten the life of the roofing by fifty per cent.

Cheaper and less desirable roofing materials are asphalt roll (generally used on sheds but sometimes on flat roofs and decks), fiber glass, and plastic. The last two are used mainly over patio areas, carports, or permanent awnings, and sometimes over greenhouses. Some of these materials are poor in thermal resistance and, if not installed properly, are subject to leaks at the joints and nail holes.

Checking exterior walls

If areas in the siding show signs of water infiltration, besides correcting the cause, it will help to go over the exterior with a clear sealer. For brick, a silicon sealer is usually used.

One of the advantages in buying an older house is that its exterior may be constructed of materials now extremely costly to use in new home construction, such as brick, fieldstone, stucco-and-timber, cedar shakes, and slate for roofs.

Brick houses are now very much in demand, because brick has a lifetime finish and requires minimum maintenance. Also there is a graciousness and permanency about brick that has especial appeal in today's rapidly changing society.

The bricks should be examined to see if any have come loose, or if the mortar is cracked or loosened. If loose, bricks must be pointed up with new mortar, a costly job. It may also be worth-while to go over the surface with a clear silicon sealer, for protection against moisture penetration. But if you have an ivy-clad brick house, no matter how charming the ivy looks, better pull it down. The roots eat into the bricks and pock the surface. The same is true of other climbing vines.

The Tudor-style stucco-and-timber houses of the 1930s and 1940s are now much in demand, perhaps because of their old-fashioned appeal. Stucco is a dying art; few masons are trained to apply it. This is one disadvantage of such houses: when the stucco is in need of repair, it will be difficult to find someone to do the job properly, and when found, his services will not be cheap.

If your house now has a frame (clapboard) siding and you are debating whether to fix this up or add a new siding over it, the first step should be to examine the wood. See if it merely needs a good paint job, or if the wood itself is in bad condition. If all it needs is painting, the many easy-to-apply paints now on the market make this a good do-it-yourself job. If you do not have the time or inclination for house-painting, it is the kind of summer job students can handle.

But before painting, carefully look for moisture damage around windows, doors, under downspouts and eaves, at the bases of porch columns, around exhaust vents, and so on. Old paint that has cracked, peeled, or "alligatored" should be scraped or sanded off, and cracks and scratches filled and sanded before new paint is applied.

For use on natural wood, oil-base paint is better than latex paint, because the latter does not always bond well to wood. Also, oil-base paint has more elasticity to withstand the dimensional changes of wood in different seasons. This does not apply necessarily to reconstituted wood—Masonite (textured hardboard), or particle board. If a painting contractor is hired, the contract should specify which paint or paints are to be used, not only the type, but brand name and style number, and exactly what surfaces are to be refinished. Sometimes a new coat of paint will peel because it is of slightly different composition, produced by a different manufacturer, than the original coat.

If the siding is of redwood, cypress, or cedar, and these woods have been left unpainted to weather to natural grayish tones, they may need nothing more than a coat of sealer for protection. If you are not satisfied with the weather-grayed color, a stain may be applied to bleach the wood lighter or make it darker in tone, or the siding may be painted. Some stains also weatherproof (seal) the surface. Check the label to determine this.

Wood is rated the best of self-insulating materials. So even if upon inspection you decide the siding is too far gone to be worth the labor cost of extensive scraping, sanding, and perhaps replacing sections with new clapboard, there is no reason to take it down. Put insulation over the old frame exterior, and the new siding on top of that, and retain the advantages of the natural insulation of wood and the added exterior insulation. Even if the old wood is rotten or infected with termites, it can be treated to rid it of the insects, and bad sections can be filled in or replaced with construction-grade lumber.

Other types of siding

Exterior siding is available in easy-to-install panels made of reconstituted wood products of various kinds as well as several types of so-called maintenance-free materials. The reconstituted wood includes hardboard (Masonite is the best-known brand name), and particle board. Both are moisture-resistant and easier to saw, nail, put in place, and paint than natural wood. Many homeowners elect to do the painting even when the siding is put up by a contractor. Plywood is also available in exterior sidings, some with redwood veneer.

Among the many "maintenance-free" sidings on the market, aluminum continues as one of the most popular, though costs for all metal sidings have soared. Many new textures and finishes, in over twenty colors, are offered. The colors are baked on, a two-coat permanent finish which never needs painting (though if your house already has aluminum siding, and you do not care for the color, it can be covered over with a latex paint).

Some aluminum panels look so much like wood that they must be examined carefully to detect the difference. Good-quality aluminum siding should last thirty to forty years without attention.

The thermal property of aluminum is debatable. Some claim that it is poor, inferior to that of reconstituted wood or solid vinyl, and much below that of natural wood. Others assert it has good thermal resistance because of its reflective qualities. Used with three-and-one-half-inch wall insulation, it is more than adequate. Aluminum does often show dents, and color may fade on the sides with southern exposure, but a single panel can be replaced without having to redo an entire wall and with a fresh coat of paint applied all over, the siding will look like new.

Other "maintenance-free" siding materials include solid vinyl in clapboard effect, asbestos shingles, and compressed mineral fiber, of which Stratolite is one brand name. Vinyl siding is proclaimed to have better insulating properties than aluminum, and to be dent-resistant, though it must be installed with care to avoid warping due to expansion. The manufacturers of Mastic, one brand of solid vinyl siding, point out that it can be washed with soap and water to remove stains, does not absorb or retain moisture like wood, or sweat like metal, helps to deaden sound, and is fire-resistant. The Stratolite manufacturers say of their siding that it will not rot, shrink, curl, or split; can be put up with simple carpenter's tools (the same used for wood); and that it, like vinyl siding, is fire-resistant and vermin-proof.

Builders are experimenting with other siding materials, including masonry walls, precast concrete panels, and solid cement blocks.

To insulate masonry sidings effectively, walls totaling ten to twelve inches in thickness are urged, with an outer wall four to five inches, an inner structure (which could be of cement blocks) three to four inches, and a cavity between where poured insulation of two to three inches could be added. However, to reduce cost, walls totaling eight inches in thickness with one-by-three furring and one-inch insulation are considered satisfactory.

For brick, two-inch foamboard insulation may be used in the cavity between the outer brick wall and the inner finished wall. In a test of four exterior wall finishes, brick walls constructed in this manner proved, on a day when the outdoor temperature was at ninety-five degrees Fahrenheit, to have heat absorption only one-ninth that of a comparable structure with insulated aluminum siding.

Another method for insulating brick calls for a four-inch brick exterior, two inches of loose insulation poured into the cavity between brick and framing, and next to this, concrete or cement block four inches thick. Over the concrete blocks go drywalls attached to furring strips.

These methods are costly but might be kept in mind when planning any new structure to be attached to your home.

Checking for insect damage

While inspecting the house for energy and moisture leaks, also check for signs of insect or rodent infestation.

Termites are the greatest worry since they can seriously damage a house's basic structure. The most obvious signs are tiny mud tunnels on and inside the wood or on the masonry foundation. Also look for rotten or spongy areas in the wood. The places to examine are studs, joists, support beams, any place where wood meets earth, and especially dark, damp areas. Basement window frames, basement stairs, porch steps, porch floors and supports, and any wooden structure around the crawl space should be examined. Occasionally termites may be found in furniture purchased from a thrift shop or at an auction, or in closets through which water pipes run.

Since one seldom sees the insects themselves, the best test is to poke with a pocketknife or screwdriver around any suspicious-looking areas. If the point goes in too easily, you have probably found a termite tunnel. The only time of year when the insects themselves are likely to appear is on a single day in spring when they swarm, and if you are ever present at this time, you will never forget it. Suddenly the air is full of flying silvery insects, thousands of them. But this lasts only an hour or so, then they disappear for another year. They may, however, leave a trail of hundreds of silvery wings on sills or floor.

Many firms advertise "termite insurance," which includes annual inspection. Currently the favorite treatment is "soil poisoning"—injection of a chemical, chlordane, in the area immediately surrounding the house. This is said to be effective for ten years, even longer if the soil is relatively dry and absorbent, and if the chemical is spread properly, annual inspection should not be necessary. Chlordane can be purchased in hardware stores and injected by the homeowner, but, like any poison, it must be handled carefully and not allowed to harm children or pets. Because it is injected in the soil, the chemical could be injurious to a pet that paws up the earth.

Before hiring a professional pest-control service, whether for termites or other unwelcome intruders, carefully check its record with your local Better Business Bureau. A contract should be signed with a warranty clause of free additional treatment if infestation recurs within twelve months.

For new construction, termite-proof wood can be used in any structure near the earth. And to avoid termite penetration, make certain that there is no wood structure within six inches of the ground. This applies to siding of any material, since some wood is always used in the substructure.

Other insects that can cause structural damage include the wood borer (sometimes called a powder post beetle, because it leaves a trail of white powder) and carpenter ants, whose calling card is a pile of sawdust where there should not be any.

Carpenter ants, the biggest and blackest ants known, usually enter the house through the roof, dropping from trees, but occasionally come from the earth. Flying ants (sometimes mistaken for termites) and carpenter bees are not so much to be feared, and can be destroyed with ordinary insect sprays.

Yellow jackets, hornets, and bees are more of a threat to the inhabitants of the house than the house itself. For some people their stings can be lethal. Their mud-structured nests are usually easy to spot, under eaves or inside the wood frames of old screen. When you go after them with inspect spray, be well protected, for they will fight for their lives.

Other unwanted visitors include birds, mice, squirrels and other rodents, cockroaches, little red ants, mosquitoes, flies, and moths. The best way to keep out birds and rodents is to make sure there are no cracks where they can enter. If insects cannot be exterminated with ordinary drugstore preparations, it is best to have it done professionally.

CHAPTER 3

Preventive Maintenance:
Heating, Airconditioning, Plumbing, Wiring

In the last decade, central airconditioning has come to be considered almost as important as a furnace, depending somewhat on the region of the country.

Most homes built in the last twenty years have hot-air systems with ducts through which either hot or cold air may be directed; adding both airconditioning and humidity control to these systems is fairly simple. Next in popularity are baseboard hot-water heaters: hot water carried through copper coils enclosed in louvered baseboard units. To add airconditioning to this system is more difficult, but separate ducts can be placed alongside the hot-water units using the same routing system.

Many homeowners who are still getting along with the old-fashioned type of hot water-radiator heating system wonder whether they would be justified in changing to a new system. To add airconditioning to these older houses is extremely complicated, and to rip out radiators and install a completely new "climate control" system may prove staggeringly expensive, if not impossible. Walls may have to be torn down, the structure weakened. Even to retain radiators and add airconditioning will cost from $3,000 up to $6,000, depending on how ductwork must be routed. Usually an attic unit is installed with ducts directed down through closets and hallways. A second unit probably will be necessary for the main floor.

To replace only the furnace (the average life is twenty to twenty-five years), assuming radiators or ductwork are in good operative condition, may cost $1,000. But with today's high fuel costs, its replacement may be justified on the basis of efficiency. When the renovation is arranged through the fuel oil company, payments often are simply added to the monthly fuel bill.

A further justification for updating your heating-airconditioning system is that it will increase the resale value of your home. "Climate control" is an item that rates high on the most-wanted list with home buyers.

Types of heating systems

How long it may be before a solar-energy system is perfected for extensive use in private residences is a matter of controversy. However, it is widely predicted that by the end of the century, use of solar heat will grow as fast as did airconditioning in the last twenty-five years.

Solar units already are being used to heat the water in swimming pools and commercially by laundry and car-wash firms. One of the research scientists at the National Science Foundation has said that "if we could use 1 percent of the solar heat which falls on this country, it would equal all the energy we now consume."

In a solar-energy system, collectors trap and hold the sun's heat, which in turn heats water that can be circulated through a hydronic system; or air can be blown over the heated water in a hot-air system. But at present solar heat alone cannot do the job; an alternate fuel source is required for cloudy days, and if not properly engineered for each building, the cost of operation could be prohibitive and the results unsatisfactory as well.

Research is going forward on both the private and federal

Residential Energy Consumption

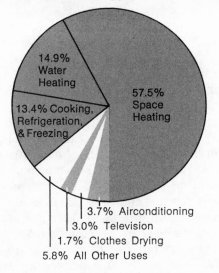

14.9% Water Heating

13.4% Cooking, Refrigeration, & Freezing

57.5% Space Heating

3.7% Airconditioning
3.0% Television
1.7% Clothes Drying
5.8% All Other Uses

Sources: Office of Science and Technology, Air-Conditioning and Refrigeration Institute

level, but clearly it will be some time before solar heat can be used in the average residence. One California builder has combined hydronic hot-water heating with the use of solar roof traps for heating apartment houses, a system that may later be adapted for private homes.

An advantage of hot-water heating systems is that they supply both heat and hot water with the same boiler. For a family that uses a great deal of hot water, this can mean considerable savings. Also, many persons believe that with hot-water heating, the air inside a house is less dry, which is better for health (unless, of course, the hot-air system includes a humidifier).

Besides hot-air and hot-water systems, some houses have radiant floor heating; others are heated by individual wall units with a separate thermostat for each room, eliminating the need for a furnace.

To change from one type of heating system to another is a major undertaking, requiring long and careful consideration. Opinions and estimates should be sought from a number of experts before taking the plunge. If the existing system is any other kind but hot air, it might be better to retain it and add an attic air conditioner with ducts routed down through the second floor.

Whatever type of furnace you have, it should be cleaned and checked for efficiency each autumn by a plumber or heating repairman. Many oil companies include such inspection as part of their service.

Electric heat, promoted widely a decade ago, is now recognized as by far the most costly of heating fuels, though rates vary in different localities. Any house already equipped with electric baseboard or floor heating must have the most thorough insulation. In addition, the thermostat should be lowered in each room when it is not in use and throughout the house during the night. No longer are separate electric baseboard or space heaters recommended for heating new additions or enclosed porches if tying into the main system is possible. The cost per room has been known to run $150 per heating season. Such heat is feasible only for a sun room, where in sunny winter weather the heat can be turned off entirely during daylight hours.

No matter which fuel is used, when a house is well insulated, spectacular savings are sometimes possible. In a test made at the National Bureau of Standards, it was proved that in a properly insulated house, with the outdoor temperature at twenty-one degrees Fahrenheit and the furnace heat turned off during the night, the indoor temperature dropped only six degrees.

The owner of a new house in Annandale, Virginia, was convinced of the value of optimum insulation when he found that in his new home, built with insulation meeting highest industry standards, his winter heating bill was only $32 a month, in comparison with monthly bills averaging $69 in his much smaller former home.

The same rule applies, of course, to airconditioning, and with the prospect of more brownouts during the summer heat waves, every precaution should be taken to reduce electric current as much as possible in the home.

Checking airconditioners

Room airconditioners and central airconditioning units should be checked before the start of the summer season. Room airconditioners sometimes acquire rust from exposure

Design for Cooler Living
Without Airconditioning

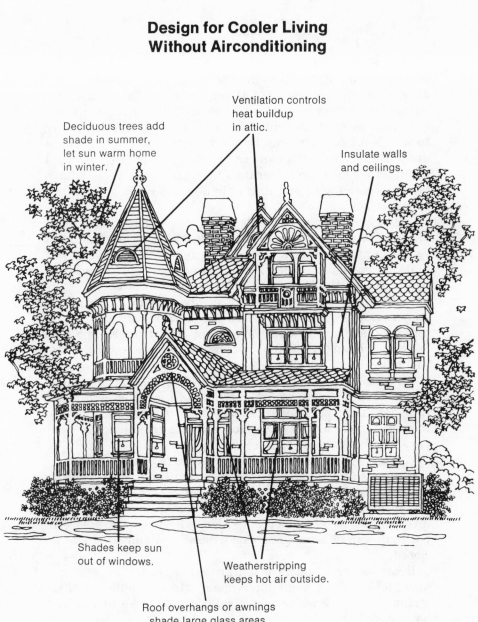

Ventilation controls heat buildup in attic.

Deciduous trees add shade in summer, let sun warm home in winter.

Insulate walls and ceilings.

Shades keep sun out of windows.

Weatherstripping keeps hot air outside.

Roof overhangs or awnings shade large glass areas.

during winter months, causing squeaks and groans when the unit is in operation. Rubbing the shaft with a rust solvent may solve the problem, but if the noise continues, the unit should be checked by a mechanic to see if there is a bad bearing or if the shaft is bent. Icing of the fins is another thing to watch out for. This can be caused by nothing more than a dirty filter, which you can easily clean yourself. Or it could mean a leak in the refrigerant system, or that the coils have become coated with oily lint. If in doubt, have it attended to by a serviceman.

Icing or a clogged filter also could cause a central airconditioner to operate at reduced efficiency. It is best to call a repairman to give the system a thorough examination if you find that rooms are much hotter than they should be according to the setting. Most warranties cover the cost of new parts for five years, and there is always a chance that a leak has developed somewhere. Also, the outdoor coils of the system may be clogged with leaves or other debris. Even slight icing cuts down the efficiency of operation, resulting in higher fuel bills.

An automatic timer that turns off the central air conditioner during the night, when temperatures drop, and turns it on again at a set time in the morning, is a means of economizing. Timers are also available on some room airconditioners; ask about this if you are buying a new one.

A simple trick to reduce energy leaks, if yours is a central system, is to cover the hot air registers in summer. If they do not have baffles that can be closed, cut cardboard to fit over the openings. One engineer believes that this can cut airconditioning costs by 10 percent. Also, whenever a fireplace is not in use, in either summer or winter, its damper should be closed.

Room airconditioners often are responsible for considerable "leakage" through their metal wings. Apply weatherstripping or glue white acoustical tile over these to keep out hot air.

Pipes and plumbing

Water damage inside a home is often due to worn-out pipes or plumbing fixtures. This may show itself first in the form of blistering or peeling paint in the ceiling of a room immediately below or on the walls adjacent to piping. To repaint, paper, or panel over such walls is a waste of time and money, for sooner or later the water damage will become so much worse that the newly finished walls will have to be redone.

As leaks become more serious, damp spots or standing water can be noticed. If left too long, the water will cause cracks, loosening of plaster, and rotting of wood.

In addition to such damage, the effect on your water bill can be costly, and if a hot water pipe is affected, your utility bill will also rise considerably. Leaking faucets should be repaired promptly. Often nothing more is needed than a new washer. Sometimes, however, the fitting is worn and a new part or even a completely new faucet is needed. These are not costly and a do-it-yourselfer should be able to make the change without much trouble.

Since there is always the possibility that a serious leak could develop in pipes or fittings, make sure that you know the location of all water valves, also of meter and control boxes for electricity, gas, and water. Never go into a flooded basement before cutting off the electricity.

Places to check for leaks are behind toilets, under wash-basins, the kitchen sink, and around the base of the washing machine and dryer. It is always possible that the fixtures themselves have aged and need replacing. But the fault is just as likely to lie with the piping.

In houses built thirty to fifty years ago, only galvanized or lead piping was used, and the buildup of rust through the years not only loosens fittings, allowing leaks at the joints, but decreases the apertures inside the pipes until only a trickle of water can get through. This affects water pressure, especially on upper floors, and especially hot water lines. (Hot water is more corrosive than cold, and hot water pipes are usually the first to become defective.) In an extreme case, when water is being used in the kitchen, none at all comes out of second-floor faucets.

If you have reason to believe the piping in your house is twenty-five to thirty years old, probably at least some of it needs replacing. This should always be done before any new bath, kitchen, or laundry fixtures are installed.

During the past twenty years, copper piping has been used exclusively in new houses and as a replacement in older houses. It is noncorrosive and will last a lifetime. Of the two types, M and L, the latter is preferable, being heavier, especially for use from the basement up to the first floor, the section that receives the hardest wear.

Increasingly in recent years, rigid vinyl (plastic) pipe is finding acceptance. It is much less costly than copper, and is popular with do-it-yourselfers because it can be cut with an ordinary saw and the joints can be connected simply by brushing both pipe and socket with special adhesive, twisting them together, and letting them set until completely dry.

It is not necessary to replace all the piping at once, though generally it pays to do so, obviating a similar job later. But if only some of the pipes are to be replaced, the horizontal ones are most important because they rust more readily (gravity pulls down the accumulated rust in the vertical piping).

In very old houses, lead plumbing may have been used from the bath tub and toilet to the main sewer stack, and when a lead pipe springs a leak, it cannot be repaired. In remodeling this type of bath, all lead piping must be replaced. However, the four-inch main stack through which all water and waste flows down is nearly always of cast iron and rarely needs replacing.

Water pipe replacement is usually begun in the basement, largely because this is where the pipes are most accessible, and begins with the line from the hot water tank. Most pipes can be snaked through the walls or ceilings, so that there is not much need to tear out walls or floors.

The sewer stack usually has a vent on the roof of the house (if it does not, it should have) and goes down to the basement, where it empties into a large drain leading to the main public sewer, ten feet below street level, or to septic fields for homes with their own septic systems.

If the water heater is more than ten years old, it probably needs replacement. Not only will it grow less efficient with age, but it will become subject to leaks and rust. For most families, a forty-gallon tank is adequate, if gas-fired, but if fired by oil or electricity, a tank with a capacity of fifty or sixty gallons may be needed. The recovery with gas heating is so much quicker that a smaller tank is adequate. A relief valve is important for any type of water heater in case the thermostat should fail to turn off the burner at any time. This will relieve pressure and prevent the water from reaching boiling point.

The tank should be drained periodically to get rid of heat-robbing sediment. This will aid recovery and also help to lower water-heating costs. Since operational cost increases with the distance water must travel, it could be a saving to have a small space water heater in the kitchen or an upstairs bathroom. Some savings is also possible by turning off the hot water heater at night; if the tank is well-insulated, there should be enough hot water for use in the morning, when the heater can be turned on for an hour, and, if no one is to be at home during the day, can then be turned off again.

Wiring and lighting

The increased use of small as well as large electrical appliances today means that in nearly all private homes, a minimum of 100 amperes and preferably 150 amperes is needed. Not more than 80 percent of the total electrical capacity should be in use at the same time. The chart on page 66, showing the amount of current required for various appliances, indicates how easily this could be exceeded.

In selecting any new appliances for your home, look for those which will give you the greatest efficiency in terms of amperes or watts used.

There is a growing movement that has as its goal the labeling of each piece of equipment with its BTU-watt ratio, to show how much energy is consumed per watt-ampere. For example, some room airconditioners provide 6,000 BTUs, yet only consume 7.5 amperes, while the usual 6,000 BTU airconditioners require 9.9 amperes.

There are many small ways of conserving energy with the appliances you already have. Three appliances that consume a great deal of energy and give off corresponding heat are the kitchen range, the dishwasher, and the clothes dryer. In summer, try to avoid using the range oven or broiler, remembering that baking and roasting will increase the cost of airconditioning your home. If you have a portable oven, use it on the patio, and do your broiling over an outdoor charcoal grill. When you must use the range, a kitchen exhaust fan will help to carry off excess heat.

Amperes Required for Appliances

Kitchen range	50
Clothes dryer	30
Hot water heater	30
Central airconditioning	30
Rotisserie-oven	15-20
15,000 BTU airconditioner	12
Iron	12
Washing machine	10-12
Dishwasher	10-12
Freezer	10-12
Toaster	11
Window airconditioner	7.5-10
Vacuum cleaner	7.5
Refrigerator with top freezer	7.5

Note: These are averages which vary according to the individual appliance.

The dishwasher gives off most heat during the drying cycle. If its door is opened, stopping the operation at this point, the dishes will dry themselves. As for the clothes dryer, you can economize in summer by hanging laundry on an outdoor line. There has been talk of the advantage of angling the vent of the clothes dryer indoors during winter so that the heat and moisture given off can be channeled into the house, but experts warn that this amount of moisture can be damaging to walls and ceiling.

The use of fluorescent light fixtures in place of incandescent wherever possible will cut down considerably on the energy load. Fluorescent lamps give off three to four times as much light per lumen (a method of measuring light capacity) as incandescents, and last ten times as long. The incandescent is, in fact, the least efficient of all bulbs. One four-foot-long, 40-watt fluorescent gives as much light as a 150-watt incandescent, and uses one-third as much electricity.

The disadvantages of fluorescents, besides their initial higher cost, are that they are not interchangeable, each size requiring its own special socket, and some give off light so greenish or bluish that colors, including human skin color, are distorted. The type of fluorescent called "soft white" gives a pinkish glow that emphasizes reds and pinks, but it

Use of Electricity by Appliances

	Average Wattage Consumed	Average Hours Of Use Per Year
Kitchen range	8,200	128
Clothes dryer	4,856	204
Self-cleaning oven	4,800	128
Water heater with quick recovery	4,474	1,075
Water heater	2,475	1,705
Microwave oven	1,500	200
Broiler-rotisserie	1,436	70
Portable space heater	1,322	133
Dishwasher	1,201	302
Frypan	1,196	187
Iron	1,008	144
Automatic washer	521	198
Vacuum cleaner	630	73
Frost-free freezer (14 cu. ft.)	615	2,974
Airconditioner (central)	566	887
Frost-free refrigerator (15 cu. ft.)	440	4,002
Hair dryer	381	37
Attic fan	370	786
Color TV	332	1,512
Radio/record player	109	1,000
Circulating fan	88	489

Source: Maryland Energy Policy Office

tends to gray cooler colors. Even better are those called "deluxe warm white," which are the closest to reflecting true color of any fluorescents. Ask to see a demonstration of the various fluorescent lights in an electrical supply house; this will help you to determine the best type for each situation.

If at present your electrical capacity is inadequate, having a 200-ampere line installed would be wise, for this will be ample for almost any house, even when all appliances operate electrically, and the difference in installation costs between a 150- and 200-ampere line is very small.

It is also important to avoid using appliances with high current requirements on the same circuit. The old-fashioned fuse box is rapidly being replaced with circuit breakers, because the latter cut off current instantly by thermostatic control, in case of overloads or short circuits. When the line is overloaded, a fuse will blow, but not quite as quickly, and in case of defective wiring, sparks could start a fire. Also, if too large a fuse is used for any circuit, damaging heat could build up on the line before the fuse blows.

Building codes require one outlet for every twelve feet of wall, or within six feet of any doorway, so that you should never need to use an extension cord exceeding six feet in length.

Chart the circuits

It is good to know which appliances and light fixtures are on which circuits. The easy way to determine this is to turn on all the lights at once, then one by one shut off a circuit and note which lights go off. This information should be written on a chart posted next to the circuit box. Next, obtain the same information for your appliances, but do not turn on all the heavy-load appliances simultaneously. If at some time you must change the wiring, to accommodate a new appliance or to remodel a room, you will know from this chart which circuits can take an additional load.

When remodeling a kitchen, the building code requires that a separate circuit be used for each major appliance, and even for smaller appliances that might be operated at the same time.

For each unit that operates at 220 volts, there must be a separate line to the circuit box. This would include an electric clothes dryer, an electric range, certain power tools, and also an airconditioner large enough to cool most of the first floor. It is, incidentally, more economical to operate an airconditioner of this size on a 220-volt than on a 115-volt line. Outlets for these appliances should be the three-pronged grounded type to help prevent shocks.

A main circuit breaker switch is a must for every home, because it instantly cuts off power if a short-circuit condition is caused by serious current leakage. It will, however, tolerate overloads for a short period, such as when an airconditioner or a freezer automatically switches on while other major appliances are drawing current.

Another safety device recommended for use in certain indoor areas and outdoors is a ground-fault circuit interrupter. The circuit breaker does not always cut off when leaks occur that are small enough to go through a 15-ampere fuse. Such leaks are called ground faults because the current, uninterrupted, flows to the ground through any path open to it, which could be a human body, and thus can cause dangerous electrical shocks. The interrupter can cut off such faulty circuits in as little as one-fortieth of a second, faster than a heartbeat. Such interrupters are recommended by the National Electrical Code as essential for all outdoor circuits but could be critical for circuits serving kitchen and workroom as well.

The main circuit-breaker panel should be near one of the entrances to the house so that it is easy to reach in emergencies, to cut off power, for example, in case of flooding or fire.

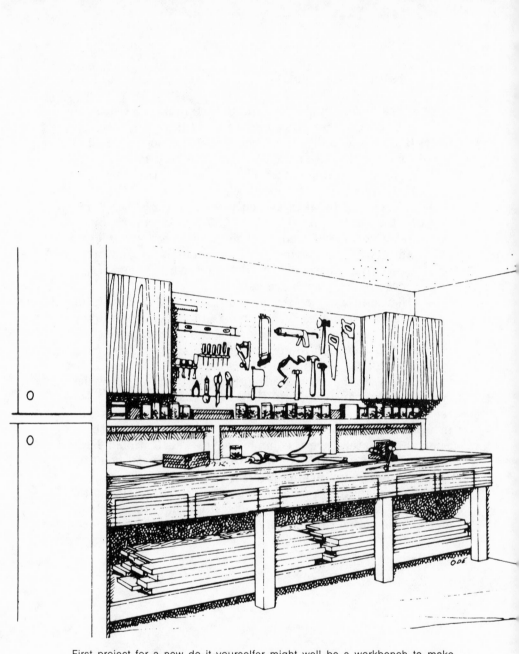

First project for a new do-it-yourselfer might well be a workbench to make future projects easier. This one is 10 feet long, and could be constructed at the back of a garage or in a basement.

CHAPTER 4

The Do-It-Yourself Revolution

A first-time visitor sitting at the downstairs bar would assume that this, like the rest of the handsome house, was the work of a custom builder. Resembling an old-time English pub, the room has walls of stippled plaster and dark-stained timber trim, a brick fireplace, and flooring of individually-laid tiles set in mortar. There is not a hint of the amateur to be detected anywhere in it.

The bar counter gleams with a nautical finish like the woodwork on a luxurious yacht, which is appropriate, as the owner is a Navy man. Rarely does one see detail work as careful as this even in the most expensive homes.

Yet everything in the finished basement was done by the owner himself with some help occasionally from his sons. The do-it-yourself project included finishing a downstairs guest bedroom, full-sized bath, and photographic dark room and utility room, in addition to the large L-shaped bar-recreation room which leads to a lower-level patio. The owner even did the wiring, plumbing, and brickwork himself, although he had no training in any of these skills. How long did it take him? Working only on weekends, approximately one year.

Rare are the do-it-yourselfers who have the combination of technical skill, patience, and persistence to complete a project of this dimension, and most should not even try. At the outset, the pleasure of creativity and the saving in labor costs are attractive prospects to a handy homeowner. But when all the work must be done in spare time, sometimes in the midst of family arguments or with young children getting in the way and raising the specter of injuring themselves in the process, even a skilled do-it-yourselfer cannot always perform effectively. And when the work is not done proficiently, the results could detract rather than add to the value of the house.

"Handyman's special"

When the young couple purchased a house advertised as a "handyman's special," they looked forward to modernizing this peeling, decrepit cottage mostly with their own hands. It was an almost square frame building, constructed originally by a carpenter for his own home. It looked like nothing much either outside or inside, but it was surrounded by an acre and a half of land, had a fireplace and four good-sized rooms with a half-bath downstairs, and four bedrooms and a full bath upstairs.

The interior walls were of the cheapest grade of plywood nailed direct to the studs, and though they bought a "textured paint," which the manufacturer claimed would cover any surface with just one coat, giving the effect of stippled plaster, they found this assertion to be decidedly exaggerated. Their plywood still looked like cheap plywood barely covered with paint. They finally paid a contractor to install new dry walls throughout the house at a cost of $1,200, though they did all the interior painting themselves.

Rewiring of the house also had to be done professionally, and cost $916. They rented an electric sander to refinish the floors themselves, but never having handled such a machine before, they found it harder to control than anticipated, and the dents it left in the wood convinced them too late that they should have hired a professional to do that job, too.

The "full bath" upstairs required complete remodeling. The slope of the roof was such that the husband could not stand up to take a shower, so they had the roof raised by means of a dormer window at an installation cost of $750. They considered themselves lucky to find a footed bathtub in a junk yard for $25. Although the tub had only three feet, it was far better than the rusted and stained existing tub. In place of the missing foot, they shored up the tub with bricks on the side against the wall. For a shower, after diligent searching they found in a catalog a spray spigot for $53 that could be installed on the wall with a bar. But when they tried putting up melamine tile board around the tub, they concluded that for this to be advertised as "easy to install yourself" was misleading.

The wife described that effort: "Here's a huge, completely rigid, curved piece that you have to hoist up onto the wall while you have thick gook running down over everything, and when you get it against the wall, you find it doesn't fit properly, so you have to take it down, gook and all, to figure out what's wrong, then start all over."

After intensive shopping, they found slightly damaged kitchen cabinets in the basement of a supply house, but installing the upper cabinets (which, even though damaged, cost $90 each) proved far more difficult than expected. Two male friends came to help, but it took the three men nearly three hours to get the two wall cabinets in place and fastened to studs, with quite a few expletives filling the air meantime.

Despite all the difficulties already encountered and those that they now realize still lie ahead, the couple feels a sense of accomplishment from having made something livable out of such an unlikely-looking house. They have rounded up friends to take part in a "painting party," to help paint the exterior of the house. A contractor has been hired to add a screened side porch, which they hope will be the first of two wings, one on either side of the cottage.

Painting is the one do-it-yourself job that anyone can do—that is, by observing the basic rules and making use of the proper equipment. This is not to say that the hundreds of other items advertised as do-it-yourself specials should be ignored, or that they cannot be used by amateurs. In a time when labor accounts for up to two-thirds of the cost of any home renovation, anything that the owners can do, and do well, is more than worth the effort. Perhaps the watchword is "go slow"—do not undertake any more than you can do without strain in your free hours; then proceed one step at a time, and each time only after careful study of the best way to do the job.

In most cases, compromise is the best solution. Hire a contractor or subcontractors for part of the work, and stick to those tasks you know you can do competently. When husband and wife have skills that can be applied to any small or large home-improvement project, they will probably lavish on it far more care and attention to details than a hired professional for whom time is money.

The importance of a good workroom

However small or large the job, it can be done more efficiently if you have a private, well-ventilated, and well-lighted place in which to work. This is true even for painting jobs. You need a place to store paints, thinner, brushes, dropcloth, paint stirrers, and any other necessary equipment, and also space in which to mix paints and afterward clean the brushes and rollers. And even a homeowner with little do-it-yourself ambitions will occasionally need to use such basic tools as hammer, screwdriver, pliers, and saw.

The best place for a workroom usually is in the basement, though it could be at one end of the garage, or in a converted pantry. A worktable (or workbench, as it is more commonly called) is absolutely essential. This can be nothing more than wide planks laid on two sawhorses, but a long table of hardboard or plywood fastened to permanent legs is better. Above this should be pegboard, or shelves, or both. Empty pickle jars can be used to hold small items such as nails, screws, and staples. If the workbench has drawers, so much the better. Or a narrow shelf could be installed underneath it, but make sure that the shelf would not interfere with knee space. Making such a workbench might be the first of a homeowner's do-it-yourself projects.

It is all too easy to go overboard when purchasing tools. Several hundred dollars can be spent without even trying, especially if one becomes fascinated by power tools. These are among the do-it-yourself specials which often benefit the seller more than the buyer. It is best for the amateur to begin with only the most essential tools, adding more as he finds he needs them. Power tools can always be rented.

Comparatively inexpensive but extremely useful equipment a homeowner should acquire includes a carpenter's level, a fold-up carpenter's rule for taking measurements, a caulking gun, a staple gun kit with inserts in assorted sizes, a tack hammer and heavy-duty hammer (and goggles to wear when hammering materials that could shatter), screwdrivers ranging from fine to heavy, and both a fine-toothed and a coarse-toothed saw. Besides brushes, you may want a sprayer for paint. Also keep on hand linseed oil and naval jelly for removing rust from tools and machine oil for lubrication. For the garden, you will need different types of pruning shears, spray guns, a hoe, and hand cultivators.

The innumerable household helps such as adhesives, insecticides, and cleaning fluids should also be kept in the workroom, in cabinets that can be locked to prevent small children from getting at any dangerous products.

The room should not only have good light, ventilation, and outlets for use of power tools, but also if possible direct access to the outdoors. Be sure to store any flammable or combustible items away from heat or other fire hazard. This particularly applies to oil-base paints, stains, and thinners. Throw out used paint rags—they are too hazardous to be worth keeping. Absorbent paper toweling in many cases can be used as paint rags and disposed of after use.

Indoor painting

There are many new paint products that do an almost magical job. But before you purchase paint, be sure that you are getting the right kind for your particular project. If the salesclerk waiting on you does not seem to know the difference, find someone else in the store who can advise you.

For interior walls, vinyl latex paint goes on easily with a roller, dries so quickly that two coats can be applied in the same day if necessary, has almost no odor, and is not flammable. However, because it goes on so easily, and is thinned with water, the tendency often is to spread the paint too thin.

Make sure that the surface is properly prepared before beginning to paint. If the walls and/or woodwork are badly soiled, they should be washed before a new coat of paint is added, using trisodium phosphate in the water. (Several preparations containing this ingredient are available in supermarkets. Soilax and Spic and Span are brand names for two in wide distribution.) Latex paint does not adhere well to dirty or chalky surfaces. If you find spots of mildew, scrub them off, using household bleach and water. In rooms subject to moisture, a mildew-resistant paint might be used.

For wood trim, doors and other surfaces where enamel is advisable, there is now acrylic or alkyd semigloss enamel, which is thinned with only a very small amount of water rather than turpentine or odorless thinner. This enamel goes on easily, leaving no brush marks—the chief drawback of oil-base enamel—and produces a hard, scrubbable surface. Such enamel and polyester-epoxy coatings are both recommended for kitchens, bathrooms, and any wood surface subject to a great deal of grime and grease, or moisture. In any home with children, make sure that all paints, including enamels, are lead-free.

Before going to the store, figure out how much paint you need, and also give considerable thought to choice of color. (The psychological and dimensional effects of color will be discussed in subsequent chapters.) Estimating the amount needed for walls is easy. Measure the perimeter of the room, that is, the total length of the four walls, and multiply this figure by the height of the room to get the total number of square feet. Do not deduct for windows unless there are more than four of them or unless they measure more than a total of 100 square feet. When estimating the amount of paint required for ceiling or floor, simply multiply the length of the room by the width.

The labels on some cans of paint tell how many square feet a gallon of the paint will cover. If the label does not give this information, ask the salesman, for some paints provide more extensive coverage than others. If the salesman does not know the answer offhand, the store will have a chart that contains this information. If one wall is to be painted a different color than others, you will, of course, calculate its dimensions separately.

The enamel for wood trim always seems to go farther than flat paint. Simply count the number of doors, windows,

What Interior Paint to Use . . . and Where

	Semi-Gloss Latex	Flat Paint—Latex	Flat Paint—Alkyd Type	Semi-Gloss Alkyd	Gloss Enamel—Alkyd	Rubber Base Paint (not Latex)	Interior Varnish	Shellac	Wax (Liquid or Paste)	Wax (Emulsion)	Stain	Wood Sealer	Floor Varnish	Floor Paint or Enamel	Aluminum Paint	Sealer or Undercoater	Metal Primer	Cement Base Paint	Clear Urethane	Catalyzed Enamel
Dry Walls	●	●	●	●	●			○				○				○				●
Plaster Walls & Ceiling	●	●	●	●	●	○										○				●
Wall Board	●	●	●	●	○	○										○				●
Wood Paneling	●		●	●	○	○	○	○	○		○	○							○	○
Kitchen & Bathroom Walls	●			●	●	○										○				○
Wood Floors						○			○	○	●	●	○	●	●				○	○
Concrete Floors						○			●	●	○			○					○	○
Vinyl & Rubber Tile Floors									○	○										
Asphalt Tile Floors										○										
Linoleum									○	○	○		○	○						
Stair Treads						○		○			○	○	○	○					○	○
Stair Risers			●	●	●	○	○	○			○	○							○	○
Wood Trim	●		●	●	●	○	○	○	○		○					○			○	○
Steel Windows	●		●	●	●	○									○		○			○
Aluminum Windows	●		●	●	●	○									○		○			○
Window Sills	●				●	○	○													○
Steel Cabinets			●	●	●	○											○			○
Heating Ducts	●		●	●	●	○									○		○			○
Radiators & Heating Pipes	○		●	●	●	○									○		○			○
Old Masonry	○	○	○	○	○	○										○	○		○	○
New Masonry	●	●	●	●	●	○										○		○		●

◉ Black dot indicates that a primer or sealer may be necessary before the finishing coat (unless surface has been previously finished).

Source: National Paint and Coatings Association

When Painting With Roller

1. Use brush to paint two-foot-wide strip just below ceiling line, and also from ceiling to floor at corner.

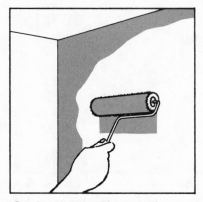

2. Beginning with upward movement of roller, paint a short distance from finished area and work toward it.

3. Move roller back and forth on area about two feet wide and three feet deep that has been coated with up and down strokes.

4. Brush paint onto areas at bottom of wall not reached by roller. Use cardboard guard when brushing near woodwork.

cabinets, and other parts to be covered. Paint salesmen are accustomed to making estimates when customers provide figures. Buy extra paint if in doubt and keep the sales slip handy in order to obtain credit if you return any of your purchases. It is less exasperating to have to take back an unopened can than to run out of paint when halfway through the job.

For some surfaces, you will need a primer coat, either to seal a porous surface, or because one coat is not likely to be enough. Metal needs a primer to protect against rust. Tell the paint salesman what kind of surface you will be painting and ask if a primer is advisable. If the surface needs a primer and you omit that step, the paint will simply be wasted—and using extra coats will not solve the problem. If raw wood is not sealed with shellac or some other clear glaze, no matter how many coats you add later, the surface may swell or remain rough, or knots in the wood may "bleed." If latex paint is applied to masonry before it has been waterproofed, the masonry cannot be successfully waterproofed later. It is important to buy a primer that goes with the finish paint, or the two might not bond properly.

Set up your equipment

Be sure you have all the necessary equipment before starting the job. This includes a ladder from which you can reach high surfaces comfortably, a large drop cloth to cover the entire floor (plastic drop cloths are quite inexpensive), a roller and a paint tray for walls, masking tape for edgings, and an assortment of good-quality brushes for woodwork and corners. Do not try to save pennies by purchasing cheaper brushes; instead, purchase the best quality, and if using oil-base paints, get a thinner or paint remover for cleaning the brushes afterward. When latex paint is used, brushes and roller are easy to wash out with water. If brushes are thoroughly cleaned after each use, the good ones will last a long time. Cheaper brushes, on the contrary, lose their bristles even when used the first time, and removing stray bristles from an otherwise smoothly painted wall can be a maddening interruption.

Before opening the first can of paint, make sure everything is in readiness. Besides washing grime and grease from the

When Painting Window

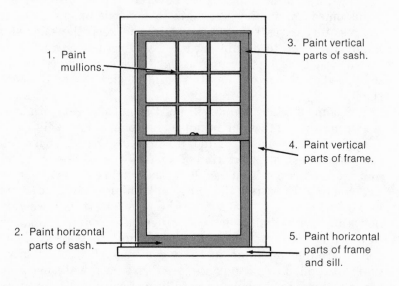

1. Paint mullions.

2. Paint horizontal parts of sash.

3. Paint vertical parts of sash.

4. Paint vertical parts of frame.

5. Paint horizontal parts of frame and sill.

surface to be painted, patch any loose places with spackle, fill cracks and nail holes with putty, and when spackle and putty are dry, sand down the surface until it is even and smooth. Fill cracks and knotholes in wood with plastic wood, which now comes in colors to match each of the most commonly used woods. Wipe off all sawdust or other loose particles with a damp cloth.

Remove all hardware before you begin painting, staining, or varnishing, whether you are working on doors, windows, cabinets, or furniture. Anything that is not to be covered completely with the same paint—even wooden knobs on cabinets—must be removed for the best results. Take all smaller objects such as drawers and cabinet doors to the workroom to be painted, where they can be left to dry out of everyone's way.

Wipe up any splatters or spills of paint before they dry. This is even more important with latex than oil-based paints, for once it is dry, latex paint has to be scraped off with a razor blade or paint scraper. This little tool should be kept handy in any case, for some spots always manage to escape notice until later, and when window frames must be repainted, some of the paint always seems to go onto the glass.

If paint is spilled on waxed wood floors, the best way to remove it is with a brush dipped in turpentine, quickly, then when the floor is dry, apply liquid wax to the spot with a clean cloth. If the paint dries on the floor, scrape or rub it away with steel wool dipped in solvent, and if this leaves whitish spots, apply Old English scratch cover very lightly with a cloth, then rub until you have removed the excess and matched the floor color as nearly as possible.

Wallcoverings

A revolution in wallcoverings has taken place in the last decade. The time was when it was all wallpaper and putting this up was a job that required not only skill, but also a very large measure of patience and fortitude. Further, the prelude often meant peeling and scraping old paper with the help of a steamer.

Today there are wallcoverings in many different materials, many of them prepasted and most pretrimmed, some with self-adhesive backing. A large number are "strippable." When any covering carries this notation, it means that when you wish to remove it, all you need to do is pull it away from the wall and off it comes like a bandaid.

Some wallcoverings require very careful wall preparation in advance; others can be put up over almost any wall that has been well washed and allowed to dry thoroughly.

Before purchasing any wallcovering, read carefully the instructions on the back of the sample. Unless a wallcovering carries the printed notation "strippable" or "dry-strippable" (which means the same thing), you can assume that removing it will be a dirty chore. Another important distinction: pre-pasted wallcoverings are not the same as those with self-adhesive backing. The former are impregnated with paste but must be dipped in water then placed on the wall while dripping wet; the latter have a paper backing that peels off.

But most vinyl-coated papers with self-adhesive backing are made to stick "forever" and when you try to pull them off, you may find the plaster coming off as well. However, certain self-adhesive wall coverings will strip off quite easily.

Some do-it-yourselfers who have papered many rooms declare that it is really easier to put up fabric-backed vinyl, applying the paste themselves, than to use any of the prepasted or self-adhesive coverings. The reason is that because fabric-backed vinyl is limp, it does not tear, and it is easy to slide into place on the wall, to fit the pattern in conformance with the adjoining strip.

The type of wallcovering you need and want will depend on the particular purpose for which you intend to use it.

Many vinyl-coated papers and fabrics are fire-resistant and are said to be "self-extinguishing." One of these would be a good choice for a kitchen wall.

There are many coverings with a shiny or reflective surface. The former is called the "wet look"; the latter is used in the same way as patterned mirror tiles. Those standing before a "mirror" paper can see a faint reflection of themselves, and the paper also reflects the room in such a way that it creates the illusion of multiplied space. They are effective for use on bathroom walls. However, such a foil or mirror paper should be put up by a professional; the wall must be very carefully prepared and a lining paper should be used underneath, for the least crack or bump will show. Further, they are so shiny that they are usually used only over small areas. (The same papers are useful for panels on room dividers, or for covering such pieces of furniture as a chest or end table.)

There are vinyl-coated papers, vinyl acrylic papers, fabric-backed vinyl wallcoverings, aluminum foil patterned papers (not the same as "mirror" papers), and papers that feel like velvet or silk. You can find wallcoverings that simulate the look of brick, stone, wood, cork, silver leaf, gold, grasscloth, burlap, moire satin, or fur. There are scenic papers to be purchased by the roll, and mural papers in sets of four panels, to transform a wall into a hazy garden scene or an oriental landscape, or give it the appearance of a hand-painted wall in a palace.

For the first-time do-it-yourselfer, it may be advisable to use either prepasted or self-adhesive paper until you get the knack of how to trim and put the paper in place.

Most papers and wallcoverings now come pretrimmed, but find out when making your purchase whether or not the width given is a pretrimmed width. Figure the amount you require by measuring the length and width of the space to be covered and multiplying those dimensions to get square feet. If the

How to Estimate Amount of Wallcovering Required

First measure the length, width, and height of the room. When you know the distance around the room (length + width × 2), use the chart to determine how many rolls of covering you will need. Deduct one single roll for every two ordinary-size doors or windows or every 30 square feet of opening. A roll of wallcovering contains 36 square feet.

Distance Around Room in Feet	Single Rolls for Wall Areas — Height of Ceiling —			Number of Yards for Borders	Single Rolls for Ceilings
	8 Feet	9 Feet	10 Feet		
28	8	8	10	11	2
30	8	8	10	11	2
32	8	8	10	12	2
34	8	10	10	13	4
36	8	10	10	13	4
38	10	10	12	14	4
40	10	10	12	15	4
42	10	12	12	15	4
44	10	12	14	16	4
46	12	12	14	17	6
48	12	12	14	17	6
50	12	14	14	18	6
52	12	14	16	19	6
54	14	14	16	19	6
56	14	14	16	20	8
58	14	16	18	21	8
60	14	16	18	21	8
62	14	16	20	22	8
64	16	18	20	23	8
66	16	18	20	23	10
68	16	18	20	24	10
70	16	20	20	25	10
72	18	20	20	25	12
74	18	20	22	26	12
76	18	20	22	27	12
78	18	20	22	27	14
80	20	20	24	28	14
82	20	22	24	29	14
84	20	22	24	30	16
86	20	22	24	30	16
88	20	22	26	31	16
90	20	24	26	32	18

Source: The Sherwin-Williams Company

wallcovering has a distinctive pattern, you will need more for matching. (Those with a geometric, plaid, or other bold design are difficult to match and usually should be put up by a professional.)

Preparing the walls

Whatever the type of wallcovering to be used, certain surface preparation of walls is essential beforehand. Any loose wallpaper must be removed and where the paper will not come off easily, the area must be sanded smooth around the edges of the paper. Fill cracks and holes with a spackling compound—these now come in cans ready to apply with a putty knife. It may be advisable to cover the paper with a coat of clear shellac or wall sizing—ask the salesman when you buy the wallcovering.

If the walls were previously painted, they must be washed down thoroughly and any loose paint scraped or peeled off. (If it is an old house, approach this job gingerly—in houses built before 1950, the paint may contain lead, so keep children out of the room until it has been cleaned up thoroughly.) If a vinyl covering is to be put up, wash the walls with a disinfectant. It is recommended that enameled walls be washed with a solution of trisodium phosphate, then rinsed with clear water.

If you are putting vinyl-treated wallcovering on any kind of plasterboard or wood (for panels that can be removed later), it is necessary to first brush the surface with sizing.

Next comes the cutting of the paper or other material. Many people cut the strips on the floor. A large trestle table will make the job easier. It may be possible to rent such a table from the shop where you buy the wallcovering. Or make use of a long barbecue table, or three card tables lined up in a row. If you plan to use a dining table, the surface should first be covered with a cloth or newspapers to protect the finish.

It is important to have all the essential tools for the job. Kits are available that include knife, trim guide, chalk, seam roller, and a wide brush for pressing the covering in place. If the wallcovering you have purchased must be pasted, make sure that you have the right kind of adhesive: some wallcoverings must be spread with simple wheat paste (formerly called flour paste) ; others with liquid vinyl adhesive; some with vinyl paste. If on the back of a wallpaper you see the phrase "use only with wallclad adhesive," it means that the adhesive is to be applied to the wall, not to the paper. Manufacturers advise that this kind of paper should be put up by a professional.

Measure the walls carefully, inch by inch, before cutting any strips. Some instructions from manufacturers stipulate that each strip be cut an extra three or four inches in length to allow for any irregularity in the ceiling or baseboards. However, some people claim that it is better to cut the strip to the exact length, because most papers stretch a little as they go on the wall, and also because it is extremely difficult to trim off several inches evenly with a razor blade while the strip is wet with paste.

Cut just one strip at a time, but before putting any on the wall, cut at least the next two strips in order to match the pattern. Lay them out in proper order ready to hang.

Spread the paste or other adhesive from the bottom to the center of the strip, with a generous amount on the edges, then fold in half to transfer the paste or adhesive to the other half, but do not crease and do not unfold the strip until you are up on the ladder ready to press it in place.

Do not overlap the strips; butt the edges, then go over them with a seam roller. There is one exception: when you come to a dividing wall between rooms or an unframed doorway, go around the corner for about an inch, then overlap with the next strip for about one-half inch. At this juncture you may need a special kind of adhesive for certain materials.

A plumb line is essential to make sure that the paper goes on straight. Tie a piece of chalk or a small pair of scissors to a piece of cord, and suspend the cord from the ceiling (attached to the molding strip) or the top of a door frame adjoining the wall. Use this to mark the plumb line and as a guide around the rest of the room. A "panel square" is also helpful to determine whether a patterned paper is going on straight horizontally, and to serve as a cutting guide for the portions that fit around a window, door frame, or cabinet.

Wallcoverings cost more initially than paint but last much longer. A new paint job is needed every three years and sometimes more frequently. A good-quality wallcovering, especially a scrubbable vinyl, will last ten years or longer.

Paneling

A man who is handy with hammer and nails and not so adept at cutting and pasting would consider paneling a room far easier than papering, especially since so many of the new panels are prefinished, require no sanding or varnishing, and are available in a four-by-eight-foot size to fit against the walls of standard eight-foot-high rooms without any trimming required except at windows and doors. When the panels do require cutting, this job can be done easily with a special paneling saw and a panel square to make sure that the edges are straight and plumb. A cutout guide for light switches and outlets is a help, too.

The choice of paneling is almost limitless. Prices, too, vary from as little as four dollars a panel to more than twelve dollars each. Some paneling looks almost like wallpaper (and some vinyl-coated papers look like wood paneling). For a room where light walls are needed, there are honey-colored panels and some are in delicate pastels. For a more masculine, Old World type of library, the dark-toned walnut panels are extremely handsome.

In some cases, panels may be applied direct to the walls with adhesive, though in most cases panels should be nailed to studs or furring strips. If walls are not completely level, panels glued to the wall might not fit tightly or might begin to come loose later. Also, when the panels are nailed on, it is easier to remove them if a change is desired later.

A "goof-proof" way to nail panels in place is by using a "whammer" nail gun. This looks like a staple gun, but instead drives nails rather than staples into the paneling. It can also be used to install molding. Its manufacturer claims that you cannot possibly miss the nail head this way, nor is there any chance of the nail bending, nor of a hammer denting the surface of the paneling. By using nails or brads colored to match the paneling, you avoid having to cover them with plastic wood.

Molding strips at top and bottom give paneled walls a more finished look, though for contemporary decor they are sometimes omitted.

Ceiling tiles

Ceiling tiles are only slightly more difficult to install than wall paneling. First take measurements carefully, then draw a grid pattern, using graph paper and ruler, allowing for either one-by-one-foot or one-by-two-foot panels. You will probably want to install one or more light panels in the ceiling, so plan where these will be placed and how the wiring will be routed. Furring strips must first be nailed to the ceiling joists. If you plan to install a new ceiling over an existing one, locating the joists may not prove easy. If you cannot figure out where they are from below, try tapping the floor boards in the rooms overhead. Wood strips are always nailed across the joists. Before you start putting the ceiling tiles in place, you should box in pipes or ducts that project below the ceiling.

Many tiles come complete with instructions for installation. If not, ask at the hardware store or supply house where you buy them if they have any available literature on the subject. Some manufacturers print instructional booklets.

Wood flooring

If your house has hardwood floors, preserve them. They will last a lifetime with proper care, and cost less than composition flooring or carpeting over a long period of time. The U.S. Department of Agriculture a few years ago estimated that in twenty-five years—the average life of a home mortgage—a homeowner with hardwood flooring in one fifteen-by-twenty-foot room could save approximately $500 on the cost of composition flooring and $750 on the cost of carpeting in the same size room—because composition flooring and carpeting must be replaced.

In recent years, many newly constructed houses have had only plywood subflooring, over which carpeting was installed. This means that when the carpeting must be replaced, either new wall-to-wall carpeting must be added, or a new finished flooring laid above the plywood.

Oak is the finest flooring, the most durable and beautiful, but other hardwoods—maple, birch, and hard pine—with proper treatment will last as long as the house. If the existing flooring is in bad condition, it can be sanded and refinished, but often all that it needs is thorough cleaning and rewaxing. Areas where there is a heavy buildup of old wax or embedded dirt need to be cleaned with fine steel wool dipped in a solvent such as naphtha or in mineral spirits (Varsol). Some nails may need to be reset, but even should it seem necessary where boards are warped or shrunken to replace certain areas with new strip flooring, it will be worth it.

A sealer should be applied to new wood and to a floor that has been completely resanded, but the best preservation for wood is paste wax, applied and buffed with an electric floor polisher. If this is done once every few months, and the floor meantime kept dusted and vacuumed, the wood will develop a rich lustrous gleam.

Much easier, of course, is to apply liquid self-cleaning or self-polishing wax. The self-cleaning wax is all right, but does not give as rich a gleam as the paste wax buffed by machine, and some of the self-polishing liquid waxes contain water, which will in time cause the wood to shrink and warp.

For a family with rough-and-tumble children, the most trouble-free wood floor finish is a coat of polyurethane varnish of the type used in bowling alleys. This provides both a high luster and exceptional resistance to wear.

Self-stick flooring

When press-and-place composition flooring tiles were first introduced, it seemed a do-it-yourselfer's dream. No need to apply any glue or adhesive; just rip off the paper backing, put the tiles on the floor, press them down firmly, and the job is finished.

In truth, the job is very easy indeed. A woman who has done a bit of dressmaking should find it a cinch to cut and fit pieces to go around the base of kitchen appliances and in corners. Strong shears are preferable to a knife for this job, and the cutting lines must be marked off clearly before cutting.

There are two cautions to be observed. First, the existing floor should be free of bumps, ridges, or uneven sections, and completely clean. The most satisfactory method is to lay new subflooring or one-quarter-inch underlayment over the existing floor, whether it be of wood, vinyl, or vinyl asbestos. However, if the existing flooring is in relatively good condition, or can be made so by repairing only a few bad spots, the tiles can be applied to the old linoleum or vinyl. Make sure the floor is thoroughly scrubbed—not a trace of grease or dirt remaining—and let it dry completely before putting the first tile in place.

The second caution is to begin laying tiles in the most conspicuous part of the room, at the doorway, or in the center of the line of cabinets, then work to either side. Press each new tile as close as possible to the one next to it to avoid any conspicuous seams. After the first row is down, again start in the center, so that each new tile is pressed tightly against the one above it, and in line, so that no seams (cracks) will show up as you go along.

Flooring tiles are available in all composition (resilient) floor finishes, from asphalt (the least expensive) to vinyl asbestos, "vinyl formula," solid vinyl, and the no-wax type, the most costly but also the most trouble-free of all. "Cushion-backed," no-wax tile, slightly more expensive, is even more desirable for foot comfort in a kitchen. All these are available with self-adhesive backing, in sheet vinyl in six-, twelve- and even fourteen-foot widths, as well as in the twelve-inch square tiles. For kitchen or bath, the seamless sheet flooring is preferable, for with tiles, there is more possibility of water settling between the seams.

The self-adhesive trend has now spread to carpeting, to oak flooring, and even to slate for the foyer.

The indoor-outdoor type of carpeting with self-adhesive backing is particularly easy to lay, and this, too, is available both in twelve-inch squares and in six- and twelve-foot widths. It is recommended for kitchens, baths, playrooms, basement rooms, porches, and patios. Women who have used carpeting in their kitchens report that it is the most comfortable of all floor finishes and not difficult to keep clean—if spills are wiped up immediately. The material is factory-treated with Scotchgard.

Some foam-backed carpeting in shag or deep pile is also available for other rooms and its manufacturers claim it is easy for the homeowner to install. It does not have self-adhesive backing throughout, but the adhesive binding is on the edges. A stretcher should be used to make sure that the carpeting is pulled taut before being pressed in place. This is what is known as tackless installation.

Before adding or replacing carpeting, the existing floor or subfloor should be gone over to eliminate squeaks, which al-

Dos and Don'ts
When Hanging a Door

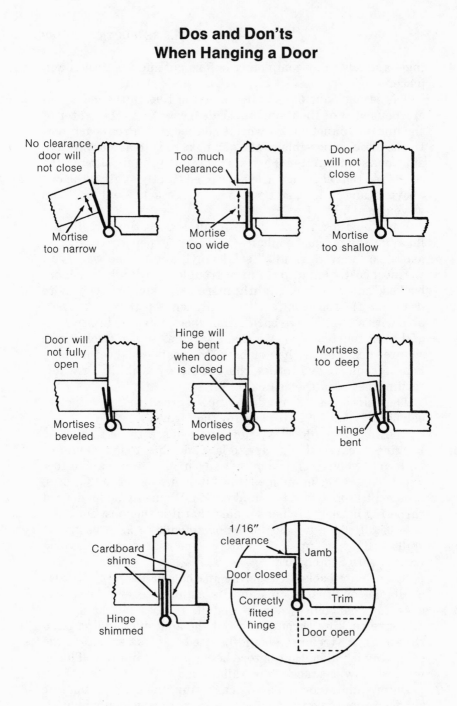

ways indicate loose boards. Squeaks are usually caused when the nails connecting floor boards or sub-flooring to the joists have worked loose. A rubber-based adhesive, which comes in ready-to-use cartridges (available at most lumber yards and hardware stores) can be applied to the joists with a caulking gun; the floor boards adhere to this as it dries. If the ceiling of the room below has been finished, it may be difficult to get at the joists. In this case, lift up the floor boards or subfloor enough to press the adhesive in place.

Oak flooring in twelve-inch-square parquet tiles with foam backing is a new product with great possibilities. These are made entirely of variegated oak strips. They are quite handsome, and may be added not only to any above-grade rooms, but even placed directly on the slab floor of a basement below ground level (assuming, of course, that the slab floor is dry and even). These oak tiles deaden sound, keep floors warmer, and with their foam backing, provide an additional moisture barrier. They are costly and not easy to find (they are so much in demand that supplies are quickly exhausted), but very much worth looking for.

Almost as good as the foam-backed tiles are laminated parquet tiles, also made of oak, but moisture-cured with a polyurethane finish. Strip oak flooring in random widths with tongue and groove fittings is not quite so easy to lay, because adhesive must be applied, and fitting the strips together is more difficult than fitting together the larger squares. However, many now come prefinished and, once laid, need nothing more than ordinary waxing and polishing. Since oak is a lifetime flooring, these tiles and strips, though more costly to begin with, in the end may prove to be the least expensive.

Slate with self-adhesive backing for foyers comes in variegated patterns in color combinations suitable for almost every decor. This flooring can be used only indoors and is recommended for foyers, not for long hallways.

Installing windows and doors

Replacing doors is not a difficult chore if you select a door of exactly the same dimensions as the one you wish to replace. However, to do the job properly you need a good planing tool, for no matter how similar the measurements seem to be, a new door never seems to fit exactly; one side or another needs to be trimmed. Also, it is of the utmost importance that the door be in line on the hinge side, for the hinges must be parallel to each other and work freely in unison. Clearance of one-eighth inch needs to be allowed at the top and bottom of the door.

Before installing a door, give it two coats of paint, varnish, or sealer. For an exterior door, an oil-base paint should be used over the primer.

Interior doors usually are easier to install than those leading to the outside. Louvered doors are especially easy to install, though these, too, usually need a bit of planing to fit exactly into the existing door jamb. Such doors are good for closets (to allow for ventilation) and for use between rooms where only semiprivacy is required. Some styles are solid halfway up, with louvers in the upper part. There are also louvered swinging cafe doors, which are attractive between kitchen and dining area—but these should be fitted with a catch, so that they can be kept open when desired.

Bifold or vinyl folding doors must work on tracks, but all come with instructions that anyone with mechanical aptitude

A skilled do-it-yourselfer can install new windows to replace old ones even if the frame is not exactly the same size. The procedure to follow for decreasing the size of the window frame is shown here and opposite.

can follow easily enough. Even sliding mirror doors are advertised as "easy to install," but as these are much heavier to handle, and more costly to begin with, they should probably be tackled only by those who have considerable confidence in their mechanical skill.

For a home handyman to replace windows requires a fair degree of skill in carpentry. It is not a job for an amateur to tackle. Yet many homeowners have done and are doing it, and the saving in labor costs is considerable.

To replace windows, it is often necessary to remove the old frame completely, then install two-by-four-inch filler studs at the sides. If the new window is shorter and/or narrower than the old one, trimmer studs or perhaps plywood sheathing may be needed to make the opening smaller. It is usually better and costs little more to order windows at the lumber yard to be made to the same measurements as the old ones.

Before going this far, it is best to make a thorough survey of existing windows, their sizes, insulating properties, and whether the frames can be utilized. If the frames and windows are of standard size, and the frames have predrilled holes for easier installation, putting in new windows may not

Corner
Nailed

How Much Paint Is Needed?

Only a close estimate of a house's square footage is needed to determine how much paint you require by dividing its per-gallon coverage into the area to be covered. Figure the siding area below the roof line by adding the length of your house to the width, multiplying by the height, and multiplying that number by two. In the example below, the square footage is (20 + 40) x 12 x 2 = 1,440 square feet.

For pitched roofs and gables, multiply the height of the peak from the roof base by half the width of the area, doing this for each peaked area; then add the area of each gable to the below-roofline siding area. In the example, this is 6 x 10 x 3 gables = 180 square feet; the total area to be painted thus is 1,440 + 180 = 1,620 square feet.

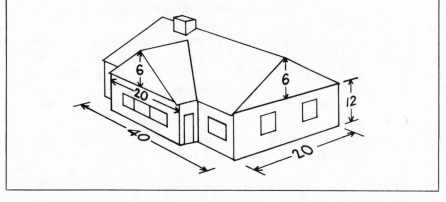

Source: The Sherwin-Williams Company

be all that difficult. How-to booklets are available with complete instructions for window installation; it would be wise to study them before purchasing any new windows.

Installing storm doors and windows involves the same basic problems of exact fit; they can be ordered in the sizes required. The "piggyback" type of storm window is not difficult to install on casement windows. However, to be sure of proper fit, it would probably pay to have this type of work done professionally.

Exterior painting

Painting the outside of a house is a far more demanding job than painting the interior. Outdoor temperature is an important factor. You should not paint when the thermometer falls below fifty degrees Fahrenheit (some experts make it forty degrees) or above seventy-five degrees, and never in exceedingly humid weather or just after rain. If it rains the day before you plan to begin, wait until the surface is completely dry. In fact, even in perfect weather, painting should not begin until the sun has evaporated the morning dew. This makes less difference with latex paint than with the oil-based type, but even latex paint will bond better to a dry surface.

Also, the surface must be very carefully prepared, and because it has been exposed to the elements, this is a much bigger job than preparing interior walls or woodwork.

Ordinary dirt can usually be removed by hosing, but some areas, especially those closer to the ground or under gutters or eaves, may need scrubbing with detergent and water, or brushing with an old stiff paint brush to get rid of dirt, dust, and chalky paint. After this scrubbing and brushing, a second hosing is needed.

It may seem strange, but the best way is to start washing the exterior at the bottom and work up toward the roof. If you start at the top, streaks that will be hard to remove will run down over the uncleaned areas. As you work up the wall, hose off the lower sections that you have already cleaned.

If you are painting the exterior of a new wing or addition —in many cases, owners elect to do this themselves after a contractor has completed the construction—make sure you use a priming coat first, especially if it is a frame structure or is made of hardboard panels.

If the old paint is blistered or peeled, it should be removed by means of a paint scraper, and sanded if the condition is extreme. Blistering, remember, is often a sign of excess moisture (unless the surface was not dry when the paint was first applied). If such peeling occurs outside a kitchen, laundry, or bathroom, you might consider installing an exhaust fan in that wall. If it is under eaves or gutters, look for leaks.

Sometimes chipping of the paint results when many successive coats have been applied over the years. You can tell if this is the cause by the colors showing through the upper surface. Scraping is the best way to remove the chips, though it is sometimes necessary to sand some areas as well.

If the surface is "alligatored" (looks like alligator leather), the condition is due to the paint having been applied when the surface was moist, or because a second coat of paint was added before the first coat was sufficiently dry. Brushing with a wire brush and then sanding is the treatment for this. Always sand frame siding along the grain of the wood.

Cracks should be filled in with caulking compound, and any bad shingles or clapboard replaced. If a fresh coat of paint is to be applied on all sides, it will not matter if the replacement is of a different color before painting.

Besides filling in cracks, areas around window frames, flashings, soffits, and fascias may need to be reinforced with putty or another caulking or glazing compound. Make sure that you buy the right type of compound for your purpose as there are so many of these products on the market. Most can be applied with a caulking gun; some come in cartridge form. But before filling in cracks, or replacing broken or split mortar, remove the old caulking or mortar, clean the surface with a wire brush, and if there is any sign of grease, remove it with a rag soaked in mineral spirits. When the surface is again dry, carefully "bead" the caulking in place and let this dry before applying paint.

Selecting paint

The best paint for wood siding is an oil-base house paint because it bonds better to wood and has more elasticity to respond to changes in weather. Many manufacturers advertise that their latex paints may also be used for wood siding. This is true, but they do not hold up as well or as long. However, the latex exterior paints are fine for almost any other surface: textured or celotex hardboard, aluminum (repainted because you do not like the original baked-on finish), asbestos, vinyl, even masonry if it has previously had a coat of sealer. (Reconstituted wood sidings do not absorb moisture or contract like natural wood, which is why latex paints may be used over them.) Latex paints can also be used on aluminum storm doors and window frames, without a primer.

Tools needed for exterior painting include an extension ladder and a shorter stepladder (for ground level), a drop cloth to protect shrubbery and any jutting portions of the building, and a four-to-five-inch brush of best quality. If your ladder does not have a shelf where the paint may be placed, obtain a big hook with which the can may be fastened to a rung of the ladder. Also, be sure to protect your face and hair with a brimmed paint cap.

It is best to begin painting at the top, dipping the brush into the paint only half the length of the bristles, and wiping

What Exterior Paint to Use . . . and Where

	Exterior Masonry Paint—Latex	House Paint—Latex (Wood)	House Paint—(Oil)	Transparent Sealer	Cement Base Paint	Exterior Clear Finish	Aluminum Paint—Exterior	Wood Stain	Roof Coating	Roof Cement	Asphalt Emulsion	Trim Paint	Awning Paint	Spar Varnish	Porch-and-Deck Enamel	Primer or Undercoater	Metal Primer	Latex Types	Water-Repellant Preservatives
Clapboard Siding		O	●				O									O		●	
Brick	O		●	O	O		O									O		O	
Cement & Cinder Block	●		●	O	O		O									O		O	
Asbestos Cement	O		●													O		O	
Stucco	O		●	O	O		O									O		O	
Natural Wood Siding & Trim						O		O						O					
Metal Siding		●	●				●					●					O	●	
Wood Frame Windows		●	●				O					●				O		●	
Steel Windows		●	●				●					●					O	●	
Aluminum Windows		●	●				O					●					O	●	
Shutters & Other Trim		●	●									●				O		●	
Canvas Awnings													O						
Wood Shingle Roof								O											O
Metal Roof		●	●														O	●	
Coal Tar Felt Roof									O	O	O								
Wood Porch Floor															O				
Cement Porch Floor															O			O	
Copper Surfaces														O					
Galvanized Surfaces		●	●				●					●			O		O	●	
Iron Surfaces		●	●				●					●					O	●	

■ Black dot indicates that a primer or sealer may be necessary before the finishing coat (unless surface has been previously finished).

Source: National Paint and Coatings Association

Suggested Exterior Color Schemes

If your house has shutters, it is best to paint the trim white or the same color as the body of the house. If there are no shutters, you might choose from these suggested colors for trim.

If the roof of your house is	You could paint the body	Pink	Bright red	Red-orange	Tile red	Cream	Bright yellow	Light green	Dark green	Gray-green	Blue-green	Light blue	Dark blue	Blue-gray	Violet	Brown	White
GRAY	White	●	●	●	●	●	●	●	●	●	●	●	●	●	●		
	Gray	●	●	●	●		●	●	●	●	●	●	●	●	●		●
	Cream-yellow		●		●		●		●	●							●
	Pale green				●		●		●	●							●
	Dark green	●				●	●	●									●
	Putty			●	●				●	●			●	●		●	
	Dull red	●					●	●						●			●
GREEN	White	●	●	●	●	●	●	●	●	●	●	●	●	●	●	●	
	Gray			●		●	●	●									●
	Cream-yellow		●		●			●	●	●						●	●
	Pale green			●	●		●	●		●							●
	Dark green	●	●			●	●	●									●
	Beige				●				●	●	●		●	●			
	Brown	●				●	●	●									●
	Dull red					●		●			●						●
RED	White		●		●				●		●		●				
	Light gray		●		●				●								●
	Cream-yellow		●		●						●		●	●			
	Pale green		●		●												●
	Dull red				●			●		●	●						●
BROWN	White			●	●		●	●	●	●	●		●	●	●	●	
	Buff				●				●	●	●					●	
	Pink-beige				●				●	●						●	●
	Cream-yellow				●				●	●	●					●	
	Pale green								●	●						●	
	Brown			●		●	●										●
BLUE	White			●	●	●		●					●	●			
	Gray			●		●							●	●			●
	Cream-yellow			●	●									●	●		
	Blue			●		●	●						●				●

Source: National Paint and Coatings Association

off excess paint against the side of the can before applying the brush to the siding.

While you are up on the ladder, you might want to paint the gutters if they need a touch-up, remembering that galvanized gutters need a special paint. However, the trim of the house should be attended to after the siding is finished.

If galvanized nails have been used in construction, they may have rusted and left stains. The best way to treat these is to reset the nails beneath the surface so that putty or glazing can be applied over them and the area, when dry, be painted or stained.

Masonry walls (stucco, precast or poured concrete) can be both primed and painted with a roller. For the finish coat on masonry, rubber-based coatings, or vinyl and alkyd emulsion paints are fine. For brick, to preserve the exterior and protect it against moisture, a clear glaze is advised. If you wish to paint brick, get a paint especially for this purpose and prime the surface first, for the most durable results. Cement, cinder block, and asbestos cement each require special paints, so be sure to purchase the proper kind.

Porch floors, steps, and patios come last. If porch floors and steps are of wood, use heavy-duty exterior varnish, or special outdoor deck paint over a priming coat. Concrete steps and porch floor can be painted white or a color if desired, with a rubber-based coating—but only after the surface has been treated with muriatic acid; otherwise the paint will peel off. There is a nonskid product that can be applied with a paint brush to steps and walks to make them safer in wet or icy weather; use this only after the finish paint is dry.

To repaint metal railings or ornamental wrought iron, first remove all loose particles with a wire brush, sand any smooth or shiny surfaces for better adhesion, and make sure all dust is rubbed off. Then go over the surface with a rust-control primer and finish with either latex or oil-base exterior paint. It is best to paint the undersides first, finishing with the topside surface.

The big do-it-yourself jobs

Persons with decided mechanical aptitude not only can handle easily all the projects mentioned so far, but will bravely enter into much more complex operations, and for them do-it-yourself kits of all kinds are on the market. These projects include installing an automatic garage-door opener, repiping a house with plastic (rigid vinyl) piping, putting in pre-fab fireplaces, installing central airconditioning, and constructing swimming pools.

To install foldup attic stairs is said to be fairly easy, though it entails cutting a hole of correct size in the hall ceiling into which the stairs spring, installing a header to hold the joists, and constructing a neatly-fitted cover that will remain inconspicuously in place when the stairs are not in use.

Kits are available to enable the homeowner to install ceramic tile around the perimeter of a bathroom or over a kitchen splashback, and thin bricks are suggested as easy to press in place with quick-drying adhesive around a fireplace or a kitchen wall. Novice do-it-yourselfers have confessed that anything that entails using glue or other adhesive is messy and not as easy as it sounds. But this, of course, depends on individual aptitude.

The two areas into which even skilled do-it-yourselfers should enter cautiously are those involving rewiring or changes in plumbing. Some homeowners can do such work successfully. But when plumbing lines are not properly hooked up, water problems may develop. Poor wiring is a fire hazard, and fire insurance may not be valid if illegal wiring is installed. A homeowner therefore should obtain a permit to do such work and have the finished job inspected.

However, those who have sufficient self-confidence, patience, and time, can save a great deal of home-improvement expense by supplying their own labor, and there is literature in abundance to show them how.

Many homeowners gain the skills they lack by attending adult education classes that cover phases of home improvement. At least one building supply company in the Washington, D.C., area holds seminars for the benefit of its do-it-yourself customers. Perhaps there are firms in your locality that offer a similar service.

Making
the Old
Seem
New

An older house that looks fresh, bright, and well-cared for has the same attraction as a new house. If a house feels comfortable, if it has that certain something that makes you want to sit down and make yourself at home, its age is of no importance, except that the years may have added mellowness to its charms.

Tasteful decoration can do wonders in rejuvenating a house, and today many of these changes qualify as fairly easy do-it-yourself projects. Like all other home improvements, however, careful advance planning is important.

A file should be kept of ideas gleaned from the pages of magazines and newspapers and the free booklets offered by manufacturers of wall coverings, paneling, wood products, paint supplies, and other products for the home.

If you prefer to seek professional help, free decorating service is offered by many department stores, furniture houses, and drapery firms. Keep in mind, though, that decorators working for a company are part of the sales force and their job is to promote that company's products.

Some independent decorators act as brokers, bringing swatches of fabric and pictures of available products to your home to help you make your choice on the spot. As they are allowed a 40 percent discount by the firms with which they deal, they may pass on part of their discount to you, in which case it may cost you little if anything extra for their services. Also, they often know of products that are not nationally advertised but are excellent buys, comparable in quality but less expensive than better-known brands.

The choice of patterns and colors today is almost overwhelming. To mix patterns is risky. As a general rule, it is safer to have just one distinctive pattern in a room, with all remaining finishes either plain or subdued. For example, if the wallcovering is in a floral or geometric print, draperies and carpeting should be in solid colors. If both draperies and wallcovering are to be of the same print, choose a delicate design, one that does not "talk back."

If you use area rugs on polished wood floors, make sure that the pattern in the wallcovering does not fight with the rug pattern. If the rug is in a bold pattern, walls should be simple or plain, perhaps wood-paneled, or have a textured covering such as a simulated grass-cloth or burlap finish, or be painted.

If you wish to hang pictures on the wall, the wallcovering should be unobtrusive. Plain painted walls, or a simple vertical stripe (against which the shapes of the picture frames form a pleasing pattern), or natural wood panels are suitable. Paintings with large white or light areas show off well against dark paneling.

Tricks with color
Color can change the shape, size, and personality of a room.

Light colors make the room seem larger; dark colors cause it to "shrink." White and pastels reflect up to 80 percent of the light; dark colors reflect only 25 to 30 percent (black only 10 percent). When dark colors are used in decoration, more artificial illumination is necessary, even in daytime.

Color has psychological effects as well. Off-whites, pale gold, and most blues and blue-greens are relaxing. The vivid "hot" colors—reds, bright yellows, orange, kelly green or

The Light Reflectance of Various Colors

Do you wish to make the most of the natural and artificial light within a room? Or do you wish to soften the glare that sometimes enters through large glass areas? Dark colors absorb light and light ones reflect it. This chart will help you to determine the colors that will best serve your purpose.

White	80%	Light Buff	56%	Light Green	41%
Ivory (Light)	71%	Peach	53%	Pale Blue	41%
Apricot Beige	66%	Salmon	53%	Deep Rose	12%
Lemon Yellow	65%	Pale Apple		Dark Green	9%
Ivory	59%	Green	51%		
		Medium Gray	43%		

Source: National Paint and Coatings Association

bright yellow- or mustard-greens—should be restricted to small areas or they will soon wear out their welcome.

Individuals have their favorite colors and their color aversions. You usually can tell when you enter a house what the owner's favorite color is because you see it everywhere.

Color needs to be coordinated from room to room, but this does not mean using the same colors everywhere. On the contrary, too much of any one color, or the same color combination repeated again and again, becomes monotonous. If the living room is in golds and two shades of green, the dining room adjoining it might be in the lighter of the two greens combined with brown and cinnamon. In the kitchen beyond, the gold may be repeated, but in a softer, lighter shade, combined with orange or rust, with porcelain enameled cookware in avocado. Or the kitchen might be in yellows and browns.

The safest colors to use are the pastels and neutrals, but yellow, though a pastel, can be very tricky. In small amounts it adds a note of gaiety, but when an entire room is painted yellow, a shade that looked soft enough on the color chart can seem garish on the wall. This is especially true of the lemon-yellows. On the other hand, when only safe, neutral colors are used throughout the house, the effect is insipid. One feels the owner must be a colorless, uninteresting person. A certain degree of boldness is needed in the use of color.

When a particular color or combination of colors is in high fashion, when "everyone" is using it this year, be wary of using it except in materials that can be easily and inexpensively replaced. That is, unless you want an excuse for redoing the house when that color or color combination is out and another is in.

In the 1950s, everyone was using aqua; later avocado was favored, followed by a combination of blue and kelly green, and now poppy is the rage, though the earth colors and combinations of brown and white are said to be moving in fast. Enjoy high fashion colors in draperies, slipcovers, or painted surfaces which can be easily repainted, but as a matter of economy, it is wise to avoid them in costly wall-to-wall carpeting, upholstered furniture, or any permanent fixtures. Because dark-stained kitchen cabinets have been so popular, it is safe to predict that their day is just about over. Besides, with electricity rates climbing sharply, lighter colors are bound to return to fashion as a means of conserving energy.

First impressions

Since the foyer of your house is the first place visitors see, it may be a good place to begin redecorating.

The flooring should be of water-resistant material, because water and mud inevitably are tracked in. If you have gleaming wood floors, and want to keep them that way, at least place a sizable mat just inside the entrance—not a carpet which may fade with repeated cleaning. A slate entranceway is a more practical solution. Colored slate with self-adhesive backing is very easy to install, and is especially appropriate for the area just inside the front door.

For a larger foyer, or one that becomes part of a hallway, vinyl tiles would be more practical. And again, the self-adhesive tiles are easily installed. If you are going to economize by putting these down yourself, purchase of the no-wax vinyl is worthwhile; the labor saved by not having to wax the hallway can be applied to other home-improvement projects.

The foyer should set the tone for the rest of the house and reflect your life style. If you prefer traditional styles, you may decide on black and white marbleized tiles for the floor, and for the walls, an embossed paper or fabric wallcovering in a rich, dark shade, with a hanging wrought iron or gold-plated light fixture, or a prismed chandelier. If you lean towards the modern and functional, the flooring may be of no-wax tiles in two colors set in a geometric pattern, the walls wood-paneled in a light stain, and lighting directed toward the ceiling from a cove. Or you may have a large skylight, which could be lighted around the perimeter, to be seen from the outside as well as in.

The lighting is important. You will, of course, have a light control switch just inside the door, preferably a triple switch; one should turn on outside lights, a second the indoor hall lighting, and a third to light the living room beyond. If yours is a long hall, you may want several recessed ceiling lights, "high hats," or panel lights, depending on how much illumination you feel is needed.

A display case recessed in the wall gives a small foyer a feeling of greater depth. The case could hold statuary, an arrangement of dried flowers, a shade-loving potted plant, a lighted fish tank, or African violets if you have the proper lighting for this delicate but decorative flower.

Mirrors can do a great deal to lighten foyer and hallway. A handsome hanging mirror above a hall table is the traditional answer, or you may want to make a "mirror wall" with mirror tiles above wainscoting, and have potted plants suspended from the ceiling at either end, or a long planter holding greenery at the base of the mirror, so that the mirror will reflect this touch of nature.

In one home, plastic mirror glass was used to cover floor-to-ceiling closet doors and did wonders in "enlarging" and lighting up the hallway. To achieve this effect, the door knobs were removed first, then the double solid doors were measured and their dimensions marked on the back of a standard four-by-eight-foot sheet of plastic mirror. The position of the screw holes was also marked with chalk. The mirrors were cut to size with a cutter sold for the purpose (or a coping saw could be used) and taped to the doors. This is the most difficult part of the operation, for once taped on, the mirrors cannot be moved again. It is the kind of do-it-yourself job that only a skilled person should try, but for those capable of mastering the technique, it can be a home-improvement miracle.

Provision for hanging wraps is very important in the foyer or entrance hall. A coat closet must be at least twenty-four inches deep (thirty inches is better) to take coats on hangers; it should be a minimum of three feet wide. If there is not space enough for such a closet just inside the door, perhaps it can be placed under the stairway, or next to a powder room, or constructed at one end of the living room, next to the entrance.

A much less expensive solution would be to hang an old-fashioned coat rack on the wall, the kind with a hat shelf above large coat hooks, or even use a turn-of-the-century free-standing coat rack. These and other Gay Nineties furniture fashions are now very much "in."

Redoing the living room

Size and comfort are the two most important qualities in a living room. If you are in the mood to do over the living room, see the suggestions for creating an illusion of greater space in chapter 6, and select new wall treatment, carpeting, and furniture (or slipcovers) with these factors in mind. Comfort is not just a matter of selecting furniture that is comfortable to sit on; the "feel" of a room has much to do with whether it is a relaxing place, and colors, space, lighting, and a view (or its substitute) all are factors in this.

In some cases, a mirror wall can "double" the size of the living room—if the rest of the room is so furnished that you wish to double its effect. Usually the best place for such a mirror wall is at the opposite end of the room from the front entrance. A reflective paper, or a wallpaper mural, or a very large painting with a vista can accomplish the same thing.

Or you may decide to open up the living room by removing a wall between it and the adjoining dining room and replacing the wall with movable dividers. This makes it possible to have one big room when you are giving a cocktail or buffet party, and to separate the dining room and living room when that suits your purpose.

A room divider suitable for this purpose is the pole type with translucent panels through which light is reflected. These partially shut off the adjoining room but do not reduce light. Floor-to-ceiling screens, like the Japanese shoji, offer the same advantage. Potted plants can be placed along the floor to throw a lacy shadow on the screens when lights are on behind the plants.

Room-divider screens are not difficult to make by hingeing together either louvered, paneled, or solid doors. The latter can be covered with paper or fabric to match walls or draperies, or with decoupage or stenciled designs. Certain types of wall paneling can be used in the same way. Or make your own panels from hardboard cut to any size you wish. Paint, paper, or hand-decorate them and put them together with hinges. Plain glass mounted on a frame can be lined with self-adhesive vinyl for a stained-glass effect.

If you cannot afford a renovation that involves installing new windows or taking down old walls, your living room can be made to seem roomier by the way it is furnished and decorated. Wall-to-wall carpeting and plain walls in approximately the same color (the carpeting just a shade darker) will "open up" the room amazingly. Big cumbersome pieces of furniture make a room seem smaller; replace some of these with smaller pieces, or pieces that fit closer to the wall, and your room will "grow."

It is a paradoxical fact that a room with furniture in it can seem larger than an empty room, depending on the size of the pieces and the way in which they are arranged. Moving a big sofa from one part of the room to another can sometimes make a difference, especially when by doing so the view through the windows is unobstructed.

The choice of wallcovering can also affect the "size" of a room. A paper with a bold pattern, especially a floral pattern, "shrinks" a room. One with a less obtrusive pattern and a light background, or with a scenic view on just one wall, "expands" it. The smaller the room, the more important it is that the walls be comparatively plain and light in color. For darker or bolder decor, you need more space.

Wall treatment pointers

Never before has home decorating been so easy, and with such a wealth of materials to choose from. Paints go on with a roller, dry in minutes, have almost no odor, and are scrubbable. Wallcoverings can give rooms a rich, luxurious effect. Paneling can completely change the personality of a room.

Vinyl-coated wallcoverings that are soil-resistant and wipe clean with a damp cloth are especially welcome in a household with children. Many fabric wallcoverings have matching forty-eight-inch material which can be used for draperies or slipcovers—but be careful not to overdo it, for too much of the same print can be both monotonous and overpowering.

A combination of wainscoting and paper is especially attractive in dining rooms. To make wainscoting, or a "chair rail" as it is sometimes called, you could use paneled doors laid on their sides (but be sure to choose doors with a symmetrical pattern). This makes wainscoting two-and-one-half to three feet high, depending on the widths of the doors. Another way is to use wall panels on their side, but as the standard size is four by eight, this would give you wainscoting four feet high. Hardboard panels designed to resemble eighteenth-century British oak paneling with inlay stripping are particularly handsome used this way. To finish off the wainscoting, lay molding strips at top and bottom. A scenic wallpaper above such paneling can be quite striking.

A series of "historic" designs in hardboard panels has been so beautifully executed, it is hard to believe at first glance that the panels are not of carved wood. Used all around a room which is to be furnished with Victorian antiques or reproductions of Hepplewhite or Queen Anne style furniture, they can provide a truly sumptuous air. Other paneling in French provincial style goes beautifully with chintz slipcovers and ladder-back chairs.

It is possible to "make" your own panels of plain overlaid plywood, forming the "panels" by nailing on inexpensive molding strips, and painting it all in soft off-white or cream.

Paneling is also available that looks like stippled plaster but its baked-on vinyl finish is far easier than genuine plaster to keep clean. This is particularly appropriate for a family room in Mediterranean style. With these simulated plaster walls, install dark-stained fake exposed beams across the ceiling, hang decorative wrought-iron objects on the walls, and place carpets of woven fiber or matting over flooring of either black and white "marble" vinyl squares or red and black Moorish-style tiles. The white walls provide an excellent contrast for colorful pillows, couch cover, and hassocks, and either vivid striped draperies or indoor shutters painted dark red. If there are large windows with a southern exposure, all you need to complete the Mediterranean "feel" are potted geraniums hanging from the dark beams.

Hardboard panels in French provincial style provide an attractive wallcovering for a dining room. The panels have also been used as floor-to-ceiling doors for a china closet built into the wall.

For some people, a room like this would be too quaint to be comfortable. Brick, both simulated and real, is a popular interior finish for rooms where informality is the keynote—not for a large expanse of wall, but perhaps around a fireplace, or on the wall adjoining patio doors. Panels of fireproof material resembling brick are offered in brown, red, rust, white, or "old white"; simulated fieldstone panels are available in white or gray. These can be used even around an indoor barbecue grill.

For children's rooms, wallpaper patterns in which well-known nursery characters are depicted come not only pre-pasted but dry-strippable so that they can be easily removed when the children are older or when the house is put on the market. For teen-agers, wild pop art patterns are available. Or, one wall of a teen-ager's room could be finished in cork tiles on which collected signs can easily be pinned. The cork also would serve as a sound-deadener for the benefit of parents.

Decorating with light

The placement of portable lamps and permanent light fixtures can make a vast difference in the appearance of a room. Table lamps placed near a wall give off much more light than overhead fixtures in the center of the ceiling, because the wall—particularly a white or pale one—reflects the light. Also, a wall with a semigloss or highly varnished or "wet look" finish reflects more light than one with a dull finish or a soft texture, such as fabric. Often, a table lamp next to a white wall must be fitted with a dark shade to avoid unpleasant glare.

The way a room is lighted has an immediate psychological effect. If lighting is diffused and indirect and yet illuminates the room adequately, the room becomes a far more restful place. When the only lights are overhead and too glaring, it becomes difficult to relax.

There are two categories of light fixtures: those intended to give diffused light to the entire room, and those to throw light directly onto a specific area. Most rooms need both, though in a hallway, diffused light alone may suffice, and some people do without an overhead light in the living room.

Stairways should always be well-lighted for safety, but

with the lighting so placed that it never glares into your eyes, for this could cause missteps. An attractive arrangement is to have recessed lights in the wall, at spaced intervals, as well as a ceiling light at the top of the stairwell.

Fluorescent lighting

Fluorescent lights enclosed behind a cornice or cove can light a room softly and are particularly suitable for a modern decor. For a cornice, the light fixture is mounted to the ceiling rather than the walls, with the top and front of the wood frame enclosing it, to throw light downward over walls covered with drapery, books, or panels on which trophies and awards have been mounted. The wood frame to enclose such a light fixture should extend four inches out from the wall, two inches beyond draperies. A cove is the opposite; it is enclosed at the bottom to throw light up toward the ceiling. Both of these types have valances (board coverings) across the front.

For the best color rendition, fluorescents in deluxe warm white are recommended. However, if the color scheme is mostly in cool colors (blues and greens), cool white will enhance it; if the furnishings are mostly in warmer colors, soft white will give a pleasant pinkish glow, which brings out reds and pinks but makes cool colors seem gray.

Hanging lamps

Recessed or panel ceiling lights are most appropriate for a rec room or playroom, hallways, kitchen, and bathrooms. If there is no overhead light in the living room, the wall switch should be wired to turn on a floor lamp or table lamp. But in the entrance hall and dining room, decorative hanging lamps or chandeliers seem more appropriate, especially with traditional decor. With a contemporary decor, white modular hanging shades that throw light downward in an arc are attractive, as are translucent globe lights.

Lamps that throw spots of light downward give a room a cozy atmosphere. For use over a dining table, a reel lamp is practical: it can be lowered or raised according to the occasion. At mealtime, the light should be thirty-six inches above the surface of the table. To throw light into the corners of the room, the fixture can be thrust upward, and to concentrate light on something like a jigsaw puzzle or homework, it can be pulled down lower.

Also attractive over a dining table is a cluster of hanging lamps in groups of three or five, especially those with cutouts in the shades that throw snowflake patterns of light over ceiling and walls. Over a snack bar or island counter in kitchen or family room, a row of hanging lamps is both decorative and practical.

For reading, the light should be sixteen inches to one side, preferably coming from over the left shoulder. If it is a table lamp, the base should be high enough so that light is thrown all across the pages of the book, magazine, or newspaper. The best type of light for reading in bed is one with an open shade at both top and bottom, throwing light simultaneously upward and downward. Hooded lamps, which throw the light only downward, are harder on the eyes. If these are used, another light should be turned on somewhere in the room.

For a study desk in a youngster's room, the best type of light is one fitted into an open shelf sixteen inches above the desk top, so that it throws light both above and below this shelf. Fluorescent lights are not recommended for study; incandescent are preferred, because the color is more nearly that of natural light.

In any room where small children will be playing, avoid having portable lamps or any low-placed electrical outlets. Panel ceiling lights or lamps hanging well out of a child's reach are best for such a room.

There are a number of new types of wall switches. The feather-touch switches, which need to be barely touched to turn on the light, cost more initially but are so long-lasting they almost never have to be replaced. There are also push-button switches with tiny lights beside them, making it easy to find them in the dark. And dimmer switches include some with several levels of light that range from quite dim to very bright.

There are also the photoelectric switches that will turn on certain lights in the house at a set time every night, whether the family is at home or not, and turn them off at dawn, or at whatever hour is preset. This is a good safety device, especially if lights are set to go on and off in different parts of the house at various times.

Adding a personal touch

Sometimes the defects in an old house can be imaginatively disguised. A couple in Massachusetts, taking over an old rambling house of pre-1914 vintage, liked the giant-sized bathroom on the second floor and dreamed of such future luxuries as a wall-to-wall vanity, a sloping picture window and, of course, new bath fixtures. But meantime, with all the unexpected expenses of making the place livable, they had to make do with what was already there, including a built-in floor-to-ceiling linen closet, which had been many times repainted.

The old-fashioned linen closet, they soon discovered, was a great convenience. It held not only all bath and bed linens, but also out-of-season clothing. For the fun of it, they decided to decoupage the doors. Cutting pictures of fish, birds, kings, and princesses from an outgrown children's book, they pasted these to the doors with white glue and used a strip of wallpaper "molding" around the edges. Then they covered it all with two coats of polyurethane clear glaze. They were so pleased with the effect, they decided never to replace the old linen closet.

Decoupage is the current rage in hobbycraft studios, popular because it does not require skill at sketching or painting, only care in making paste-ups and applying the covering glaze or lacquer. This type of decoration can be used to brighten up old chests, nursery furniture, kitchen cabinets, and even the walls of certain rooms, such as a child's room or a basement powder room.

Using stencils or decals is another easy way to decorate old furniture, fireplace mantels, closet doors, screens, and window shades. Kits with complete instructions for use can be purchased in hobbycraft studios; lessons in various decorating crafts are given in adult education centers and also sometimes in the shops that sell craft materials. For those with a little more self-confidence in design techniques, freehand scrolls, leaves, flowers, and hearts can be painted on old bookcases, kitchen cupboards, or sideboards, copying one of the Pennsylvania Dutch or Colonial patterns.

Another way to rejuvenate furniture for the bedroom, playroom, or bath is to paint (enamel) each drawer of a chest a different color, then add new wooden drawer pulls painted in a color that goes with the others, to make it a "fun" piece. For example, the bottom drawer of a chest of drawers might be painted a deep royal blue, the next drawer green, the drawer above that aqua, and the top drawer pale pink. The door knobs might be dark red. The frame might be white, or any one of the colors used on the drawer fronts. This multicolored technique can also be used for chairs and desks.

Antiquing has become such a popular hobby and such an easy way to beautify old furniture that antiquing kits with instructions for use are available wherever paints are sold.

In most cases, it is best to restrict hand decoration to personal possessions rather than any part of the permanent house structure, because what is amusing and decorative for you and your family might not please potential future buyers of your property.

Decorated furnishings, on the other hand, including screens, window shades, and ceramics, can probably be disposed of in a garage sale if you decide to move, and may bring you a profit.

Anything that makes your home more comfortable and attractive can be considered home improvement. And even when future buyers may not fully appreciate your artistic touches, it may give them an idea of how they can change things to their own taste.

Repainting furniture

Certain basic rules are important in repainting any furniture. First, make sure that any paint you use is lead-free and also contains no traces of antimony, arsenic, cadmium, mercury, selenium, or soluble barium. All these are potential poisons, even in minute amounts, and especially dangerous if young children are around.

Then clean the furniture, removing all hardware, and make any necessary repairs, including reglueing. The great attraction of the latex furniture paints—including antiquing, "wet look" or lacquer finish, and "color over color"—is that they can be applied over the existing surface. However, all dirt, wax, and grease must first be removed, and if the present surface is slick (varnished, waxed, or lacquered), or if it is flaking or chipping, it must be sanded down to ensure that the new paint will adhere properly.

Some furniture can be spray-painted. This is the best method for covering steel mesh, outdoor furniture, or any wooden pieces with rungs, spindles, or carving. The best place for spray-painting is outdoors, under the protection of a patio roof or in a garage with the doors and any windows wide open. Either newspaper or a drop cloth should be placed underneath the articles to be painted, for the spray will leave its mark on the surroundings.

Often it is worthwhile to have old furniture stripped by a professional, who will dip each piece in a "strip bath" and in less than an hour have it ready for refinishing. However, some pieces may be weakened by this high-strength "bath" and may even come unglued, so it is wise to get professional advice first as to whether such a dipping operation is safe for each piece of furniture you wish to redo.

When furniture has been sanded as part of the cleaning process, wipe off all loose particles with a tack cloth before adding a stain, glaze, enamel, or lacquer. If more than one coat is necessary, always let the first dry thoroughly before adding the second. Usually, more sanding is necessary to smooth down the finish, after which the piece should be given another good wiping with the tack cloth before the second coat is applied.

Reupholstering furniture.

Reupholstering is a far more difficult operation than painting furniture, but if an upholstered piece is structurally sound and the springs are in good condition, taking off the old fabric to replace it with new is easier than making slipcovers. The old fabric can be used as a pattern to cut out the new pieces, which are then pasted in place around the edges with white glue. When the glue is dry, upholstery tacks are added to strengthen the adhesion. The only difficult part of this operation is in stretching the fabric as you fit it so as to avoid wrinkles or looseness.

A special staple gun for attaching fabric can also be used for reupholstering or for stretching fabric over fiberboard or plywood panels.

For an old couch or upholstered chair that will receive hard use, vinyl upholstery material might be a good choice. A new type of leather-looking vinyl with tiny "pores" is more comfortable to sit on than the early vinyl finishes. Some of this new vinyl has a suede finish; others have a "wet look." Some vinyl cloth has the look of damask; others are in plaids. It comes in a fifty-three-inch width, and can be used for covering padded benches or stools as well as upholstered furniture.

Many canny shoppers are now buying old furniture in preference to new, because it is sturdier in construction and less costly. There is also the gambling lure that in purchasing junk furniture you may just happen to acquire a valuable antique.

Often it is possible to purchase an old table whose legs are in bad shape and replace the legs. New legs are available, ready to screw on, in several styles and various heights. What was originally a dining or refectory table can be transformed into a coffee table, simply by replacing the tall table legs with short ones. Or, conversely, a large coffee table might be transformed into a dining table.

If you plan to spray-paint some furniture, you might find other objects around the house or in a junk yard which could be rejuvenated with the same spray, such as discolored venetian blinds, a mail box that could go on the kitchen wall to hold receipts and letters, or a bird cage to be turned into a planter by removing the screening. Art objects made from junk are in the height of fashion just now.

CHAPTER 6

Ways to Expand Living Space

Whatever the size of your home, there never seems to be sufficient space for storage, and most families dream of how nice it would be to have an extra room to spread out in, whether they call it a family room, rec room, or den.

In a good many households, as the size of the family increases, more living space becomes a necessity not just a dream. As children grow older, they need a place where they can get away by themselves, and so do their parents.

As a first step, whatever your future plans or aspirations, adding more closet and storage space is the simplest way to make your home seem roomier. Having places to put the excess clutter that all too quickly fills every home can make rooms suddenly seem less cramped.

Putting up shelves is one of the easiest do-it-yourself tasks, especially in these days when ready-to-assemble units are available in every kind of finish, color, and style, in wood, metal, and glass, with matching or contrasting supports and braces. Many are prefinished and can be assembled with just a screwdriver. These, of course, are the most expensive types. Walking through a store or supply house that carries a full line of such component units is a do-it-yourselfer's dream.

From heavy, dark-stained, Tudor style shelves with equally heavy wooden or wrought iron supports, to glossy units in bright colors, to those with expensive teak or walnut finish, the range of units allows one to make such items as a complete entertainment center, a combined storage unit and study center, a home office unit, or a room divider.

Unpainted furniture departments and stores also carry a complete line of bookcases, cabinets, hanging shelves, and chests, all sanded ready to stain, shellac, wax, or paint.

The many units that can be put together with a screwdriver are, of course, the easiest and quickest, but it will cost less to buy shelving, plywood, or particleboard and make your own storage units, cut to the exact size you need.

Types of wood products

It is valuable to understand about the different grades and varieties of wood products. Hardwoods are used mainly for surfaces which get hard wear, such as floors, cabinet fronts, and counter tops. Oak, birch, beech, walnut, maple, and certain varieties of pine are hardwoods. Softwoods include yellow pine, Douglas fir, cedar, cypress, and redwood. The soft woods are easier to work with because they can be sawed and planed more quickly and smoothly.

Grades of lumber range downward from A to D: Grade A is virtually free of defects, but even Grade D may be used for painting if the surface is properly prepared. *Common lumber* is used for construction and in places where it will not show; it is graded downward from Number One through Number Five.

When lumber is dressed—the surfaces planed and smoothed on sides and edges—its size is less than it was when it left the sawmill, but the sawmill size is still used. This means that a two-by-eight-inch board is actually more like one and five-eighths by seven and five-eighths, or possibly one and three-quarters by seven and one-half. Standard lengths in board lumber always come in multiples of two: two by two, two by four, two by six, and so forth. (But in finished panels, the widths are in multiples of four feet. When a panel width is given as four by eight, this is the finished size, ready to install.)

In selecting dressed lumber, make sure that it is completely dry, for when green lumber is used, it shrinks and warps. This is frequently the cause of structural defects in hastily built, low-cost housing, and even sometimes in costly houses that have been put up by a contractor trying to cut corners. One way to test lumber for dryness is to tap it sharply: it should give off a hollow sound.

"Reconstituted wood products" include plywood, particleboard, and hardboard, and within each of these categories there are varieties and grades. *Plywood* comes in veneer core and lumber core. The former is made of thin veneers (very thin layers) running parallel, glued together. Lumber core is made with narrow strips of sawn lumber with crossbands and faced with veneers. Each type is available in four grades, and made with different varieties of wood. Grade One is used where appearance is of prime importance: for cabinet fronts, siding, furniture, and such. "Utility," the lowest grade, is used for subflooring or backs of cabinets, and other places where the wood is concealed.

Particleboard is made of sawdust and particles of wood— fragments gathered from the floor of the sawmill, compressed with glue and resins under pressure to make a rigid, cohesive layer three-quarters of an inch thick. It has a smooth surface, resists moisture, denting, cracking, and splitting. It is easier to saw than either natural lumber or plywood, has no grains or knots, and is much easier to paint. It should be sealed with a primer before adding any latex paint.

Hardboard also is made of sawdust, glue, and resins, but does not contain the larger particles. It ranges in thickness from one-eighth to three-eighths inch and is up to eight feet in length. The most common width is four feet. It, too, has a smooth surface, unless textured to resemble natural wood for use as siding or wall panels, and is resistant to moisture. Some hardboard panels are decorated so as to resemble carved oak, teak, or other hand-worked finishes.

Celotex hardboard is a composition containing other fibers besides wood sawdust, and is also compressed with resins and glues.

Sheathing plywood is used as a subsurface for exteriors and under floors. It is one-half or five-eighths of an inch thick and is put together with an exterior type of glue for durability, but it is not suitable for a finished surface.

Gypsum wallboard, also called dry wall, is the cheapest material for interior walls. It can be cut easily with a knife, and has tapered edges. It can be painted or papered, or used behind panels to straighten uneven walls. It is available in three thicknesses, three-eighths, one-half, and five-eighths of an inch, and in four-by-eight-, four-by-ten-, and four-by-twelve-foot panels.

All of these but the wallboard are available in many grades and finishes, some for exterior use, down to utility grades which may be used for any concealed work. All are available in standard sizes, precut and prefinished, and in any home renovation project, time will be saved by buying precut sizes that conform as nearly as possible to your required measurements.

Selecting nails and screws

Selecting the right nails and screws for each of these wood products and for each use is extremely important. Your hardware dealer can advise you on this. Nails are measured by the "penny": ten-penny nails are the big ones. In some instances, copper nails must be used rather than the galvanized type. Brads are nails with almost no head; they need to be countersunk—beneath the surface—then covered over with plastic wood. The new plastic wood does not shrink and comes in colors to match natural wood, such as birch, maple, walnut, and so on. When dry, plastic wood must be sanded so that the surface is again completely smooth.

Screws, too, are available in many different types and sizes. "Molly" screws are used to attach shelves or cabinets to plaster or dry wall: these screws expand after they are on the other side of the wall, which provides better holding power. Molly screws come in different sizes and strengths, some strong enough to support heavy shelves or objects hung from the ceiling.

The best way, always, is to locate studs in the wall and nail or screw objects to the studs. To find the studs, tap the wall lightly with a hammer; when the sound is not hollow, you probably have located one, but try above and below that point to be sure. When one stud has been located, the others should all be spaced exactly sixteen inches apart.

Wood for shelving

When selecting wood for shelving, use standard precut sizes as much as possible, supplemented by pieces cut to order at the lumber yard. Shelving comes in six-, eight-, ten,- twelve-, and sixteen-inch widths, and only needs to be cut to the required length (but remember, these are sawmill dimensions and the dressed size will be slightly narrower). Such shelving can be put up with simple metal arm brackets which hook or screw onto lengthwise metal braces screwed to studs in the wall. Paint shelves and the supports to match the wall and they look built in.

Look around the house for any spots where closets, shelves, or boxed-in storage units might go. Under the stairs is one possibility. Or along the stairwell from first floor down to the basement is another. Fill all available wall space with a combination of narrow shelves and cabinets with sliding doors, paint them off-white or pale yellow to lighten the area, and

Under-eave space can be used for a plywood built-in storage unit. It is especially suitable for use when remodeling an attic. By cutting the sides to the proper angle, the unit can be made to fit any ceiling slope.

install overhead lighting to flood the corners with light. You will be amazed how many things can be stacked away in this otherwise unused space.

Under the eaves in a converted attic or a one-and-a-half-story cottage is another natural spot for a combined closet and storage unit. Often cabinets can be built in the thirty-inch-high wall space beneath windows, fitting together shelves and/or drawer units. These units can be purchased at unpainted furniture stores in various sizes, some with four drawers to a unit, others with only two drawers. The drawers can be installed also in existing cabinets by using nylon tracks available at the same stores.

Some windows, especially bay or bow windows, have space for a window seat, under which you can build a concealed storage chest. Pad the seat with one- or two-inch-thick foam rubber and cover it with washable Scotchgarded fabric. Similar concealed storage units can be placed under corner benches built around a dinette table, or in the family room, or in one corner of a screened-in or enclosed porch.

If you need more closet space, consider adding a unit across one wall of a bedroom, dividing it into three sections. In the center, put drawer and shelf units. This may eliminate the need for a separate chest of drawers in the room. At either end install poles for hanging clothes. If you add full-length mirrors to the closet doors, or install sliding mirror doors, the room will seem even larger than before. Plastic mirror-glass can be cut by a careful handyman to fit plain doors and glued or taped in place, though attaching with screws is better for bifold doors. Louvered bifold doors also are attractive for a closet, and open to give a complete view of what is inside, besides providing ventilation.

Instead of using a hard-to-reach narrow upper shelf inside a closet, take down the fascia above the closet door and make a separate storage unit in that place, or several units, each with its own door. This space can be useful for storing blankets, suitcases, and out-of-season clothing, and is easier to get at than upper shelves in the traditional closet. You might want to line these with cedar paper, which not only protects against moths but gives the clothing a nice fresh scent.

Other closets can be installed next to or around jutting portions of walls, such as those enclosing a chimney or duct work. A space twenty-four to thirty inches wide can be turned into a kitchen pantry or bathroom linen closet. If you install pullout shelves in these closets (on nylon tracks with ball bearings), it will be much easier to locate things at the back. A louvered door is a good choice for a narrow closet.

One advantage of creating your own storage units is that you can make them to fit whatever space is available. But there are a number of ready-made unpainted pieces that can be used in many ways, and often will cost little if anything more than ones you make yourself. For example, bookcases and hanging shelves may be exactly the size you need for filling an empty space. Such pieces are sometimes available on sale at very reasonable prices. The shelves come in a number of sizes, with two, three, or four shelves, and can be as decorative as they are useful. They come ready to stain, wax, or paint.

In a bedroom, make a storage unit at the head of the bed, consisting of shelves above and at either side of the bed, with a concealed reading light beneath the overhead shelf. These shelves provide a place for books, magazines, alarm clock, telephone books, writing materials, and other paraphernalia.

Wall units in the family or rec room may serve as complete "entertainment centers," holding TV, stereo, games, magazines, and glassware and other accouterments for serving refreshments. In the rooms of school-age youngsters, a wall unit may serve both as a study center and for clothing and storage. In a nursery, a wall unit is an excellent place for storing toys and so teaching little ones neatness at an early age.

Inspect the lumber

When purchasing lumber or plywood to make storage units, shelving, or cabinets, inspect each piece to be sure it is free from defects such as wormholes, warping, spongy areas, or knots. This applies as well to unpainted furniture. If the wood is to be painted, it must first have a prime coat of shellac or clear glaze; otherwise it might "bleed" later. Shellacking is unnecessary if the wood is to be given a wax finish, but remember that once it is waxed, it cannot later be painted.

Because of its smooth surface, particleboard is an excellent material for making your own cabinets, especially if you plan

Side-step storage unit made of plywood panels provides children with a desk as well as an attractive place to keep toys, games, and books. Latex or enamel paint can be used in several bright colors to finish the unit.

to paint them. However, for the beauty of natural wood finish, plywood with hardwood veneer is preferable. You might combine the two: use particleboard for the frame and the plywood with birch, walnut, or maple veneer for door fronts and counter top. You will need narrow molding around the edges of the counter top to conceal the veneer layers of the plywood.

Patterns and detailed instructions for making various kinds of built-ins, and also furniture, decks, and sheds, are provided in many books and booklets. A list of these, with prices and addresses from which they can be ordered, will be found at the back of this book.

Hanging space

Hooks and pegboard can greatly increase storage facilities in many rooms of the house: kitchen, workshop, playroom, laundry, sewing room, hobby room. Pegboard comes precut in two-by-two, two-by-four, two-by-six, and two-by-eight-foot sections, or it can be cut to order in any size. It must be mounted on the wall so that it extends out one-quarter inch, allowing space for the hooks to go into the holes. Pegboard can be painted any color, and special pegboard hooks come in all sizes and in shapes designed to hold many different types of tools and utensils.

Even simpler, for hanging storage in garages, attics, or basements, is to use eight- or ten-penny nails set at an angle in exposed studs or rafter beams. Two such nails a few inches apart will hold garden tools such as rake, hoe, or rolled-up garden hose. Sports gear also can be suspended in this way, as can many of the larger workshop tools.

Hanging tools not only saves drawer and closet space, but makes it much easier to locate them when needed.

Creating the illusion of space

A room can be made to seem larger by the way in which it is furnished and decorated and by the amount of light it receives.

Window walls are popular largely for this reason. A small room seems larger when it looks out over a garden or expanse of lawn. A change in window treatment can let in more light. Use drapes that when pulled back fully expose the glass area. This may mean installing the rods on the wall or ceiling, not the frame of the window. To make sure that the pull of the curtain's weight will not force the brackets from the wall, a furring strip should first be nailed to the studs, and the brackets for the rods screwed on this. The furring strip should, of course, be painted to match wall or ceiling.

Another way is to install louvered indoor shutters, the type that fold back completely in daytime and can be closed over the windows at night. Or, use draperies at the side of the window merely for decorative effect, and for privacy at night use a pull-shade of fiber glass, or a roll-up bamboo shade, in a width to cover the entire glass area.

Another trick is to treat two side-by-side windows as one unit, with draperies pulled back all the way to the corners of the room in daytime. Over the top of the two windows add a scalloped cornice or a swag to help the two windows seem one.

Many rooms are unnecessarily darkened by overgrown shrubs just outside the windows. Pruning this greenery will let in more light.

A porch with heavy columns or posts can make a living room seem dark and cramped. This is particularly true of cottages built in the 1920s and 1930s with heavy narrow porches across the front of the house. Replace the heavy columns with lacy wrought-iron posts, or remove the porch roof and the columns or posts and turn the porch into an open terrace set off by planters or shrubs. It is astonishing to see how much a change like this can "enlarge" the room just inside.

Replacing narrow windows with new ones of a different size or shape can also make a room seem far larger. Bow and bay windows are again enjoying popularity for this reason. If there is a view to be enjoyed on any side of the house, a wide picture window to encompass that view will seem to expand the entire lower floor. Such a window need not be in the living room. If the view is on the side of the house where the dining room and the kitchen are located, let either of them be the room to be opened to light and sun.

Similarly, any room that opens onto a garden or patio can be expanded with sliding doors. A kitchen with patio doors can become a delightful place in which to prepare meals. Psychologically, the cook feels "liberated" with a wide-open door before her. A dinette or dining room opening onto the patio becomes an indoor-outdoor dining area where even in midwinter one can enjoy the feeling of being closer to nature and in summer the barbecue grill is just a few steps away from an indoor dining table.

Mirrors also create an illusion of greater space. Mirror tiles are less expensive than plate glass and can be easily installed by do-it-yourselfers. However, you must not only measure the wall space carefully, but be sure it is smooth and plumb. You may have to limit the area to be covered to avoid any bulges. Or, better, buy plain plywood or hardboard in panels, glue the mirror tile to this, and then attach the panels to the wall.

Shop around for mirrors in secondhand stores, Salvation Army warehouses, and other such outlets. Almost any mirror can be used. If you do not like the frame, paint or antique it. Or you may like the frame but find that the glass is discolored or spotted. In this case, either the mirror can be reglazed, or inexpensive plastic mirror-glass can be cut to fit the frame. Most mirror tiles are made of this plastic material.

In some rooms, a skylight will help to bring in more light. Such a skylight might be needed at the top of an open stairwell, in a dim library in a one-story house, or in a dark kitchen. Acrylic plexiglas is the best material for skylights; it lets in light but not the glare or heat of the sun.

Panel lights set in between ceiling tiles can serve the same purpose as a skylight, in a narrow dark hallway, for example, or in a below-grade family room. Or overhead lights in the same large panel shape can be installed on an existing ceiling.

The manner in which a room is painted can make it seem larger. Light colors expand space; dark colors contract it. If a room is long and narrow, paint the side walls a light, delicate pastel and the end walls a deeper color. Or use paper on the end walls in a pattern that adds to the illusion of width.

A scenic or pictorial paper on just one wall creates more feeling of space than if the same paper goes all around the room. The same is true of striped papers. Vertical stripes, of course, make a room seem higher, while horizontal stripes make it seem longer. But the horizontally-striped paper on just one end of a narrow room, with the other walls plain, will do more to make the room seem wider than if the striped paper is used on all the walls.

Light rather than dark furnishings also help to make a room seem larger. This does not necessarily mean throwing out what you have, but it could mean recovering or repainting certain pieces.

Dividing and respacing rooms

Without changing the exterior of the house at all, you may be able to rearrange interior rooms to create a more spacious living pattern.

Today the trend is toward openness, and virtually no main floor room is considered to be too large. Rather than separate living and dining rooms, walls are torn down to make one big room with separate functional areas.

Room dividers often are used for this purpose. The idea is to retain a feeling of openness, yet partially "wall off" one part of a large room from another.

For example, suppose an old house has a dark small foyer, a long dark hallway, and a living room opening off the hall that is of a nearly square shape. By removing the wall that creates foyer and hallway, the living room instantly becomes much larger. A storage unit in what was the foyer provides space for hanging wraps, and provides some privacy for the living room—the front door does not open directly into the living room, yet there are no doors. Dowels can be run from the top of the storage closet to the ceiling, and floor-to-ceiling dowels or poles beyond the closet unit create a kind of "open wall."

The stairway in the hall can be made a decorative part of the living room by having open treads, no risers on the steps, and potted plants on the walls or stair landing, or both. It may also be possible to have a skylight at the top of this open stairway to introduce more light.

Between dining area and kitchen, a room divider can have cabinets that open on both sides. The base cabinets serve as a pass-through, with cabinets overhead also opening on either side. Or, easier for a do-it-yourselfer, open shelves might be installed above the lower cabinets, with decorative pottery, and glassware, and porcelain on the shelves.

For the woman who prefers more privacy in the kitchen, the area above the base cabinets might be constructed of one big panel which can be papered, with a pass-through cut in the center. So it will appear on the dining area side, at least. On the kitchen side, shelves can be attached to the panel. This would be anchored with floor-to-ceiling poles at both ends.

Multicolored plywood panels are combined with cabinet units to make this decorative room divider with storage space. Two panels are hinged to provide fold-down desk tops.

Even easier to construct is a room divider with cabinets and shelves in units prefinished and ready to assemble.

A room shared by two children can be effectively separated by a divider that includes cabinets, shelves, and let-down desks. Some of the cabinets could open on one side, some on the other; each child would have his or her desk and his or her side of the divider. But this unit need only extend two-thirds of the way across the room, so that both children could continue to use the existing doorway.

An inexpensive way to make one part of a room usable for sleeping is to install a folding vinyl door across one end, so that the area can be closed off at night but opened during the day. This is not as satisfactory as having a separate bedroom, but as a temporary expedient, such as accommodating a house guest, it is preferable to having someone sleep in the living room without any privacy.

Nicer than a folding vinyl door is a solid door that disappears into a wall, but this is a more costly solution, as the door itself costs more, and a special wall must be built into which the door can slide.

If a bedroom is large enough to divide into two rooms with separate entrances, you might want to use a new type of do-it-yourself partition system for putting up walls. This consists of metal studs and modules that fit together; the studs are adjustable in height, up to nine feet, and there are holes through which electric wiring can be run. Plywood, hardboard or vinyl panels, or regular dry wall, can be applied to the studs with liquid mastic or tape adhesive. The wall system is suggested as particularly useful for dividing basement rooms, but can be used in any part of the house. A likely place is a semifinished attic that is now just one big room.

Sometimes the size of a room can be increased by extending the wall above a bay or bow window, or beneath such a window if it is on the second floor.

In one Kansas City house the walls were extended below the second-story bay windows on each side of the house. A Dutch-style house with an overhang across the entire front could have the walls of the lower floor extended out the same distance, creating a larger living room in front and perhaps allowing room for a new storage area near the front entrance.

Sometimes it is possible to take down enough walls on the

main floor to make two large airy rooms out of three small, less useful rooms. However, removing walls calls for supervision. You must be certain that it is not a bearing wall, also that if you remove it you will not run into problems of mismatched flooring or differing ceiling heights. And what about heating ducts or radiators? Will they have to be rerouted? This kind of renovation can be very tricky and may in the end prove far more expensive than you anticipated, for when walls must be torn down and floors torn up before new work is begun, labor costs are doubled. Also, this becomes a custom job in the truest sense, and custom work always costs more.

Enclosing a porch

Enclosing an existing porch is the easiest way to add on a room. The difficulty of the job depends, however, on the dimensions of the porch and where it is located in relation to adjoining rooms. Side and rear porches are the easiest to change; front porches are usually the most difficult.

Many side porches prove to be too narrow for comfortable arrangement of furniture. The solution to this problem is to

BEFORE: The add-on porch, which is not even suitable for summertime entertaining, gives the house a dark and forbidding appearance. See the transformation on facing page.

extend the wall out two or three feet—if this can be done in accordance with zoning restrictions. To avoid changing the existing roof, put a skylight over the portion where the roof ends and the new outer wall stands. This will bring in more light besides avoiding a costly roof alteration.

Another problem may be that the floor of the porch is on a different level (usually lower) than that of the adjoining room. The best way to solve this is to add a new floor system: first install two-by-four sleepers, add insulation with a vapor barrier between, then raise the level with joists until it matches that of the adjoining room, and cover with five-eighths-inch plywood. If heating ducts will be needed in the newly enclosed area, they should, of course, be put in before the new floor is installed. Over the new subfloor, you may add vinyl, wood, or carpet tiles. Besides raising the floor level, this will help to keep the new room much warmer in winter.

If you wish this to be an "indoor-outdoor" room, it will need windows that provide the maximum light and air. The three most popular styles for this purpose are awning, gliding, and vertical casement windows. Of the three, for an en-

AFTER: With the porch remodeled into a family room, the whole house takes on new character and charm. The casement windows bring the outdoors in, yet close snugly to seal out winter cold.

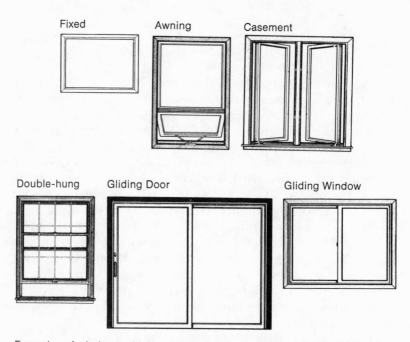

Fixed   Awning   Casement

Double-hung   Gliding Door   Gliding Window

Examples of windows which may be used in enclosing a porch. The awning, gliding window, and vertical casement styles are the most popular. A combination of fixed windows with other types is an alternative.

closed porch, the new type of vertical casements are probably the most attractive architecturally, and provide the greatest degree of ventilation as they open all the way.

When an enclosed porch is intended for use as a bedroom, or as an extension of the living room, regular walls and standard-size windows will probably be preferred. The difficulty in transforming a porch to this use lies in matching the existing siding, or at least in making the new room look like an integral part of the house design, unless all new siding is to be added anyway as part of the renovation. If the room is to be used as a bedroom, since it is on the main floor and adjoining the living-room area, furnishings should be in "studio" style: a studio couch or sofa bed and built-ins that can serve as storage units for clothing but do not look the part.

Turning a garage into living space

Similar to a porch enclosure is transformation of a garage into a family room. This works out especially well when the garage is on the same level as main floor rooms, but it can also be done effectively in a split level or raised ranch style of house, or even when the garage is below grade level. A carport can be attached to the side.

One advantage in converting a garage to such purpose is that its exterior matches that of the house, and it already has a foundation and roof (or ceiling, if it has been built under other rooms). To take the place of the wide garage door, you could install either a patio door or a regular exterior door with windows on each side of it and contrasting trim, such as face brick, textured stone, or stucco and stained timber, to fill the space.

In filling in the space formerly occupied by the garage door, it may be necessary to change the grading or to build up a protective wall to avoid water seeping in during periods of heavy rainfall.

New flooring will have to be installed over the slab floor of the garage. As garage floors usually slant four to six inches, it may be necessary to build it up with sleepers, insulation, and a subfloor of five-eighths-inch plywood. Windows will have to be added to the sides, and perhaps a doorway in the back, leading to the garden. If plumbing is needed immediately or is planned for a future bath, pipes should be laid before the finished flooring and wall panels are installed.

Even a one-car garage can be converted into a spacious room, with its own bath, and a two-car garage (twenty-by-twenty feet) might be turned into one large room or two smaller rooms with bath.

Another way to create more living space is to expand a one-car garage, adding storage space and a workroom at the back, so that basement space now being so used can be converted to other use.

Sometimes an existing garage becomes the foundation for a new wing, with two bedrooms and a bath built above it, and the roof line made an extension of the existing roof line.

A far more ambitious and imaginative project won an award in the Kansas City HOMEE contest in 1974 for the "most dramatic change." In this case, a small split-level house, with a garage located in the lower level, was completely transformed. The space that had been occupied by the garage became an activities room for the children, and in the new wing built at the rear, a combined kitchen-family room with fireplace and a separate dining room were added, all looking out

The attached garage shown in the photograph has been converted into a guest bedroom with bath, as shown in the floor plan. The front stoop was retained, but windows were installed where the garage door had been.

Converted Garage

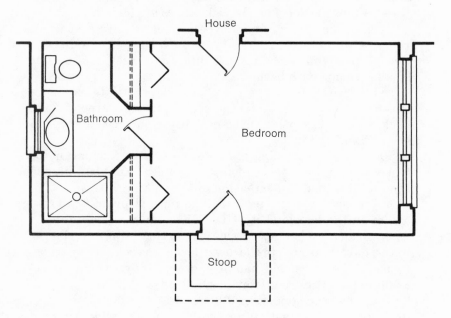

over the new patio. A new master bedroom and bath occupy the second floor of the new wing. The exterior of the house was face-lifted with solid vinyl siding and, to replace the garage, a carport was added.

Basement renovation

The basement is most often the do-it-yourselfer's big project. It is out of the way, which makes it easier to do the work piecemeal over a long period of time, and if there are no water or humidity problems, turning it into a recreation, family, or play room can be fairly simple.

But before embarking on even the simplest of basement renovations, certain factors should be carefully looked into. The first, of course, is dampness. Because it is below grade level, the air in a basement more often than not tends to be overly humid. But assuming that this is not a problem or, if it once was a problem, has been corrected, the next things to consider are: 1) the ceiling height—it should be a minimum of seven feet high, preferably higher; 2) how the area will be heated; and 3) the ventilation.

Even if the basement is used for nothing but a laundry area and workshop, ventilation is important. If the number of windows is inadequate, or if they are difficult to open, an exhaust or ventilating fan should be installed. Two exhaust fans may do a better job than one; these can be installed in windows or walls. They need not be turned on except as needed, but should be used on wash days, whenever the basement has been occupied by a group of people (at a party, perhaps) or when it is used for sleeping quarters. A dehumidifier in addition to exhaust fans will keep the air free of mustiness.

Another consideration is plumbing. If you wish to install a downstairs toilet, now or in the future, before going ahead with any other work see about having piping laid. Make sure that the sewer stack goes well below house level. In most houses it does, but occasionally a situation will be encountered where it drains into pipes at a level that will make it necessary to have waste from a below-grade toilet pumped upward to the sewer line, and this can be expensive.

If there is a laundry area already in the basement, there must be a drain for the washing machine, and therefore the

This basement recreation room is the handiwork of a do-it-yourself family. No-wax vinyl flooring in a brick pattern, papered and paneled walls, and acoustical tile on the ceiling are the basics of this cheerful room.

best place for a basement toilet, powder room, or full bath would be close to the laundry area, to connect to the existing drain, or to the main stack coming from the upstairs bathrooms.

Unless the basement is exceptionally well insulated, it will probably need more heat than can be obtained from overhead heating pipes, especially as these, after being boxed over, will not be able to distribute heat. Also, if the area is to be divided into several rooms, each may need its own heat source. If yours is a hot-water system, a circulating pump might be attached to the boiler. If it is a hot-air system, ask your heating serviceman about having ducts run around the perimeter.

The flooring is the next thing to consider. If the slab floor is level and dry, either foam-backed oak parquet tiles, foam-backed carpeting, or vinyl "no-wax" flooring can be laid directly on the slab. The foam backing in each case serves as a moisture barrier. Otherwise, it is best to lay two-by-four sleepers before installing a plywood subfloor with a vapor barrier.

Masonry walls may simply be painted, over waterproofing sealer, if the area is to be used primarily by youngsters, but paneling will give it a more finished effect and better insulation. Select light colors or finishes for the walls unless you plan to have light floors, ceilings, and furnishings.

A trend has developed of remodeling already-finished rec rooms into more sumptuous family rooms or bars for elegant entertaining.

An interest in wine, which has become almost an obsession with some Americans, might lead you to set aside a part of the basement for a wine cellar. This would be one area in which you would want no heat at all. On the contrary, it would have to be insulated for protection against all heat sources.

Raising the roof

It sounds easy enough to finish an attic and thus create space for extra bedrooms, but often this proves to be the most difficult of renovations.

First, the existing ceiling height at the peak of the roof must be at least seven feet, preferably seven and one-half to eight feet, or even with the addition of dormers, the space will not be suitable, because the height decreases sharply from the peak downward.

Second, if there is not an existing permanent stairway, a space measuring three by thirteen feet will be needed to install one. A disappearing stairway needs half this space, but it cannot be made permanent. A spiral staircase requires only five feet in diameter, but if the attic room is to be used by children, this is not advised: in their exuberant haste, they are too likely to stumble and fall down the narrow treads.

Sometimes the only way to add a stairway is to relinquish space from an existing bedroom on the floor immediately below. If you must lose one bedroom to add two, is it worth the cost and effort?

Also to be considered: heating, plumbing, and wiring will have to be routed to the attic from the basement. This could put a strain on water pressure, and the extra wiring might entail a separate circuit. However, attic rooms require less heat than downstairs rooms because heat always rises and the attic ceiling will be low.

If an attic has ample headroom and a stairway, it could provide the best and least expensive way to add bedrooms. One contractor, by adding a long dormer to the attic of a one-story house, found it was possible to put in three bedrooms, including a fourteen-by-twenty-foot master bedroom, and a full bath, where formerly there had been just one big loft-like room. As the house already had a full bath and two bedrooms downstairs, the owners were able to turn one of the former bedrooms into a family room.

Sometimes simply replacing two small narrow dormers with one long one opens up the attic area amazingly. If two long dormers are added, one in front and the other in the rear, the former attic may have almost as much usable space as the floor below.

But remember that adequate insulation and ventilation are essential. Windows are not enough. Ventilation must be provided in the enclosed area behind knee walls, to avoid condensation. Vents in the soffit under the eaves are important, and so is a louver with vents in the peak of the roof, above the finished ceiling.

The slope of the ceiling offers space for built-in storage areas. The more closets, cabinets, and drawer units built in, the less furniture will be needed, which in turn makes a room seem larger.

Make sure that windows in the renovated area are the kind that require little or no exterior maintenance and can be washed easily from the inside, with removable sashes or those that tilt inward.

In some cases, an entire new second floor can be constructed above a one-story house, especially a ranch or rambler style with a low-peaked roof. This kind of addition is more costly but it also creates more living space than adding dormers. Since this type of house usually occupies a greater land area, finding space for a stairway should not be as difficult as in the cottage type of house.

The chief problem for an entire second-story addition is often one of exterior design, to make this second floor look like an integral part of the house. A run-of-the-mill contractor is not likely to have the style sense or skill to do it properly. Probably plans should be designed by an architect and the work carried out by a reputable contractor already experienced in this type of renovation.

Adding a wing

When not enough extra space can be realized with one of the previously described methods, the best solution may be to add a completely new wing. In one sense, this alternative is more costly because a new foundation, new exterior walls, and a new roof are necessary. But when extensive changes are made inside an old house, especially when it involves rearranging walls, double labor costs are involved. In such cases, a new wing could turn out to be the less expensive way.

Can a clever home handyman add a wing to his house? It has been done. One couple living in New Jersey needed a playroom for their children and decided it would be satisfactory to remove a side porch, which they rarely used, and add a room that would be right off the kitchen and dining area. They hired an architect to draw up blueprints—necessary before they could get a building permit—and hired a bulldozer operator to clear the ground and excavate for the crawl space. But the only other outside help they had was from plumbing and electrical subcontractors. It took the couple four months to complete the job, working part-time. Before they finished they decided to do a little more than originally planned, extending the vented soffits under the roof overhang all around the house.

To use the masculine gender in referring to do-it-yourselfers is unfair to the many women who are learning such skills as carpentry, papering walls, installing floor tiles, and even roofing. One Oklahoma City housewife proved so adept at shingling, the contractor agreed to let her work beside his men and paid her two dollars an hour. Further, he declared she was faster than most men at the job. She had begun by helping to raise the walls and lay bricks.

One of the difficulties in adding a wing to an existing house is achieving conformity in style. The original siding has been on for some time. Can the wing be added without replacing all the existing siding, roofing, and windows? And when the wing is finished, will it look like an obvious afterthought, or will it blend unobtrusively with the design of the original house?

Most added wings are only one-story high, yet the cost of making a two-story addition may not be a great deal more.

When a family in Virginia presented their contractor with an architect's blueprint for an extension to their brick raised-ranch house, the plans called for a twelve-by-twenty-one-foot room above a carport, the new room to adjoin the existing upper-level dining room and kitchen. Bids for this work were about $12,000. The contractor, after studying the blueprints, suggested that for an additional $1,500 he could make a twelve-by-thirty-eight-foot addition in brick to match the existing house, with an enclosed heated garage on the ground level and above this the twelve-by-twenty-one-foot room they wanted, plus an open nine-by-fourteen-foot deck at the rear. The new room has sliding patio doors opening onto the deck. In the rear of the garage, below, is a sizable utility room, a workshop, and a garden room. Stairs lead from the deck to the garden in the rear.

An added wing, whether one or two stories high, must have the same foundation and roof, and the cost of additional siding and windows for the second floor is not great. The interior finish of the overhead rooms can always be delayed if the budget does not permit finishing them now.

When one couple consulted an architect about adding a wing to their Tudor-style house (in place of an old side porch with sloping roof), they intended to have a simple family room, but the architect pointed out that there was a lack of closets in the house, and suggested adding a story above the new family room for use as a large dressing room for the master bedroom. This made it possible to have two immense closets and, at the rear, a desk beneath a window that overlooks the garden. The new wing was finished with a siding of stucco and timber to match the upper portion of the adjoining structure, with roofing of cedar shakes as on the old roof, so that when completed, it seemed an integral part of the house.

Reading blueprints

Learning to read blueprints is an important part of home improvement. If any of the symbols or technical language are beyond your comprehension, take the trouble to find out exactly what they mean. The blueprints must indicate the materials to be used, details of construction, and dimensions not only of rooms, but of stairwells, walls, and other parts of the structure.

When looking over the blueprints for a new wing to your house, make sure that the foundation includes footings going down at least two or three feet beneath the grade level of the masonry walls. These footings are the basic supports of the structure and, if too shallow or improperly constructed, could be the cause of settling or slanting of walls later.

Also, there must be four-inch drain "tiles" of perforated plastic pipe or "poroswall" around the perimeter laid in a bed of gravel and slanted to carry the runoff of water into a dry well or over a graded slope that will direct the water away from the house. The foundation walls, which probably will be of cinder block, should be pargeted (spread with mortar or cement), then covered with tar, and then possibly with a vapor barrier such as rigid polystyrene panels, before the earth is replaced.

If you plan to have a slab foundation, make sure that a bed of gravel four inches deep is laid over the excavated portion of earth, then over this a vapor barrier of polyethylene, before the concrete is poured for the slab. Bluestone in fairly large size is recommended for the gravel base; small gravel will compact too easily. After the slab is set and dry, it should be covered with waterproof sealer, as should the finished inside masonry walls. Remembering the importance of wall insulation, described in chapter 2, you will also have to make sure that both the masonry foundation walls and those above ground have adequate insulation, three and one-half-inch fiber glass or its equivalent.

If the new wing is to have a crawl space, it is essential that a vapor barrier be laid over the earth beneath and a sufficient number of air vents be added to the foundation walls. Also, any wood structure should be eighteen inches from the earth to avoid termite infection and dry rot. If you are going to the expense of having a new wing added to your house, making sure it will be free of moisture and well-ventilated should be considered part of the insurance on your equity.

CHAPTER 7

Turning Unused Space to Profit

The Bensons enjoyed their rambling five-bedroom house when their children were growing up, and had even added a downstairs bath and den by enclosing one end of the wide porch that lined three sides of the house. The den doubled as a TV room and sleeping quarters for visiting relatives and their children's friends.

After their youngest daughter married, the Bensons began to talk of selling the big house and moving to a smaller place, but for a number of years, while three of their four married children and the multiplying grandchildren were nearby, it was a pleasure to have bedroom space sufficient for family reunions over the holidays.

Then one by one the children moved farther away, transferred by the companies for which they worked. When fuel bills shot up and it became increasingly difficult to find anyone willing to do yard work, once again the Bensons talked of moving to a smaller place, perhaps even to an apartment.

But they enjoyed the neighborhood; the house was comfortable; and when they looked around at condominium apartments and town houses, which would relieve them of maintenance worries, they were appalled by the purchase price and mortgage interest rates. Besides, what would they do with all their possessions, the accumulation of decades of marriage and raising their children? Since their old house was completely paid for, they had only taxes and upkeep to worry about now that they were living on retirement income.

Finally, they called in a contractor who had done renovation jobs for them in the past to ask him whether they could turn a part of their big house into a rental unit.

The den with its adjoining full bath seemed ideal for this purpose, especially since it already had its own entrance onto the porch. But, the contractor warned, local zoning restrictions for their neighborhood would not permit them to turn theirs into a two-family house—and any separate unit with cooking facilities falls into that classification.

The Bensons could circumvent the ruling by omitting a kitchenette, he suggested, and he assured them that there are many single persons who are not interested in cooking, who simply want a place with privacy, like a hotel room but in a more residential atmosphere.

Further, the contractor told them, it is not necessary to get a building permit if no exterior changes or plumbing installations will be made. He suggested that a portion of the hallway be cut off and, by moving a wall, be made part of the den, enlarging the den by three feet. Within that area, a built-in unit could be placed that would be a combination closet and storage area. Closing off the hallway would also give their tenant complete privacy.

He also advised them to purchase a refrigerator with simulated wood-grain exterior, which would look like a piece of furniture in the rental unit. Some of these refrigerators have outlets into which small cooking appliances can be plugged. Some also have miniature sinks. For these, a plumbing hook-up is required, but when there is an adjoining bathroom, this is a simple operation. Since a unit of this kind is a "snack bar," not primarily for cooking use, it would not contravene the zoning regulations.

The Bensons liked the idea of making the rental unit completely separate so that they could maintain a formal relationship with the tenant. They redecorated the enlarged room with new carpeting, paneled walls and a built-in wall unit stained to match the paneling, and provided some dishes and appliances so that their tenant could get his own breakfast.

They had no trouble finding a tenant willing to pay $125 a month (eventually they were able to raise this to $150), a businessman who had to spend a great deal of time in the city but whose family home was in a distant suburb.

It took only a short time for the rent they received to cover the cost of the renovation and thereafter the rental went toward their own taxes and maintenance costs.

Later the Bensons learned of a university student who needed a room and they made an arrangement to let him live in one of their spare bedrooms at nominal rent if he would cut the grass in summer and clear the walks and driveway in winter. They found his presence in the house a pleasure, almost like having one of their own sons back again, and even encouraged him to bring his friends to the house.

Check zoning laws

Before going to the expense of converting any part of your house to a rental unit, the first step must be to check your local zoning laws. In some cases, there is no barrier, as long as building codes are observed. But if the neighborhood is zoned for one-family dwellings, those who try to bypass such a regulation and get caught, not only have to turn out their tenants and lose the expected rent, but must also pay a stiff fine.

When a separate garage is converted into an apartment with a kitchen, it may be a different situation. If the apartment is not under the same roof, even though a "second family" (which can mean just one person) lives in another building on the same lot, the two-family rule may not apply.

There are, as the Bensons and others with extra space in their homes have discovered, many people seeking attractive rooms to rent who do not demand cooking facilities. Most, however, want some kind of light-housekeeping arrangement for preparing breakfast and snacks. This need can be filled by a portable refrigerator unit and small electric appliances such as a teakettle, a hot plate, and a toaster or toaster-oven. The washbasin in the bathroom can double as a sink. Not an ideal arrangement, but it can suffice. The refrigerator need not be a fancy new unit. A secondhand model can be purchased, and kept hidden in a corner behind a screen or an ell formed by two pole room dividers.

Renting out a room

If there is ample bedroom space available, and the homeowners are willing to forego some of their privacy, they might simply rent out a bedroom and perhaps permit the roomer to have kitchen privileges. In any such arrangement, however, personality factors can be crucial. It is even more important to investigate thoroughly the background of a roomer who will be right in your house, perhaps invited into your living room on occasion, than a tenant in separate quarters. Even if the roomer provides good references, there can be clashes. A young person who comes in frequently at 2:00 A.M., or who leaves the kitchen in a mess, or keeps a radio turned up to a piercing range, can drive the homeowner-landlord to distraction. The initial arrangement should be so written out that the landlord can give the tenant two weeks' notice to leave should things not work out well. Also, there should be agreement in writing as to exactly what privileges are and are not granted. With luck, the arrangement might prove both profitable and pleasant.

Jane, a divorcée with two children under the age of twelve in her custody, not only found that her alimony payments were inadequate for covering living costs, but felt terribly tied down, not being able to afford a baby-sitter when she wanted to go to a movie or have dinner with friends. Since the divorce settlement had given her the family's four-bedroom house, she had a spare bedroom, and so advertised for a roomer.

The first person to reply to the advertisement was a girl who had recently taken on a local secretarial job. Elsa was away from her family for the first time in her life, and liked the idea of living in a private home. Besides, she could not afford to rent an apartment by herself and did not yet know any other young women in the area.

Elsa was quite willing to baby-sit two or three nights a week. She and Jane made an agreement that they would work out in advance whichever nights were most mutually conveni-

An unused room can be turned into a rental unit, with or without its own entrance. In this room, hardboard paneling with an inset resembling hand-carved decoration is used for the walls and for the doors of closets at each end of the daybed. The flooring is of resilient no-wax vinyl tile. This same decor could be used in the conversion of a one-car garage.

ent. While the initial arrangement was that Elsa would use the kitchen only after Jane had finished with dinner, they got on so well that Elsa frequently joined Jane and the children at table and they cleared up the dishes afterward and watched television together. It was an arrangement that lasted three years, and after Elsa left to share an apartment with a girl friend, she returned for frequent visits and would baby-sit whenever Jane needed her.

Another woman, Rosemary, felt an agonizing loss when her husband died. Her first impulse was to sell their house and move to an apartment. But the prospect of getting rid of so many possessions that had sentimental value was appalling. She decided instead to rent out two rooms as a bed-sitting room arrangement. She did not advertise, only told friends that she was looking for someone.

Finding a tenant in this way took longer, but within a month she had learned about another woman, also widowed, who had given up her home to move into an efficiency, only to find that she could not bear being in such tiny quarters and alone evening after evening. As Rosemary's new tenant, this woman had a comfortable bedroom and a sitting room where she could entertain visitors.

In this way each woman had ample privacy. They arranged schedules for use of the kitchen, but frequently ended by dining together, as they got on well, and even went out in the evening together to movies and plays which each would have been reluctant to attend alone.

Nearly all would-be roomers are single. Many are university or business school students (schools maintain lists of students needing rooms) ; others are young people taking on a first job away from home. Bachelors or widowers who do not want to be bothered even with light housekeeping can be quite agreeable tenants and ask for nothing but a clean and quiet bedroom and an adjoining bath, preferably one that need not be shared.

To have a roomer is not the same as running a rooming house. There is no law that bars making use of a spare bedroom in this way. Older couples who enjoy having young people around may welcome a bit of noise and feel refreshed by being brought once again in contact with youthful outlooks on life. It all depends on how well individuals happen to get along. But when it does work out, it can be the easiest way to make a partially empty house help pay for itself.

Converting unused space to an apartment

Where zoning laws do permit two-family dwellings, the basement is often converted to use as a rental unit. If there is no separate entrance to the basement, usually one can be made at the side of the house with steps leading down. When a house is built on a slope, the basement may even open onto a lower level. If this opening is at the rear of the house, a walk will have to be laid leading to it, but this is a comparatively simple change.

The essentials mentioned in chapter 6 for any basement renovation apply doubly to a basement made into a separate apartment. It must be dry, the ceiling must be a minimum of seven feet in height, preferably seven and one-half feet, and it must have good ventilation. It will need a separate heating unit with its own thermostat.

A room that seems dry enough for a rec room or playroom may not be sufficiently dry for use as full-time living quarters. A dehumidifier somewhere nearby, if not in the apartment unit itself, is advisable. A ventilating fan also is beneficial, even if there are windows—unless one side of the basement is at ground level.

New flooring should not be laid over the concrete slab until any moisture problems have been solved. If there is only a concrete slab, over this should go a vapor barrier (rigid insulation board preferably) and two-by-four sleepers, then subflooring of plywood, and finally finished flooring of vinyl, carpeting or wood. Paneled walls are advisable both for insulation and ease of maintenance. Plain wallboard can be painted or papered; the latter is advantageous, especially if a vinyl-coated strippable paper in a light "grass-cloth" or textured finish is used.

If there is already finished flooring, and it is satisfactory, it may be possible simply to cover it with parquet, tile, or carpeting—carpet tiles or room-size widths. In most cases, however, it pays to put down new subflooring and to cover this with no-wax vinyl, for ease of maintenance, or foam-backed indoor-outdoor carpeting. The latter provides a warmer floor and also helps to make a below-grade-level

How unused space can be made profitable is demonstrated by before and after photographs of a basement in which an apartment was constructed.

room seem more like a living room. On the other hand, many patterns in the no-wax vinyl are quite elegant—some resemble parquet, others look like Mediterranean ceramic tile—and no matter how careless your tenants may prove to be, such a floor can take all kinds of punishment.

Lighter colors will help to make a basement room brighter and more cheerful. If natural wood paneling is the choice for the walls, it is particularly important that the flooring be lighter in tone.

Creating a small apartment

A "studio" or "efficiency" apartment can be created in a surprisingly small area.

One four-square frame house built on a hillside had an unused garage along one side of the basement. Because of the ten-inch-wide foundation wall, the garage was only eleven feet wide and twenty-three and one-half feet long. (Because it was so small and the slope leading down to it so steep, it had not been used as a garage for many years.)

The owners had been using the garage area of the basement only for laundry and storage. When they approached contractors for opinions as to whether the space could be used for an apartment, most of them simply shook their heads and walked away. But Kitty Jackson, whose husband had had to retire early from his job because of poor health, was determined, as they badly needed some source of additional income. At last she found a contractor who was able to install a bathroom with a shower, a six-foot kitchenette unit, and a built-in storage unit in the living area—which was only ten by eleven feet when finished—and a closet under the stairs. The apartment thus had everything necessary for a single person. The fact that the room already had a large expanse of window that overlooked the garden and also provided a distant view made up in large measure for the limited space.

The kitchenette unit came in one piece, including an under-counter refrigerator, a stainless steel sink, and a four-burner range (available in both gas and electric models). Above this unit they installed cabinets of steel finished in white porcelain. Pegboard was mounted, floor to ceiling, on the adjoining wall for hanging pots, pans, and other small utensils. An eating bar, jutting out beside the kitchenette unit, served both as a room divider and counter space when needed.

For lighting fixtures, the Jacksons decided on two matching reel lamps hung from the ceiling for the living area, one over the studio couch, the other over the eating bar. In the kitchenette area a recessed panel light was installed in the ceiling of white acoustical tiles, and a fluorescent tube placed under the upper cabinets. A scenic paper in delicate pastels was used over the wall opposite the kitchenette unit to make that area seem less cramped.

In the bathroom, which had an area of only five and one-half by six feet, a one-component shower unit was installed. (The washing machine and dryer were moved to a place under the stairs, opening to the other side of the basement. This meant walling off part of the space, for plumbing installation, which otherwise might have been used entirely for the apartment's bath.)

Sliding windows were installed in the thick foundation walls where fixed windows had been previously. Where the garage door had been, a double-hung window and an entrance door with a large glass area added still more light and air.

The built-in storage unit served to hold the tenant's clothing, books, television set, record player, and other items. It was painted an off-white, with louvered cabinet doors, and the inside and open shelves were finished in a pale shade of blue-green.

The rent the Jacksons were able to command for this efficiency unit paid off the improvement loan in three years, and thereafter was enough to cover more than half of their own monthly mortgage, taxes, and insurance costs.

Only a little more difficult than converting a basement into an apartment is to convert a garage, either an attached garage or a separate building. As noted in the Jackson case, it is even possible to make a complete rental unit from a one-car garage, but in a two-car garage, quite a spacious apartment can be created. If the garage has a slab floor, before laying new flooring, two-by-four sleepers and a vapor barrier should be placed over the slab, then the subflooring, and last the finished flooring. This is true whether the floor is above or below grade level. Plumbing installation may present a problem if fairly long plumbing lines must be laid, but at

Converted Basement

The basement rental unit shown in these before and after floor plans was formerly the furnace room in a row house. The kitchenette opens into the room and the dining area is at the bay window. The bathroom, with shower, occupies a space measuring only 5½ by 4½ feet.

Before

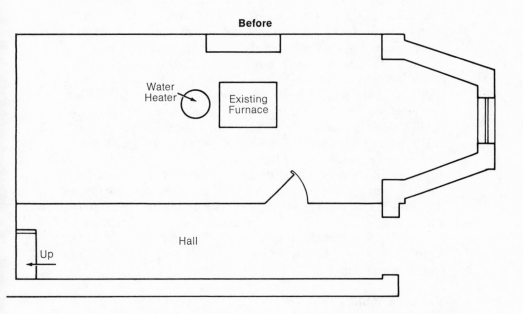

After

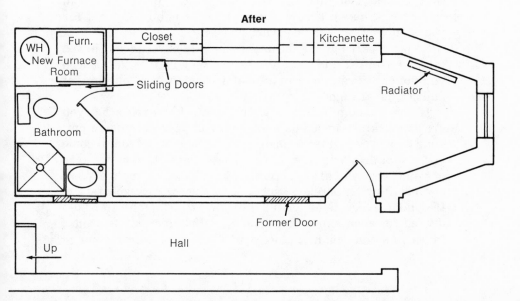

least nothing has to be torn down to make way for them.

Separate meters

It is advisable to have separate meters, gas and electric, for any apartment tenants, even if the rental includes utilities. The time may come when the landlord-owner concludes that it would be better to have the tenant pay his own utilities, even if the rent is lowered proportionately. Tenants who pay for utilities are much more careful about consumption, and a careless use of facilities can even present a fire hazard.

A rental unit must have its own completely separate entrance, and for this reason, it is usually restricted to the ground floor or below. Converting an upper floor to a rental unit requires adding an outside stairway or closing off a formal foyer from the rest of the house, with the stairway to the upper floor on one side and an entrance to the downstairs opening from it. The objection to the outside stairway is that it makes it obvious that the house is a two-family residence, and in some neighborhoods, regardless of zoning, there may be objections to this. As long as you intend to remain in the neighborhood, some consideration of how your neighbors feel is important.

Making a hobby pay

Many people look forward to retirement with the thought that then at last they will be able to indulge themselves in spending as much time as they like at a hobby enjoyed for years only on weekends or vacations.

Sometimes what has been merely a hobby can be turned into a business, and if you have retirement income to keep you going at first, you can afford at least to take a fling at it and see how things go.

If you can convince the Internal Revenue Service that you are embarking on a business venture with serious intent, your expenses and investment may be deducted from income tax, and a proportion of all expenses related to maintenance of your home will also be allowed. Purchase of supplies, postage (mailing costs related solely to business), transportation, telephone, all come under this heading. How much can be deducted for such expenses as mortgage payments, insurance, taxes, and home maintenance depends on how many rooms in your home are used solely for business. If you use two rooms in a six-room house for your business venture, you could deduct as much as one-third of all maintenance costs, including the cost of major structural repairs. If it is one room in a ten-room house, you could deduct only one-tenth.

Depreciation and amortization of equipment are also allowable deductions. For any equipment that is also used for other purposes, such as your car or power tools, you have to determine what proportion can be claimed honestly as essential for business use. Equipment purchased especially to set up or maintain your business can be amortized over the normal length of life of that equipment. Such items might include a desk, typewriter, file cabinet, and a reference library, or a new sewing machine, or new photographic equipment.

You must keep careful records and sell enough of your output to indicate that it is more than a hobby, but intent is the yardstick by which the IRS measures your venture. Auditors tend to be suspicious of pleasure trips made for "business" reasons, and of such ventures as breeding show dogs or developing prize orchids for sale. A woman who writes occasional features for a club magazine or local newspaper, even if she gets paid for her work, may find that she is regarded by the IRS as a "literary hobbyist." It depends primarily on whether one can prove that the activity is not just for amusement, that you are working hard to earn money.

Among the many hobbies that could well be turned into a business are repairing or making furniture, woodcarving, knitting, crocheting, hand-printing Christmas cards, taking candid color portraits of children, making custom picture frames, appliquéing pillow covers, making party aprons with embroidered names or slogans on them, and creating party favors, Christmas tree decorations, dresses for little girls, or "his" and "her" accessories.

Assess the demand

If you have been engaged in your hobby long enough to acquire the necessary skill, the next step is to investigate how much of a demand there may be for your wares and what price you should charge. Naturally, the selling price must cover the costs of production plus a small profit. The production cost will include an outlay for advertising. Where and how will you advertise, and how much is it likely to cost?

Then, if you still believe you could profit from such a venture, consider what room or rooms in your house might be turned into a studio or office. If prospective customers will be coming to view your work, the room should be easily accessible to visitors. Also, the room in which you do the actual work should afford complete privacy when you need it, and be a room that need not appear neat at all times. And, of course, your business arrangements must conform with local zoning laws.

If your business intentions are serious, the chances are good that the tax advantage alone will make the venture worthwhile even if you do not realize much of a cash income from it. You need not make a sizable profit from your former hobby for it to qualify as a business. As long as the IRS recognizes a future potential and sees that you are operating with efficiency and enterprise, the expenses and investments of the first years will be allowed even if the business shows no profit. In subsequent years, if you make a good profit for a while, then business falls off, you will be permitted to average your income over a period of several years for tax purposes.

You can get full information and advice at your local IRS office, and it is wise to do this when starting your business, to find out just what kinds of records you must keep. You can also obtain, for your guidance, Publication 535, titled, "Tax Information on Business Expenses." Other helpful publications include Number 463, "Travel, Entertainment and Gift Expenses"; Number 534, "Tax Information on Depreciation"; Number 536, "Losses from Operation of a Business"; and Number 527, "Rental Income and Royalty Income."

After looking over these publications, you will probably conclude that it is worthwhile to consult a tax expert when the time comes to file your income tax returns. He very likely will save you enough to cover a good part of his fee.

Renting out studio space

Renting out a spare room for commercial use is subject to local zoning regulations, but if the person to whom you are making the space available is in a quasi-commercial enterprise, chances are that this will be permitted even in a residential zone.

A finished basement might well suit someone who teaches arts or ballet, or almost any hobby craft.

You might even open your own studio, teaching others a skill you have mastered rather than trying to sell your actual products. For example, if you are known as an excellent cook, you might try giving cooking lessons, but first find out whether there is a need for such a school in your locality. If there are several such schools already, you may not be able to compete successfully. Also, to do it properly, you will have to invest in new kitchen equipment. Before making such an investment, you should have reason to believe that the business has at least a fifty-fifty chance of succeeding.

A retired person for whom photography has been a lifelong hobby might teach photography to beginners. A retired studio technician might set up a "sound recording studio," teaching students how to record and edit music on tapes. A retired stockbroker might give weekly "seminars" on investing. A retired accountant might start a part-time income tax service.

Even though the actual income may not be great, a home business helps to make life in retirement more meaningful and certainly widens one's group of acquaintances.

Starting a mail-order business

A spare bedroom might well be turned into a mail-order office, if you have had experience in this type of business or can obtain guidance from a qualified source.

In many cities, the Small Business Administration offers seminars in how to launch a new business. For further information, check your telephone directory under U.S. Government, Small Business Administration.

Your first step should be to determine what kinds of products are most suitable for mail-order purchase and distribution. If these products include merchandise with which you are familiar, and you know which items are most in demand, you might do very well in this type of enterprise.

A jeweler in Pleasantville, New York, who had for years provided a watch repair service in his shop, decided to give up the shop and concentrate on selling watches by mail from his home. Because of his long experience in the field, he had established contacts with several leading watch manufacturers and arranged to act as their broker.

In addition to saving money that would have been used to rent the shop, the jeweler and his wife found that they could work fewer hours in their mail-order business than they had in the shop. Because he knew his merchandise thoroughly, the jeweler was able to select watches that he knew were well made. He also knew from experience what proportion of the orders he could expect to be returned within the period of guarantee, and could thus estimate his losses.

Producing a catalog is an important aspect of any mail-order business. The catalog must present the goods attractively, with color pictures and descriptions, and offer them at prices slightly lower than those of retail stores.

To obtain a mailing list for prospective customers is not difficult. Such lists can be purchased. Having the catalog printed is a big initial investment, but once set up, it will need only minor revisions for future mailings.

Renting out office space

An office need not be looked upon as commercial rental if the tenant is a professional who does not receive clients but only needs a quiet, comfortable, and private place in which to work. For example, a free-lance writer who needs a room in which to work without interruption might pay $40 or $50 a month for such a room.

Watching the classified columns for those seeking studio or office space probably would be the best way to find such a person if word of mouth advertising is not successful.

As long as the room is used only by that one person, and there is no outside sign of commercial enterprise, there is no reason why you could not make an unused room available. It would not need any furnishings other than carpeting, shelves, possibly a long table, and a couple of folding chairs. The tenant could supply anything else needed.

It would be wise, of course, to make inquiries first, to avoid involving yourself in legal complications. If the way seems clear and aboveboard, when you list the rental income in your annual income tax return, you can also deduct the portion of your property expenses and cost of upkeep that relates to this rental. A tax consultant can advise you about this, as about any other purpose for which your home is used to earn additional income.

CHAPTER 8

Kitchen, Bathrooms, and Laundry

The one room more important than any others when a house is up for sale is the kitchen. But if you decide that this justifies redoing your kitchen, and you turn to a kitchen specialist to plan the renovation for you, you may end up with a bill of $10,000 to $15,000.

American kitchens have become so fanciful that the tendency often is to lavish more money on them than is warranted. There are many ways in which an existing kitchen can be made more efficient and more attractive at moderate cost and without extensive renovation.

This is also true of bathrooms, the second most important part of the house to most home buyers. Many homes have more than one bathroom, and the more the better. When an old house has only one bathroom, among the changes most new owners will want to make is to add at least a powder room on the first floor or in the basement. Often it is possible to add a bathroom back-to-back with an existing one without too much tearing up of walls and floors. The additional bathroom is usually constructed in a small space that had been part of an adjoining bedroom.

Common problems

Kitchens, laundries, and bathrooms present the same basic renovation problems. In each, existing plumbing must be examined before any alterations or new installations are made. If the old water pipes are galvanized and the vertical piping looks rather badly corroded, you can be sure that the horizontal piping is worse, and it is not unknown for old piping to go rapidly to pieces when new fixtures, placing new pressure on the pipes, are installed.

A talented do-it-yourselfer, using ordinary tools, may be able to put in new rigid vinyl piping. It is also sometimes possible to combine new piping with the old, though more often than not this means pinching pennies only to waste dollars. It is usually advisable to turn to a reputable plumber for inspection of existing pipes as well as installation of new piping and hookups.

Another common problem in these three areas is ventilation. Without proper ventilation, the moisture buildup resulting from steam (from dishwasher, washing machine, showers, and tub baths) will cause gradual and occasionally rapid deterioration of walls and ceiling, and sometimes flooring as well. An exhaust vent may be a more important addition than a new garbage disposer in your kitchen. Baths that do not have outside windows are required by the building code to have exhaust fans, but the trouble is that in most homes bathroom windows are not opened frequently enough for excess moisture to escape. A window should be opened, for example, whenever there is enough steam in the room to cloud a mirror. It is important that a bathroom window be easy to reach and easy to open. If it is not, either change the window or add an exhaust fan, whichever is least expensive.

The same applies to a laundry area, particularly when it is located in a basement. When there is a window in the laundry area, usually it is too high to reach easily. The frequent result is that the room receives no ventilation at all.

The same wall and floor finishes can be used in kitchen, bath, and laundry, all of which require finishes that are moisture-resistant and easy to clean. Suitable for use are latex or alkyd enamel paints, vinyl-coated wallpapers or cloth wallcoverings, laminated plastic for counters and walls (especially around bathtubs and for the sink splashback), and floorings in any of the many vinyl finishes. (For bathrooms, ceramic tile is preferable to vinyl, but increasingly vinyl and plastic products are being used for bathroom walls and floors because these coverings are easier for do-it-yourselfers to install.)

The same lighting problems apply to each of these three areas. Strong, well-diffused overhead lighting is important in each, but so is shadowless light directed at certain areas. If new lights are to be installed, consider fluorescents. They provide far more light and consume far less electricity than incandescents.

Another problem common to the three areas is wiring. Before using any new appliance, the wiring must be re-inspected—unless the replacement uses no greater wattage than the old appliance. If an extensive renovation is planned, a new electric line may be needed, and at least a new circuit box or breaker, as well as a separate line (circuit) for each appliance.

Finally, it is the equipment and fixtures for these three areas that homeowners are always being tempted to replace as new models with labor-saving or unusual gadgets are introduced each year. Not infrequently homeowners purchase a fancy new stove or washing machine, sold on its magic push-button devices, only to find that the new model does not do as good a job as the old one.

The kitchen

The feature most wanted in a kitchen is convenient arrangement. Next in importance, according to recent surveys, is eat-in space, regardless of how close and convenient the dining area may be. But it is psychologically important that the kitchen also be a cheerful, attractive, well-lighted place in which to work.

If a kitchen does not have these features, remodeling is called for. But in many cases just minor rearrangement or added storage units can make the kitchen more convenient; a new color scheme can make it far more cheerful; and an eating counter can be fitted into even a small kitchen without moving walls.

Before getting caught up in a major kitchen renovation, it is important to consider not only how much you can afford to spend, but how much you should spend. It is frequently claimed that investment in kitchen renovation always pays off in added resale value of the property, but this is true only up to a certain point. If you put a $10,000 kitchen in a house in the $30,000-$35,000 price bracket, it will not automatically raise the selling price of that house to the $45,000 level. The surrounding neighborhood should be taken into consideration, for a luxurious house surrounded by homes in a much lower price range is not going to command the price it would if located in a luxury neighborhood. So when you renovate your kitchen, set a budget consistent with the overall value of your property.

Also, your kitchen should conform to your particular life style. First consider in what ways your kitchen is inadequate for you and how those shortcomings can be overcome in a manner that will gratify your tastes and harmonize with the rest of the house.

Row Kitchen

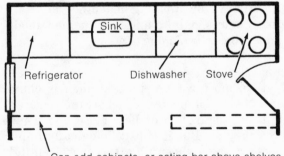

Can add cabinets, or eating bar above shelves
as room dividers (or use movable screens)

L-Shaped Kitchen
With Adjoining Laundry

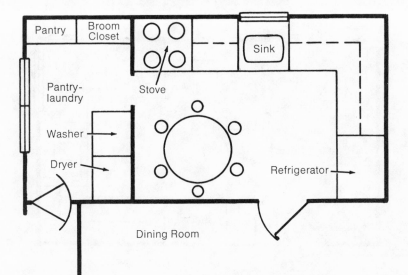

Pantry

Broom Closet

Sink

Stove

Pantry-laundry

Washer

Dryer

Refrigerator

Dining Room

L-Shaped Kitchen With Island

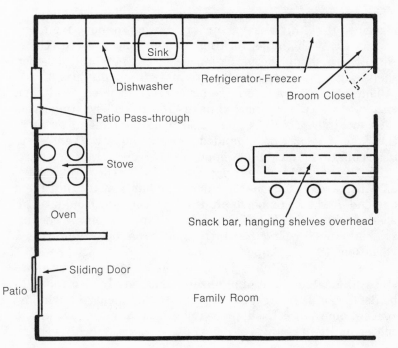

Sink

Dishwasher

Refrigerator-Freezer

Broom Closet

Patio Pass-through

Stove

Oven

Snack bar, hanging shelves overhead

Sliding Door

Patio

Family Room

U-Shaped Kitchen

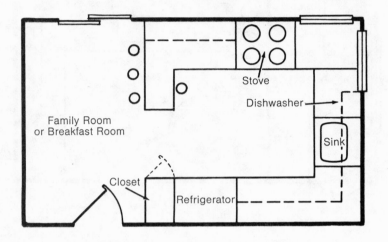

As for convenience of arrangement, appliances should be placed so that only a few steps are needed to move from one to another, with ample working counter space between them. Also, there should be ample space in cabinets and on open shelves for storing the equipment most frequently used.

There are six basic arrangements recommended by kitchen specialists (see drawings on pages 162-166). The simplest is the row kitchen. This is found mainly in apartments or vacation homes. It may be expanded by removing a wall and placing room-divider cabinets opposite the row arrangement.

The L-shaped kitchen is popular and versatile. It may have an eat-in area in a corner, or an eating bar that juts out from one end of the L, or be combined with a pass-through or an island looking into the dining area or family room. A "peninsular kitchen," with a bar jutting out from one counter, is a variation of the L shape.

The U-shaped kitchen is also popular, but requires more steps to get from one appliance to another. It also tends to be darker, unless care is taken to provide plenty of window space. Some large U-shaped kitchens have an island in the center for step-saving.

Corridor (Galley) Kitchen

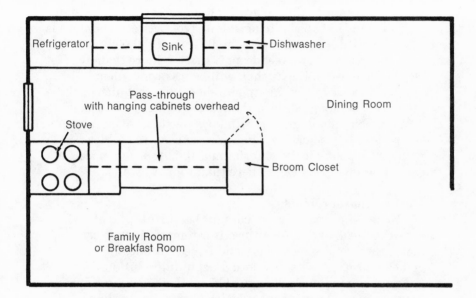

The corridor kitchen (sometimes called a galley kitchen) is the most compact arrangement, but it gives some people a feeling of claustrophobia. The parallel kitchen is probably the best of them all. It is as compact as the corridor type but offers a greater feeling of space, especially when adapted to the popular open arrangement with kitchen separated from dining area or family room only by double-cabinet room dividers, a half wall, or the projecting arm that forms the other side of the parallel.

In almost every kitchen, one of these six basic arrangements already exists or can be created. Note in the drawings that all have certain things in common. The sink always has counter space on both sides (the dishwasher can go under the counter either to right or left). The refrigerator is steps away in one direction, the stove steps away from the sink in the other, or directly across the corridor. If there is a wall oven, it must have counter space beside it on which to place hot dishes or pans. For either the corridor or parallel arrangement, the space between counters should be neither less than three feet nor more than four feet. This allows more than one person to be in this space at the same time, yet counters and cabinets are all within arm's reach, a great saver of steps.

In L- and U-shaped kitchens, four feet between counters is recommended, requiring a room at least eight feet in width, as cabinets are all two feet deep. If there is more than five feet between counters, the kitchen will be less convenient.

Take a look at your existing kitchen and see which of these plans can be adapted with the least tearing up and moving around. Existing doors and windows must be taken into consideration, but sometimes it is less expensive to block up a window or door (if the exterior siding is to be changed anyway) and place them elsewhere than to move walls.

The question of cabinets

"Model kitchens" always contain beautiful cabinets which have the finish of fine furniture. It is tempting when remodeling to throw out old cabinets and have new ones installed. If you can afford it, this is indeed a beguiling solution.

But take another look at the old cabinets. In a good many cases, they can be rejuvenated with nothing more than a little carpentry and redecorating, which could save you as much as two or three thousand dollars, since new cabinets, especially if they are custom-made, can cost as much as three thousand dollars.

Parallel Kitchen

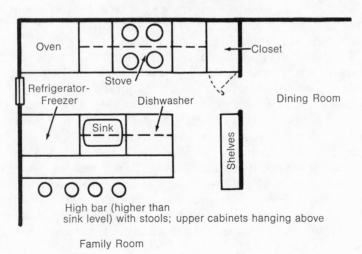

Oven — Closet

Refrigerator-Freezer   Stove   Dishwasher   Dining Room

Sink   Shelves

High bar (higher than sink level) with stools; upper cabinets hanging above

Family Room

If appearance is the chief drawback of existing wood cabinets, they may take on quite a respectable look if you do nothing more than thoroughly clean the surface and replace the hardware. Wash the wood surface with a special woodwork detergent, or with an ammonia solution, to remove all grease and grime. This may require rewashing several times, rubbing after each wash with a soft cloth and then scrubbing hard-to-clean areas with fine steel wool dipped in mineral spirits. When the wood is thoroughly clean and dry, apply clear polyurethane glaze for a hard, scrubbable surface.

A more ambitious way to beautify old wood cabinets is to apply varnish remover and strip down to the bare wood. Do this only if you feel sure that the wood is of good quality and worth the effort. Remove doors and drawers, and strip these in your workshop. You will, of course, remove all hardware as well. You may find it worthwhile to have the doors and drawers done by a professional (ask about this at an antique shop) while you work on the built-in frames. Use a paste varnish remover for vertical surfaces, and a liquid type for horizontal surfaces. When doing this job wear rubber gloves and keep children and pets out of the kitchen. Give the remover plenty of time to "cook" the old surface, then peel it off with a paint scraper or putty knife. When most of the old finish is off, rub remaining spots with coarse steel wool, and finish by sanding and using a tack cloth. When all this is done, you can decide whether to add a clear glaze or varnish, or to use a varnish-stain. The first coat of glaze or varnish will also have to be rubbed down. A final coat of epoxy varnish will give the wood a rich, handbuffed look.

A much easier method is to give the cabinets a fresh coat of paint—after removing the hardware and cleaning them. The semigloss acrylic enamels are easy to use: they are thinned with water, leave no brush marks, dry quickly, and have almost no odor. The polyester-epoxy coatings are also highly recommended but trickier to use, for these are mixtures and must be thoroughly blended. You might try painting doors and drawers one color and the frames another. Or paint the wood all one color and add wooden knobs painted a contrasting color.

Metal cabinets with a baked-on enamel finish can also be painted, but for better adhesion, the surface should first be sanded. Changing the hardware can provide an effective face-lifting, but if possible find knobs and drawer-pulls that match existing screw-holes. This will avoid having to fill in the old holes and drill new ones with a metal coping saw.

Another, more costly way to salvage existing cabinets is to have them entirely covered with laminated plastic. This is a service now being offered by a number of firms, whose representatives will come to your home to give a free estimate in advance. The laminate is available in a simulated wood grain or in a choice of colors. Some of the colors are quite handsome: for example, if a dark red laminate is used on the cabinets, add Colonial-style hardware and paint all woodwork white. For the counter tops, a marbleized pattern in a pink-red grain or off-white might be used.

Perhaps your existing cabinets are usable but there are not enough of them. If you have sufficient space to accommodate more, keep the existing cabinets, add new ones, and then treat old and new in one of the following ways:

1. If the exterior design of the new cabinets is identical or similar to that of the old ones, paint or stain and glaze all the cabinets to look alike.

2. Have a new "face" of laminated plastic installed over all the old and new cabinets.

3. Forget about making them all look alike, and deliberately create contrasting cabinets.

Attractive solution

The Marshalls, a young couple with more imagination than money at their disposal, moved into a fifty-year-old Pittsburgh house that had an L-shaped kitchen containing a single crude millwood cabinet with completely flat door and drawer fronts. This cabinet was on the shorter kitchen wall, which had an archway opening into the dining room. The Marshalls considered taking down the old cabinet, which was nailed directly to the wall, but when they discovered how much even the least expensive cabinets cost, they decided to keep the millwood unit. For additional cabinets, they chose the simplest design they could find in stock units with a birch veneer finish.

Marshall assisted a carpenter in installing the new cabinets, then he and his wife covered the base part of the old millwood cabinet and its flat door and drawer fronts with scrubbable vinyl wallcovering to match the covering on the walls adjacent to it. They removed the doors from the upper cabinet, papered the frame attached to the walls, but painted the open shelves yellow, which was one of the colors in the wallcovering pattern. They selected a matching yellow shelf-liner for the new cabinets, and also put a yellow fiberglass pull-shade at the window, with a valance covered in the wall-covering to frame the top of the window. The same new hardware was used on the papered millwood cabinet as on the new stock cabinet.

The overall effect was bright and unusual. They placed dishes and glassware, with cups hanging from hooks, on the open shelves of the old cabinet, and as this was steps away from the dishwasher, they found the open shelves a boon.

Custom cabinets are far more costly than stock cabinets, even though both are manufactured in much the same standard sizes. Custom cabinets, besides having a more elegant exterior finish and hardware, are made of better quality wood, are more carefully constructed, and have attractive interior space-saving features, such as divided drawers, pull-out shelves on nylon ball-bearing tracks (especially useful for getting at things stored in the back of cabinets), corner turn-around units for base cabinets, and vertical dividers for holding large pans and platters. All of these except the turn-around units, which range in price from $90 to $500 each, are easy enough for a carpenter or clever do-it-your-selfer to make and install. They can be made of particleboard or hardboard to fit whatever space is available, and may be put into upper corner cabinets as well as base cabinets.

But rubberized (actually vinyl-coated) space-savers of all sorts are also available in hardware stores and housewares departments in sizes designed to fit standard-size cabinets. Particularly useful are the round turntables for holding condiments, spices, and smaller cans and packaged goods.

Counter tops on old cabinets can be replaced with new laminated plastic. The installation can be quite costly, but a skilled homeowner may be able to do the job with a well-equipped workbench and the space for gluing parts together. Detailed instructions are contained in giveaway leaflets in the building supply houses that sell the material.

While fixing up the counter tops, it might be a good time to replace the sink if this should be necessary. There are stainless steel sinks in all sizes, both double and single, which it is claimed can be bolted in place with no other tool than a screwdriver. A new faucet, such as the single-lever movable type with spray attachment, is also easy to install in either a new or an old sink.

If the only thing wrong with the old sink is that it is badly discolored with yellowish rust stains, these can be removed completely with Tub 'n Sink jelly, and the appearance of an eroded chrome edging can be improved by the use of naval jelly.

Drawers that stick or nearly fall out when more than half opened might be worth rehabilitating with new warp-free nylon or metal track guides and ball-bearing rollers. The latter can be purchased with the proper screws and other attachments for installation on existing drawers.

Finding more storage space

Every kitchen needs a broom closet and a pantry for the large items that cannot be fitted into base cabinets. If there is not sufficient space to fit either or both such closets along one of the walls holding cabinets, consider another wall space where a closet no more than twelve to sixteen inches deep and no wider than fifteen to twenty-four inches might be added. Width is more important than depth for this purpose; remember that it is often difficult to reach items at the back of the normal two-foot-deep closet. A pullout pantry no more than twelve inches wide can be fitted between other cabinets or on the wall next to a refrigerator. Or shelves eight inches deep can be attached to a wall adjoining a doorway, boxed at the sides with plywood or particleboard, and fitted with louvered doors; the entire "closet" need extend no more than twelve inches from the wall and can be as wide as whatever space is available.

Broom holders fastened to the wall help to make a narrow broom closet neater. Hooks or pegboard on the back of the door can be used for hanging small cleaning equipment, such as brushes, cloths, and vacuum attachments.

Pegboard is a great space-saver, whether applied to a wall or behind doors. And do not forget the great space-saving

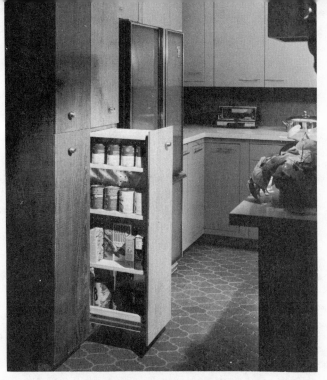

Narrow pullout pantry shelves made of plywood, located next to the refrigerator, hold an abundance of canned and packaged foods.

value of cup hooks. These can be screwed into the bottom of upper shelves or hanging shelves. On them can be hung not only cups, but small utensils such as can-openers, wire whisks, and small sieves, thus saving drawer space.

Work out your own space-saving plan for kitchen storage. Put the utensils you use most in easy-to-reach places, and the least-used items on high shelves. Keep everyday dishes as close to the dishwasher as possible, so that transferring them from the dishwasher to the shelves will require nothing but arm movement.

Try to find space somewhere in the kitchen for a desk, even if this is only a pullout shelf above a base cabinet with drawers. Such an "office" is useful not only for making out shopping lists, planning menus, and writing checks, but also when using cookbooks. If there is a place for an open counter, underneath which a stool can be placed, so much the better. A telephone in the kitchen can save money: many times a meal has been saved because the cook, while talking on the telephone, was able to reach out and snatch a pan away from the heat before the food burned. Be sure to order a telephone with an extra-long extension cord.

Narrow hanging shelves on kitchen walls can be a help. Look for any empty wall space where such shelves might go—perhaps above chairs in the eat-in area, or on a wall adjoining the door where there is no space for cabinets. These shelves can be purchased in unpainted furniture shops sanded and ready to paint or stain. They are available in several widths, with two, three, or four shelves.

"Bookcases" for the kitchen

Unpainted bookcases can provide additional storage space and more counter space in the kitchen. These units have depths of eight, twelve, or sixteen inches, and those that are thirty inches high range in length from thirty-six inches to sixty inches. If you purchase one measuring thirty by forty-eight by sixteen inches, the sixteen-inch depth will hold most small electrical appliances, even a broiler-oven or rotisserie. To make the unit a little higher, two- or four-inch supports can be added at either end, using bricks or blocks of wood for this purpose. A counter top thirty-two or thirty-four inches high is useful for certain food preparation chores, such as chopping vegetables, pounding meat, or rolling out pie crust. It might be topped with a "butcherboard" counter, made of hardwood planks glued together, with a one-inch overhang back and front.

Or such a "bookcase" might be combined with a snack bar to be set between kitchen and family room. You might make a counter top of laminate to cover both "bookcase" and bar. The bar part of the counter can be supported by wrought iron or steel supports attached to the back of the bookcase, though it would look better and be stronger if a vinyl-coated panel were installed over the plywood back of the bookcase, and the supports were attached with long screws extending well into the wood of the bookcase end panel.

Major and minor appliances

Before replacing a major kitchen appliance, shop around a long time and check consumer publications to learn as much as you can about the pros and cons of various makes and styles. When you finally make your choice, try to resist gadgetry and the latest fashion colors. (Colors show their age too specifically when they are no longer "in.")

The more gadgets and automatic features on an appliance, usually the more it costs to operate and the harder it is to repair when breakdowns occur. Gadgetry is often little more than a sales pitch. If manufacturers did not continuously add something new, many families would rarely replace their possessions.

Among the hard-to-resist features on new kitchen ranges are continuously-cleaning ovens and one-piece smooth ceramic cooktops. These innovations do indeed make kitchen cleanup quicker and easier. However, both self-cleaning and continuously-cleaning ovens increase the electric bill, and the newer spray-on oven cleaners are easier than ever to use. In some cases, using the ceramic cooktop requires buying new pots and pans.

Microwave ovens are popular, their attractions being the speed with which they bake and the fact that they emit very little heat, a boon in hot weather. They are also useful for instant heating of leftovers or frozen entrées. The question may be, if the kitchen already has two ovens, one in the wall, the other a standard oven in the free-standing range, is a third really necessary? And how much baking do you do? In most households, at least three-fourths of the cooking is on top of the stove.

Automatic self-defrosting refrigerator-freezers are fine in large households where the refrigerator door is opened frequently, for otherwise defrosting once a week is a big and messy chore. For economy of operation, however, the old style of refrigerator which must be defrosted manually has its merits. Often such a refrigerator in good working condition can be purchased secondhand for as little as twenty dollars, a very good buy for a couple setting up housekeeping. The easiest way to defrost is to turn the refrigerator off at night, removing frozen food from the freezing compartment and wrapping it in newspaper to keep in the refrigerator overnight. The drop in interior temperature will not be enough to thaw the wrapped frozen foods nor to spoil other foods inside. The full tray of water will be ready to empty in the morning, and then the dial can be turned back to its normal setting.

Purchase of a separate freezer may prove a great convenience for a large family, but the claim that large-quantity purchases will help the freezer to pay for itself has been proved erroneous. Also, foods "lost" in the bottom, buried in frost for months, deteriorate in flavor, quality, and nutritional value.

Dishwashers, like airconditioning, have progressed from "luxury" to "necessity" classification in less than two decades. If a kitchen does not have a dishwasher, the installation cost of a new one may run to $100 in addition to the purchase price. Even to replace an old dishwasher with a new model may cost $60. There is no installation fee for a portable dishwasher, and sometimes it is possible to cut out a space for it to be pushed under the counter next to the sink, with hose attachments coming up from the back of the counter where they can be hooked up to sink faucets as needed.

For a space-saving arrangement in a small kitchen, a dishwasher can go beneath an electric cooktop, with an upper oven above it, or the dishwasher can be placed beneath a wall oven.

Adding a dishwasher to a kitchen where there has not been one before can put a heavy strain on plumbing, so make sure that your existing pipes and plumbing system can take it. Otherwise you may have a big plumbing repair bill on top of the installation fee.

The same warning must be applied to garbage disposer units. While some of these are advertised as easy for do-it-yourselfers to install, it is important to make sure in advance that you have adequate drainage facilities. Generally disposers are not recommended for use in homes that have a private septic system. Also, some people in using them fail to turn on the cold water long enough to force the ground food particles down the waste pipe, and as the waste builds up, the pipe can become clogged and eventually damaged.

Exhaust is important

Keep in mind that it is important to have some form of exhaust in the kitchen. A range hood with a charcoal filter does not fulfill this need; it absorbs some of the cooking grease, but otherwise is not particularly useful. Far better is a hood with ductwork leading to the outside. However, it is important that such ductwork be carefully installed and protected with fireproof material because of the chance of accumulated grease in the ducts catching fire.

If your kitchen does not have some form of exhaust, be sure to open the window whenever the dishwasher is in operation, or when several things are cooking on top of the stove at the same time, or when meat is broiling and sending smoke into the kitchen.

Your kitchen should have ample electrical outlets: a double outlet on each wall and so wired that no two small appliances need be on the same circuit simultaneously. A toaster, electric frypan, rotisserie, electric iron, certain high-speed blenders, and any kind of portable oven all use enough current to warrant a separate line. If two are plugged into the same line at once, it could blow a fuse or cause a shutoff on the circuit breaker.

Air and light

The kitchen needs not only good overhead lighting but side and hanging lights so placed that the cook need not ever work in his or her own shadow. A strong ceiling light is needed, and in addition area lighting immediately above working surfaces. Small fluorescent tubes placed under upper cabinets, one for each main work area, are the least expensive and most effective means of throwing light directly on counter tops. A curved plastic shield over each tube will protect it from grease and grime. Recessed ceiling "eyeball" lights, which can be turned to direct light exactly where it is needed, are also useful. A dimmer switch makes it easy to soften all the kitchen lighting at mealtime, which is desirable when the kitchen opens into a dining area.

No amount of artificial light, however, can make up for lack of windows. The more windows the better, and all should be easy to open. A window pass-through between kitchen and patio is a convenience in summer.

In many kitchens there is only one window and that one right above the sink. Actually, this is not the best place for a window, for splashes from the sink cause spots on the glass, necessitating frequent window-washing.

Wherever a kitchen window is located, it is psychologically important that it frame a pleasant view—of greenery, a patio, or an attractive street scene. This helps anyone who must spend a good deal of time working in the kitchen to feel closer to the world outside the kitchen walls.

Kitchen walls and flooring

When cabinets are dark-stained, it is particularly important to use light colors for walls and floor. Resilient flooring in a light color is actually easier to keep clean-looking than a dark color—that is, if the light finish is flecked, marbleized or textured. Solid colors, whether in light or dark shades, show many spots, dents, and discolorations. The same applies to laminated plastic counters in solid colors.

There is an enormous choice of flooring materials for the kitchen. No-wax cushioned vinyl is undoubtedly the easiest to care for, though perhaps the most expensive in initial cost. It can be installed fairly easily by two men, for it can be cut with ordinary heavy shears and most of it has a self-adhesive backing. However, there are differences in "no-wax" finishes. Some "never need waxing"; others "will not need waxing for years." It would be wise to consult an up-to-date consumer report on the various brands before purchase. Some have press-on adhesive backing; others must be applied with adhesive; and some can be installed with the same kind of double tapes at the edges as used for tackless carpeting.

No-wax, like other less expensive types of resilient flooring, can now be purchased in six-, nine-, twelve-, and fourteen-foot widths, so that it is now possible to have seamless installation in kitchens of almost every size. If the flooring does not have a built-in no-wax finish, it can be covered with a protective sealer, which gives a much longer-lasting shine than the acrylic wax finishes.

Unless the existing vinyl or linoleum flooring is in very good condition, free of bumps, cracks, or broken portions, it is best to lay subflooring of one-quarter-inch plywood or hardboard over the old flooring. This will insure a level, smooth finish, which will wear much better.

What is called "seamless flooring" is something else entirely. This is poured on, in several coats or layers, with the color supplied by a combination of vinyl chips. The subflooring must be absolutely level and clean and in most cases professional application is recommended, though this, too, is a do-it-yourself possibility for those who are careful and thorough. This is a permanent installation, never needs waxing, and is easily cleaned with a damp mop. But once installed, it cannot be changed. "Seamless flooring" can also be used out of doors; in California it is often used where kitchen and patio are designed to serve as parts of an indoor-outdoor unit with glass doors between.

Kitchen carpeting is growing in popularity. There are now several makes available; some are the close-woven indoor-outdoor type, others have a deeper pile. Both types are available with cushioned backing, treated with Scotchgard. Such carpeting is especially attractive when family room and kitchen are combined. However, for those who do a great deal of cooking, or in a household with young children, it must be recognized that the carpeting is not as easy to keep clean as vinyl. Both "carpet tiles" and yardage in widths of six, twelve, and fourteen feet are available; in general these are considerably less expensive than no-wax vinyl. They are also easy to install, and may be laid directly over old flooring that is in reasonably good condition.

There is usually not a great deal of empty wall space in a kitchen when all the cabinets, appliances, and hanging shelves are in place; but this is all the more reason to brighten up any walls that show. The strippable vinyl-coated papers or cloth coverings are comparatively easy to put up, especially the "wall tiles," and help a great deal to make the kitchen bright and cheerful.

There are also many different kinds of paneling especially recommended for kitchen walls, with a vinyl-coated surface resistant to water, stains, and household chemicals. Simulated brick panels are now quite popular, often combined with a paper. Some "bricks" of plastic put up with adhesive and mortar (applied from a tube) are considered easier to handle and to keep clean than real brick. Ceramic tiles, sometimes combined with other finishes, are especially recommended for a sink splashback.

However the walls are finished, painted, papered, or paneled, the important thing is that they should be easy to wipe clean or to wash frequently to get rid of grease and grime without marring the surface finish.

If the paint on a kitchen wall is peeling and/or chipped, use a scraper to get rid of all the loose paint. Then fill in any holes or cracks and sand smooth all rough surfaces. Ideally you should then cover the wall with a primer-sealer (your paint dealer will recommend the best type for the purpose),

BEFORE: Dreary kitchen lacked eat-in space and opened onto ramshackle porch. See facing page for results of prize-winning renovation.

but some people skip this step. When the wall is clean and dry, add fresh paint, preferably acrylic or alkyd enamel, or the wall covering of your choice.

Major kitchen renovation

If your chief dissatisfaction with your existing kitchen is its small size, you might consider whether there is a wall that could be removed to enlarge it.

A home in Kansas City, Missouri, had a kitchen that was dark and lacked eat-in space. The kitchen opened onto an old porch which was little more than a lean-to. The contractor was able to double the size of the kitchen by removing the wall of a pantry closet. The porch was rebuilt to make it wider and deeper, with a raised roof so that it could serve for outdoor dining in warm weather. Leading to this porch are patio doors. The sink was moved to the side of the room nearest the porch so that a pass-through exists from the sink and its adjoining counter space to the porch. At the end of the room where the old pantry had been, there is now ample space for a round table and six chairs, and a large window which can be opened for cross ventilation.

AFTER: Kitchen after pantry and closet were removed. Patio doors lead to rebuilt porch for outdoor dining. This renovation in a Kansas City home won an award for the contractor.

Another kitchen renovation involved moving interior and exterior walls. The problem here was not only that the kitchen was too small, but the only access to it was by way of the dining room. More kitchen space was wanted for a table and chairs, and the owners also wished to have an entrance to the den as well as to the dining room.

At the rear of the house was a narrow porch with steps leading down to the garden. The architect who was consulted decided to use the foundation of the narrow porch as the foundation for an extended wall of the kitchen. This meant removing the existing exterior wall, but it added three feet to the length of the room, and by changing the counter arrangement, an area was made available for a kitchen table in the corner, next to the new doorway to the den.

On the other side of the kitchen wall had been a powder room, facing the den. The powder room was moved forward, into the space that had been the entrance into the kitchen from the dining room; the new dining room entrance was opened at the end of the kitchen "galley." Altogether these changes turned what had been an eight-by-twelve-foot kitchen into an eleven-by-fifteen-foot room, with more counter space, better traffic patterns, and more light—from facing corner windows at the new end of the kitchen, overlooking the garden. New wooden steps were constructed at the rear so that there would still be direct access to the garden from the kitchen.

Another possible way to extend a kitchen towards the rear would be to add on a six-foot extension, with a patio door and windows all across the rear. The new extension can be used as a dining area, with the former cabinet wall transformed into a pass-through or island room divider. Narrow shelves could also be added against the side wall for pantry storage, dishes, or an entertainment center. For even greater light in this new extension, a sloping skylight could form the roof, which would make it like a "Florida room" year-round, a place to grow plants and enjoy the sun in winter.

Another and much more elaborate kitchen was created by remodeling the two-car garage of a ranch-style house. The family decided that they could manage with a one-car garage, and for the remaining space, their architect designed a semicircular kitchen. For the area behind the garage, where there had been an enclosed porch, he planned a large dining room.

This was designed for a large family, several of whom were often in the kitchen at the same time, so two sinks, one on each side of the kitchen, were installed. The circular eating area, with space to seat eight persons, has a skylight overhead. A second skylight is in the living room, above the family's grand piano.

The great advantage of making a kitchen an integral part of the adjoining room, whether it is labeled family room or dining room, is the feeling of expanded space. In any major kitchen renovation today, the kitchen is planned as part of a larger unit, opening either into a family room or den, or onto a patio, deck, or porch.

Bathrooms

If you feel that your house needs another bathroom or powder room, the first step should be to find enough space to install additional facilities as close as possible to existing plumbing lines.

Sometimes it is possible to add a second bath back to back with an existing one, by making the existing bath smaller and at the same time taking space from a bedroom or closet by moving walls. Or a large bathroom might be turned into two smaller bathrooms, or into a full bath and a half-bath. One of these could open into the master bedroom, the other into a hallway. For this type of renovation, it is important to consult with an expert, either an architect, or a contractor who specializes in this type of work, or a plumber.

One innovative design created by an architect included a curved wall between the bathroom and a small closet on the bedroom side. This made the bathtub area less cramped than would have been the case with the normal square-cornered walls of an indented closet.

The smallest possible area in which a full bathroom (with tub) can be installed is five feet by seven feet. A bathroom with a one-component shower unit, toilet, and washbasin can be squeezed into slightly less space. But most people want more elbow room than this, and it is a great convenience to have a linen closet, or at least open shelves on which linens can be placed, in the bathroom. The smallest space for a powder room is four feet by four feet. (It is possible to squeeze a toilet and a tiny washbasin into an area measuring two by five feet, but this would not be suitable for guests.)

If a small bedroom that is close to plumbing lines can be sacrificed, it might be transformed into a bath and dressing room with a combination clothes and linen closet on one side of the room and a long vanity with twin washbasins on the other.

The proximity of plumbing lines is always important, because installation of extended plumbing lines is extremely costly; it involves tearing up floors. Another disadvantage is that, because of the extension of lines, water pressure might not be satisfactory.

An existing bathroom on an upper floor can sometimes be expanded by adding a five- or six-foot dormer, in which a sunken tub can be placed, so that a person of normal height could stand in the tub to take a shower. Instead of the traditional shower overhead, it is easier to install a spray attachment which fastens to the wall with a flexible cord. Sliding glass doors at the entrance to this dormer-tub area would help protect the rest of the room from steam and splashes.

A skylight can serve as a good source of light and air in a

Vinyl-coated hardboard, called tileboard, is probably the least expensive water-resistant paneling for a bathtub area. Color-coordinated moldings are fitted around the tub, in the corners, and at the top of the panels.

bathroom on an upper floor or in a one-story house or wing. The skylight may or may not replace a regular window. If it serves as a window, there should be a chain to pull it open from below. If the skylight is of fixed glass or plexiglass, an exhaust fan will be needed for ventilation.

To give a feeling of greater space in a small bathroom, use the mirror trick. Fill in as much wall space as possible with a built-in vanity and above the vanity have one large mirror. Plate glass in this size is quite expensive but plastic glass can be cut to size, even by the do-it-yourselfer, using a fine-toothed saw. Or use mirror tiles, which also are made of plastic glass, as are most mirror doors now. Installation of the glass—getting it mounted on the wall so that it is even and level—is the trickiest part. Even when using one big sheet of glass, it would be well to glue it to a panel, then screw the panel to the studs in the wall. Alternatively, you could put up a "mirror paper" on the wall above the tile; this is especially effective in a small bath or powder room.

Lighting in the bath

In the bathroom, as in the kitchen, you need a strong, well-diffused overhead light and supplementary fixtures to spot-light specific areas. However, a large mirrored medicine cabinet with its own light fixture may be sufficient.

Around the vanity mirror, there should be lights on each side and also overhead. Vertical fluorescent tubes can be attractive, using two together at each side. The overhead tube needs to be shielded so that light is directed downward over the mirror but not into your eyes. Usually this light is installed behind the soffit. But be sure to use deluxe warm white fluorescent tubes in order to see cosmetics and clothing in their true colors.

If incandescent light is used, the most effective way to illuminate a vanity mirror is with twin fixtures, one at each side of a large mirror, and thirty inches above the counter top.

There are attractive ready-made vanities in a wide range of sizes and prices. You may be able to find just what you need and be able to install it yourself for much less than having one custom-made. But by making use of unpainted drawer units and paneled doors, a skilled do-it-yourselfer can custom-make one in the home workshop. Ideally the vanity should be in three parts: at one end, a four-drawer unit; in the center, where the drain from the washbasin takes up some space, a single shelf narrow enough to fit in front of the drain; and on the other end, a cabinet with several shelves. It may be possible to keep all the linens needed for this room in the vanity, in addition to cosmetics, medicines, and the other small clutter that almost always accumulates in a family bathroom.

Each bathroom needs at least two electrical outlets, for an electric shaver, hair dryer, electric toothbrushes, and, if there is no fixed heating unit, a space heater.

Bathroom walls and flooring

Ceramic tiles will last much longer than any other material on bathroom walls and floor and give the room a richer look. However, the tiles must be correctly installed, and in most cases it pays to have them put in by someone who specializes in this kind of work.

"Tub kits" of ceramic tile are available for what is described as "easy installation," but this calls for very careful work. First wire lath must be nailed to studs in the wall. Then two separate coats of cement must be applied, the tiles being set in the second coat. Finally the tiles are further cemented in place with mortar caulked around the edges of each tile. Any excess mortar must be cleaned from the surface before it sets. If not properly installed, the tiles will work loose. But the fact that ceramic-tiled walls and floors in bathrooms forty and fifty years old are still in use, with little else wrong than loose grouting, is a good indication of why it pays to have the best. Since the cost of ceramic tiles is high, select the color combination with care, keeping in mind that this is a "lifetime" addition.

There are various types of waterproof wall panels which may be used satisfactorily around the tub and on the walls. If you do not have much to spend, and the panels are for a bath in the basement or attic, the easiest to install are the plastic-coated hardboard panels, sometimes called "tile board." The finish is baked on and these are more durable and water-resistant than earlier versions. But for a more lasting finish, either laminated plastic or fiber glass panels are preferable. The latter can be purchased in the form of a complete "bathtub cove" to fit around the tub, with soap dish and towel racks as part of the kit.

All these wall panels are proclaimed to be easy for the homeowner to install, though not all home handymen would agree with this claim. The kits include moldings, nails, and three panels designed to fit around a five-foot tub and all the way up the wall, or only above the shower-head level, if preferred that way. Holes for spigots and shower heads are cut out with a keyhole or saber saw. While the panels can be attached over old tile walls, it is extremely important to prepare the walls properly first and to remove any cause of moisture behind the walls, such as leaking fittings.

Sheet vinyl is second only to ceramic tile as a wall-to-wall, seamless flooring for a bathroom. Vinyl tiles are not recommended for a full bathroom; water will work into the seams and in a few years cause them to curl up. But for a powder room, where water damage is less of a problem, vinyl tiles are fine and are available in attractive patterns.

Often a bathroom can be made to seem new without replacing any of the old ceramic tile. If the grouting has come loose but otherwise the tiles are in good condition, scrape out the old mortar and use your vacuum cleaner to remove all loose particles. Then pack cement grout or mastic grout into the joints and scrape off the excess with a putty knife. (When grout is firm and dry, sponge with clean water and wipe dry with a cloth; allow to cure for several weeks before using the shower.)

For use around the tub, you could buy new ceramic bathtub edging; a kit that includes straight pieces, mitered corner and end tiles, a tube of caulking compound, and instructions costs less than five dollars. New spigots for tub and washbasin and a shower head are easy to install in place of old ones to give the room a fresher look.

Sometimes water from the shower has loosened the wall tiles and even rotted the wall behind them. Plaster is porous and when water gets behind the tiles, it is absorbed into the walls. In this situation, just fixing loose tiles is not enough. It would be better to remove the old tiles and patch the walls first. Then you can decide whether to apply the tiles or replace them with panels of water-resistant material all around the tub.

A quick and inexpensive way to cover up old tile floors that are discolored or uneven is to buy the colorful plush bath carpeting available in five-by-six-foot and six-by-eight-foot sizes to be cut to fit with ordinary scissors. These can be cleaned in the washing machine and fluff-dried in the dryer. But more satisfactory is indoor-outdoor carpeting (the seamless widths in preference to carpet tiles) with self-adhesive backing. This type of carpeting cannot be removed for washing, but the material has been treated for resistance to soil and moisture, and is less troublesome than plush carpeting, though equally luxurious.

Permanent bath fixtures

The bathroom is one place where vivid colors and offbeat decorating ideas can be applied extravagantly, but it is best to restrict unusual colors to replaceable objects and materials. It is an unwise investment to buy permanent fixtures (tub, toilet, washbasin, or vanity) in high fashion or uncommon colors. Shocking pink may be your favorite color, but a shocking pink toilet could so repel a potential buyer that it could cause the house sale to fall through.

If you feel that bathroom fixtures in color are a definite asset, select those in delicate or neutral colors. Blues, blue-greens, gold, or buff are the safest. A washbasin of royal blue or turquoise set in a white vanity is very attractive, but the toilet and tub should be white. Black fixtures look luxurious, especially with gold spigots and hardware, but some people may find them too exotic for daily life.

White fixtures are the least objectionable and the least expensive, and can be combined with any other colors you like. Use such combinations, if you wish, as orange and yellow, Chinese red and delicate green, aqua and purple—but only for shower curtain, towels, carpeting, or strippable wallcoverings. Light fixtures could be unusual: a Tiffany shade hanging from the ceiling, carriage side lights beside the vanity mirror, or a lamp on the vanity counter top made from an old kerosene lantern.

The best way to cover up exposed pipes in the bathroom is to box them over with hardboard, then paint or paper the outside to match the upper portion of the walls. Among younger people it is now fashionable to buy an old footed tub to replace the standard built-in style, but a footed tub will not be an asset when you wish to sell your house.

New recessed tubs can be purchased for as little as fifty dollars (of steel finished with acid-resistant porcelain), and fiber glass tubs, while more expensive, are lightweight enough for easy installation by the homeowner.

There are tub enclosures of sliding glass available in a price range from about twenty-five to one hundred dollars, not including the cost of installation. The cheapest are made of plastic; the more expensive ones of tempered safety glass; and the most expensive have mirror doors with anodized aluminum frames.

Inexpensive folding polyethylene tub panels or tri-door panels are recommended for a bathroom in which small children will be bathed, because of easier access to the tub from outside.

For a basement bathroom, or in any small guest bath, fiberglass modular showers can fill a real need. These come complete with floor drain, translucent door, curtain rod, and soap holder. For an open shower with ceramic or laminate walls, there are tempered glass doors, six feet in height, in various designs and widths, some as narrow as twenty-five inches. A shower can be installed in a space only thirty by twenty-eight inches, but thirty-two by thirty-two inches is preferable.

If the toilet needs replacing, consider the new types designed to conserve water. They use a maximum of three and one-half gallons per flush, or thirty percent less than standard two-piece toilets. Several companies now manufacture these. There are also water-saver kits, which can be "easily installed, without tools" in existing toilets. With a water shortage now threatening many communities and predictions that this situation will become more widespread, any means of saving water is important.

A new toilet seat can be an inexpensive improvement: plastic seats in a wide range of colors, guaranteed for five years, cost less than ten dollars. For a luxurious note, a plush toilet seat could be installed. Nylon pile covers, matching loose floor carpeting, serve to dress up a toilet lid that is peeled, scratched, or otherwise marred.

For a very small powder room, there are washbasins in

modified oval shape measuring only fifteen and three-quarter inches from front to back, and available in colors for under thirty-five dollars. These can be fitted into built-in vanities or hung from the wall.

Even when a bathroom has outside windows, a ceiling ventilator with a built-in light and heating element can be a great asset, especially on chilly winter mornings.

Storage in the bath

There are many ways in which to supplement the storage space of a medicine cabinet, which is often the only storage space available in an existing bathroom.

Pole shelves fit over the toilet in a space that otherwise is usually wasted. The poles are adjustable to ceiling height, and usually support two open shelves and a six-inch-deep cabinet with sliding doors.

Hanging shelves can be attached to the walls, but be sure that they are securely fastened—attached to studs or with molly screws—and do not place excessively heavy objects on them. These can be found in bath shops in all sorts of designs, made of a wide choice of materials—rattan, chrome, polystyrene plastic in vivid colors, gold-plated metal, black wrought iron, even wood. Matching accessories in the same materials include hampers, dressing stools, and freestanding towel racks. There are also cabinets designed to slide under a washbasin that cost less than one you could make yourself.

If there is space enough in the bathroom, a floor-to-ceiling open-shelf unit could be built in to hold linens. Paint the frame a color to match shower curtains or carpeting and let towels, washcloths, and patterned sheets on the shelves add their notes of gay color.

Another place where storage might be introduced in the bath is at the end of the tub opposite the shower. A removable board that fits across one end of the tub could hold such things as bath oil, bubble bath, scouring powder (to clean the tub), creams, lotions, and, of course, soap in a soap dish.

A new, larger medicine cabinet to replace an existing one could also increase storage space and if the cutout for the existing cabinet is too small for the new one, there are some cabinets that need not be recessed and can be placed on the wall where the old one used to be.

In installing a recessed medicine cabinet, be sure to place sound-deadening insulation in the back. Otherwise, the cabinet can serve as a sounding board, carrying noise from the bathroom into the room adjoining it.

Triple mirrors on a medicine cabinet are a helpful fixture for any close-up inspection of complexion or hair. Or you can make your own triple mirror from three short shutters hinged together: apply plastic mirror glass over each shutter, just inside the frame. This can be hung on the wall above the washbasin, in place of the medicine cabinet, and medicines and cosmetics can be kept on the shelves of a pole cabinet.

Compartmented baths

When a bathroom is divided into compartments, two or more persons can use it at once without disturbing one another.

For example, the toilet may be in one compartment, the tub and vanity or washbasin in another, with a door between. The door may be louvered or it may be one that slides into the wall.

"His" and "her" separated areas in the bathroom for a master bedroom can be luxurious. Each would have his and her own vanity and storage cabinets or drawers. There would be a shower unit separate from the tub, so that one could be showering as the other bathed. Such a double unit could prevent some of the petty rows caused by such things as uncapped toothpaste tubes and scattered cosmetics. A double bath of this kind requires a lot of space but not as much as two separate bathrooms.

A private bath for the master bedroom has risen close to the top of items "most wanted" by home buyers. When this bathroom adjoins a dressing room, underwear and nightwear can be kept conveniently at hand. Such a dressing room could also include a floor-to-ceiling linen closet.

The ultimate in bathroom luxury is to have a private deck opening off the bathroom for sunbathing, screened from the view of neighbors by a latticework wall covered with vines. The shower is then close by when it is time to wash away suntan lotion and get dressed.

A "twin" children's bathroom is also a fine idea. Here double washbasins are useful, so that two children can clean themselves at the same time. Each child can have his or her own storage compartment in a built-in vanity beneath each washbasin. For younger children, bath toys could be kept on shelves above the tub.

Big hampers for soiled clothing are important in any bathroom, but especially in one used by children. Even better is a laundry chute close to the bathroom, so that clothes can be dropped in to fall directly into the laundry room.

Somewhere near the bathrooms, a plumbing kit should be kept for emergencies. The kit should include a plunger and "snake" (auger) for cleaning out clogged-up drains, extra washers for faucets, a wrench for taking apart sections of pipe where trouble is suspected, and an ever-useful screwdriver.

Laundry area

In most homes the washing machine and dryer are in the basement, primarily for lack of space elsewhere. In one respect, the basement laundry room is advantageous: soiled clothes can be placed out of the way until there is time to wash them. But just because it is in the basement is no reason to neglect this room. Good lighting, ventilation, and cheerful colors will relieve it of its grim aspect.

Instead of simply placing washer and dryer side by side on a slab floor where there happens to be wall space and a drain, turn the laundry room into a bright, finished place and make it a multipurpose room. A combination laundry and sewing room makes sense. An iron and an ironing board are needed for dressmaking and mending even more than for laundry. With attractive vinyl asbestos tiles on the floors, walls painted a delicate pastel or paneled in a light finish, and a comfortable chair with a floor lamp or overhanging reel lamp in the room, you may be inclined to mend clothes there while you wait for another wash cycle to be completed.

A tub or sink for washing things by hand should be nearby, as should a good-sized table for folding and stacking permanent-press items, towels, and socks. The same table can double for cutting out dress patterns and marking the pleats in draperies and curtains. If it folds up, it could be carried upstairs and out of doors to use as a barbecue table.

Storage cabinets in this multipurpose room could hold not

only laundry aids, but supplies for home decorating jobs, sewing, and hobby crafts.

Sometimes in a finished basement the washer and dryer are concealed behind louvered folding doors in a corner. In this case, one section of a storage wall might be designed to contain the ironing board, sewing machine, laundry aids, sewing supplies, and so on, with the big room then indeed becoming an "activity room." Music from a record player in its "entertainment center" would make laundering and sewing more pleasant activities.

Another possible place for washer and dryer is next to the kitchen, so that the laundry may be put through its cycles while food preparation is in progress. However, some women object to such an arrangement because they dislike having dirty clothes associated with food preparation and psychologically prefer the laundry to be somewhere out of sight and mind.

Other convenient spots for washer and dryer are in or next to a bathroom in the bedroom area. The compact portable washer and dryer that can be rolled out of a closet and into the bathroom whenever needed are ideal for such an area.

These compacts use much less water than the permanently installed, completely automatic machines, and also complete a big wash in less time. The compacts were in use throughout Europe for some time before being introduced here. Both washer and dryer can be plugged into any outlet with a fifteen-ampere fuse. A grounded outlet to take a three-prong plug should be used, but if there is not one in the bathroom, you can use the adapter plug that comes with the machine. The "turbo-jet" action completes the washing cycle in just four minutes and the spin cycle leaves clothes damp-dry in two additional minutes. The water is emptied into any convenient sink or tub. There is no special installation, wiring, plumbing, or venting required. Clothes must be removed from the machine after the wash cycle for the first load is completed if a second load is to be added to the same wash water. This is assuming that the lightly-soiled and white or permanent color items are washed first.

In comparison with the forty-five to fifty-five or more gallons of water used for a normal automatic load, the portable washer, so the manufacturer of one compact claims, uses only about eleven gallons to wash and eight or nine gallons to rinse. Since the cycle is so short, several loads can be completed in about one-half hour, no longer than one big load in an automatic.

When the laundry is finished, the washer is unplugged, rolled back to its closet, and the dryer rolled out to be plugged into the same outlet. This, like other late-model dryers, has several different heats, including one for permanent-press.

The compacts are convenient to use where space is limited or on an upper floor, and also wherever water consumption is a problem. Families who have their own wells and septic systems may be able to use the compact washer when the standard automatic type cannot be used.

The several heats provided by the new washers and dryers are quite important for today's "miracle" fabrics, and when an old machine lacks these, even when it is still in good operating condition, purchase of a new model may be justified. Among other things, the new dryers make ironing almost obsolete.

CHAPTER 9

Fireplaces

For some people, a house is not a home unless it has a fireplace. Yet if one is to be added to your property, it is definitely a luxury item. The average cost for a traditional fireplace is $2,500.

However, if you are willing to settle for a prebuilt fireplace and do some of the work of installation yourself, a unit that looks like a conventional fireplace may cost no more than $900, and a prefab may cost as little as $300.

When a house does not have a fireplace, adding a chimney can be very costly and, further, there are now few skilled masons with the ability to construct a chimney with a good draft.

Prebuilt fireplaces are not only much less expensive to install (even when the installation is done by outsiders, the total cost is approximately half that of a built-in fireplace), but they are guaranteed to draw well and circulate heat back into the room. In a conventional fireplace, about four-fifths of

Prebuilt fireplace consists of a metal form around which masonry is applied, with grilles and ducts to project warmed air into room. The unit includes a multi-walled metal chimney.

the heat goes up the chimney. In the air-circulating prebuilts, most of the heat is blown back into the room through ducts.

Prebuilts are not the same as prefabs. The latter term is applied to units that are free-standing—attached to a wall or out in the room—and have visible metal chimneys.

The prebuilt units come complete with a triple-walled steel chimney in sections, a rain cap, a damper with chain control, and the air-circulating double firebox with ceramic base and ducts on each side. Some units also include a mesh screen with sliding door and a grate. When enclosed with bricks or other fireproof facing material, they look like conventional fireplaces; the firebox, ductwork, and chimney are not visible. The unit is boxed in with two-by-fours, then covered over. A mantel can be added if desired, or the entire wall can be built out so that only the framed firebed opening shows.

Sometimes it is advisable to install a prebuilt in an existing fireplace in an old house, both for better heat distribution and for safety (loose bricks or mortar in an old chimney can be a fire hazard). Consult a mason to get his opinion. It may be possible to lower the metal chimney inside the brick chimney, hooking the prebuilt unit up from below, and installing air ducts on either side.

Cold air is pulled into the prebuilt ducts by means of the lower intake holes, heated by the fire in the firebox, then forced out through the upper outlets. The principle is based on Benjamin Franklin's earliest "Philadelphia fireplace," perfected before he invented his better-known Franklin stove. It is really one unit (the firebox) within a larger unit, with space around it for the ductwork. In a small house, or a country cabin, this type of fireplace unit can sometimes serve to heat the entire structure, with ducts leading off into nearby rooms on the same floor.

The air intake and outlet holes on the sides of the unit can be faced with ceramic tile, slate, stone, or brick, or the facing used around the firebed opening can be extended far enough to each side to frame the duct openings.

These units are as safe as any fireplace can be, because of the triple wall of the chimney. Even so, safety codes demand a two-inch gap between the metal of the outer wall and any possible contact with wood. The firebox itself is wrapped in a roll of thick fiber glass. Some units are built on a base of concrete and firebrick like conventional fireplaces, but most have their own built-in ceramic base or bed and so can go directly onto a wooden floor or, better, on a raised hearth built one foot above the floor. The raised hearth offers a better heat source and also a better view of the burning logs. Because the unit is so lightweight, being made entirely of steel, it does not require the special floor supports used for a conventional fireplace.

If a mantel is desired, it is worth searching for an old one in junk yards or in houses about to be torn down. Sometimes handsome marble mantels can be picked up for very little.

Many styles offered

Prebuilts and prefabs are now made by twenty-one major manufacturers in more than a dozen styles. All come complete with chimneys; some can be attached to the wall in a corner or on a side or end wall. Others stand out a foot or more from the wall, with the flue pipe going up to a hole in the ceiling and from there to the chimney, which may be on an outside wall. Or the flue, encased in the metal chimney, may go straight on up through the roof; this results in a better draft. There are circular prefabs which can be placed in the center of a room to be viewed on all sides. However, their draft is not as reliable as in those that open only in front.

In a one-story house or wing, the fireplace can be placed in almost any spot desired, if a hole can be made in the roof overhead for the chimney. In a two-story structure, it may be better to place the fireplace on an exterior wall, boxing in the chimney on the outside so that it looks like a traditional chimney. Most prebuilts and all prefabs can be installed in half a day, not counting the addition of decorative facing, paneling, and the hearth which must extend into the room.

A fireplace with ducts can also serve as the source of a hot-water heating system. Instead of a regular grate, galvanized or steel pipes containing water can be used to hold the logs. As the fire heats the water, it is carried by smaller pipes to baseboard radiators in adjoining rooms. Such a system is, however, recommended only for country cottages. Obtaining sufficient firewood to heat a city house all winter would be both impractical and outrageously costly.

In any period of fuel shortage or utility breakdowns, a fire-

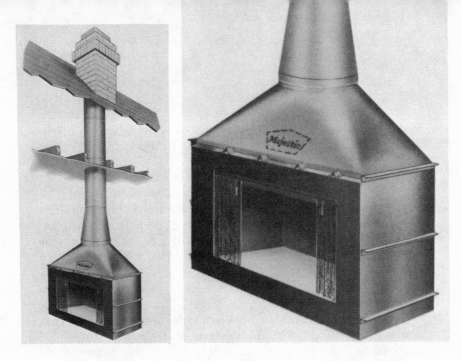

Prefabricated fireplace is an all-metal unit that comes complete from hearth to chimney top. The unit may be installed in any part of any room, and choice of exterior trim may be made from a virtually unlimited range.

place in the house can be worth every penny of its cost. This is especially true for those living in outer suburbs or in rural areas where a blizzard or ice storm sometimes causes a breakdown in electricity (for neither gas nor oilburning furnaces can be operated without electricity to control the thermostat). At such a time, the fireplace may have to provide not only the only heat source, but the only place for cooking.

A drawback of a fireplace in a house with central airconditioning is that the heat it generates can sometimes throw the thermostat off balance, causing other rooms in the house to cool off too much. It is advisable to lower the thermostat when the fire is lit, or, if the fireplace is used frequently, have a special thermostat for that part of the house which is most affected.

Prefabs and Franklin stoves

While some of the wall-hung prefabs look very much like contemporary fireplaces—especially so if a hearth of slate or ceramic tile is constructed beneath them—most prefabs are in reality more like Franklin stoves.

The authentic Franklin stove is a cast-iron unit, with or

without a viewable firebed, which extends into the room with its flue pipe above it angled into a hole in the wall that opens into the brick chimney.

The prefabs all have open firebeds. Some prefabs are square; others are circular, cone-shaped, or rectangular. All have mesh screens to pull shut when the fire is burning. The simplest type of prefab costs less than $200, not counting installation, but it is most appropriate for a country cottage or cabin, or an informal family or recreation room, not for a formal living room.

As a heat source, prefab fireplaces or Franklin stoves are more efficient than built-in fireplaces. Franklin stoves have become so popular that some companies are manufacturing new ones in the traditional designs, but the old stoves are more in demand for their antique value. Other types of old cast-iron stoves are also in vogue, including the big, black kitchen range (for country cottages) and the coal stoves with glass fronts which in the first decades of this century graced many a front parlor.

For those who like the look of a fireplace mantel in a living room, but want none of the fuss of building a fire or cleaning out ashes, there are both electric and gas fireplaces whose plastic logs appear to burn with a natural flame. These range in price from about $100 up to $250. They do not require a chimney, and can be turned on or off with the flick of a switch. Some models also direct fan-forced heat into the room.

Checking a fireplace

Despite the work involved, many homeowners still prefer to have a traditional fireplace. Those who have had little or no prior experience in dealing with a fireplace should keep in mind that the most important feature of a fireplace is its draft. No matter how handsome it may look, if the fireplace billows smoke into the room, or has such a poor draft that the most promising of fires peters out after a short time, it is not worth much.

When considering the purchase of a house that already has a fireplace, you can test the draft easily by lighting some waste paper in the hearth. Paper burns more easily than wood but it also gives out more smoke. A more serious test is to check whether there is a usable damper in the chimney. To add a damper to an existing chimney is rarely successful. Also, the condition of the bricks and mortar should be checked. If bricks are loose or the mortar cracked or broken, the condition presents a fire hazard and can require an expensive repair job.

Still another place to check is the lintel, the metal piece that supports the bricks above the opening of the fireplace. If there is a wide crack between the lintel and the overhanging mantel above it, and the crack is wider at the lintel side, it could mean that the lintel is weak from rust and age, and is beginning to sag. To replace the lintel could be expensive, and if it is in bad shape and is not replaced, this, too, could be a fire hazard.

Improving the draft

Generally speaking, if a fireplace has a poor draft it is because of poor construction, and you may never be able to make it work as well as you like. But you can try several treatments.

The most obvious place to begin is the damper. It may be stuck with rust or with a carbon buildup. The purpose of the damper is to close off the chimney to prevent leakage of air when the fireplace is not being used. But the damper should be fully open when a fire is lit, to allow smoke to escape up the chimney. Try scrubbing the surface of the damper on both sides with a wire brush and then oil the pivots. This means poking your way into the narrow space of the chimney, which can be a back-twisting and dirty job, but this treatment may make the damper turn more easily. If not, the alternative may be to remove the damper and block up the firebox opening in some other way when the fireplace is not in use.

Next is to examine the height of the chimney above the roof line. It should be two feet higher than the peak of a pitched roof, three feet above a flat roof. Making it taller by adding bricks to the top may help the draft. Even when the chimney is the proper height, surrounding trees or nearby higher buildings could interfere with the wind flow. Capping the chimney top may help, and this will also prevent rain or snow from entering the chimney.

Another possible cure may be to change the size of the firebox opening. Since this will make a difference in the outward appearance of the fireplace, test the idea first. Build a fire and when it is going well, hold a wide board or sheet of plywood against the top of the opening and gradually lower it. When smoke stops billowing into the room, measure at what place this occurs. A metal hood in a size that will cover the opening down to this level may correct the problem. Another method would be to build up the base or firebed. Test this by placing layers of bricks across the bottom. If this works well, make a permanent bed of bricks and mortar to the required height.

Sometimes the reverse is needed—to make the firebed lower in proportion to the height of the opening. This can be done only by building the fire directly on the hearth instead of laying logs on andirons or a grate.

In most cases, however, well-balanced andirons or a grate contribute to a better draft because this permits air to enter under the fire.

The way a fire is laid can be critical in determining how quickly the fuel ignites. First make a base of four or five well-crumpled balls of paper, then add plenty of dry, well-splintered kindling in a crisscross pattern so that air can get through, and finally lay three logs over the kindling. For some reason, three logs always burn better than two or four. When only two logs are left, it is time to add a third in the middle.

A good bed of ashes, three or four inches deep, will help to keep the fire going longer (because the hot ashes or embers keep the wood hot and therefore more flammable) and throws more heat into the room. Meticulous housekeepers often object to keeping ashes in the fireplace between fires because the ashes may scatter into the room and get ground into the carpet. But this is the only way to accumulate a deep bed; it cannot be done with just one fire. A fire screen of fine mesh not only prevents ashes from scattering into the room between fires, but prevents sparks from flying out when the fire is lit.

Even better, but many times more costly, are the fire doors of tempered glass called "glass screens." These fit completely over the opening, but can be opened wide for building the fire, then closed as the fuel begins to burn. The tempered glass helps to radiate heat into the room, and the flames may be watched through the glass doors with complete safety.

Chimney cleaning

Having the chimney cleaned at regular intervals is an important safety factor, though it is doubtful whether this has any direct bearing on the draft. If the fireplace is used frequently—as much as five or six times a week throughout the winter and occasionally in other seasons—it should be cleaned once a year. If used only once or twice a week, cleaning every three or four years will probably suffice. If used sporadically—only a few times in the winter—it can go without cleaning for up to seven years.

It is best to have a professional chimney sweep do the job, though it can be done by the homeowner and a helper. The old-fasioned way is to lower a small cedar tree down the chimney from the top, swishing it up and down. More practical is to use the combination of a vacuum cleaner, with extra-long hose and suction attachment, and stiff wire brushes for the area where the soot is caked more heavily.

Burning only hardwood kindling and logs will help to keep the chimney clean. Among the best fireplace woods are apple, locust, beech, birch, hickory, oak, and maple. Hardwood is superior in every way; it burns longer, creates less smoke, and gives off more heat. But make sure that it is well seasoned. If green, it gives off very little heat, and the fire is likely to go out easily because of the sap still in the logs. Soft woods, especially pine and other evergreens, are good for a fast, hot fire, but burn out rapidly and give off black smoke, and their tar and resins form a highly flammable accumulation that is hard to clean off the chimney wall. Never burn dry evergreen branches or Christmas trees in the fireplace; this is exceedingly dangerous.

When a fireplace is used for barbecuing, the fire should be of wood (instead of using an electric or gas barbecue unit in the hearth) because wood burns up the grease completely rather than allowing it to attach itself to the chimney. If charcoal briquettes are used, add them as the final layer to a fire of dry hardwood kindling.

The deck is almost as important as the pool itself, as most of the time passed
in the pool area is occupied in sunbathing, eating, and entertaining guests.

CHAPTER 10

Swimming Pools

More than five million American families now own private swimming pools. Although at least two-thirds of these are above-ground pools only four feet deep, the total represents a trend as symbolic of the American lifestyle as the family car.

A twenty-five-foot in-ground swimming pool costs from $7,000 up to $10,000, and could run to $25,000, depending on landscaping and decking.

A good quality aluminum above-ground swimming pool with deck will probably run at least $1,000, counting installation and landscaping, though a do-it-yourself job of decking around an inexpensive vinyl pool on a steel frame might cost no more than $450 to $500.

Above-ground pools are becoming ever larger and more elaborate, with decks and landscaping to make them look like permanent fixtures. Many are equipped with heaters and other costly extras, for the backyard swimming pool has become the center of family summertime activity, as well as an object of pride and status.

A built-in or in-ground pool is recognized as a capital improvement, and financing for it can be extended over a seven-year period. But county assessors also recognize it as adding to equity, which means property taxes are likely to be increased by $50 to $175 a year, depending on the size of the pool and local tax rates.

Above-ground pools are regarded as portable, not permanent improvements, and so are not subject to taxation. Not only the initial cost but the upkeep are far less than for in-ground models. This plus the fact that a great deal, if not most, of the installation can be a do-it-yourself operation accounts for their popularity.

Before investing in even an inexpensive pool, there are many factors to consider.

First, where are you going to put it? This decision is likely to depend on local zoning laws (which specify how close to boundary lines a pool may be placed, the height of the fence required around it, and drainage hookups), building codes, safety codes, and other regulations. These differ not only from state to state but even within a township or community.

The cost of the pool itself, even when a number of accessories are included in the price, is sometimes just the beginning of the expenses. For an in-ground pool, if there must be blasting, excavating costs could reach an astronomical figure, and if utility lines must be replaced or removed, and extensive regrading is necessary, the initial cost of the pool could be a mere fraction of the total expenditure.

Above-ground pools present fewer problems, and since underground utility lines need not be disturbed, it is easier to determine the total cost in advance. But even with these more simple installations, many problems may arise and the homeowner should be aware of these possible pitfalls.

Beware of sharks

There are unfortunately a good many sharks in the swimming pool business and the buyer is warned to beware of absurdly low prices and meaningless guarantees.

No group is more alarmed about shady practices in this field than the National Swimming Pool Institute (NSPI), which has drawn up a registry listing its 1,700 member firms, whose standards of workmanship have been found to be high and whose contractual records measure up to the association's code of ethics. Besides making available a standard contract, against which a dealer's contract may be measured, the institute can be consulted when special problems arise.

If not on guard, the buyer may be lured into the office of a firm that advertises $600 pools and end by spending $3,000. First there is the well-worn practice of persuading the customer that the advertised pool will be much less satisfactory than another that costs far more. In fact, this more expensive pool is usually an inferior product, grossly overpriced. Then nothing is said initially about any costs in addition to that of the pool itself—the "extras" which are in fact essentials and must be paid for separately, and a number of items that are nonessentials but which the buyer is persuaded to add. On top of this, installation costs will probably be heavily padded.

The institute asserts that any good above-ground pool larger than fifteen feet in diameter and installed by a dealer or contractor will cost at least $1,000, not $595 as the advertisements sometimes proclaim.

Then there are meaningless warranties to be on guard against. These often are worded so ambiguously that if the pool is not satisfactory, your only recourse is to contact the manufacturer, who may be located in another part of the country and who may simply ignore your complaints. Many small dealers appear in the spring of the year and disappear in the fall, only to resurface again under a different corporate name, when they can no longer be held responsible.

One of the most frequent complaints made to the NSPI concerns the vinyl liners for built-in pools. These often are improperly installed and the guarantee may apply only to seams, not breaks or punctures in the vinyl itself.

Before buying any swimming pool, the institute urges that you carefully check the reputation of the dealer or contractor with the Better Business Bureau and the Consumer Protection League. Also try to talk to some of the firm's customers to learn if they are satisfied with the pool itself and with the company's work. If a dealer or a contractor refuses to give you names of some of his other customers, you could very well regard this as evidence that he does not deserve your business.

Besides checking for yourself local codes and regulations, which sometimes even specify exactly which materials may be used in pool construction, carefully read each clause of the sales or installation contract. Do not put your signature on any document until you are satisfied. It is not unknown for dealers to be less than honest about local regulations or necessary safety factors; be on guard against this, for their lack of honesty could later lead to a big bill for drainage or fencing. Make certain of exactly what is included in the warranty and for what period of time, and who is responsible should anything go wrong.

The contract should also specify:

• Every component and material to be used in construction.

• Size, shape, color, and design of the finished pool and deck.

• Which accessories are or are not to be included in the purchase price.

• Who is responsible for installing what, and whether all labor costs are included.

• On what date the work is to start and when it is to be completed.

Final payment should not be made until the pool is filled and operating satisfactorily.

Selecting the site

It is not always necessary to have a big lot or level ground for the addition of a pool, especially for the smaller above-ground models. Some particularly attractive designs have been worked out on cliffs or hillside slopes, where only partial excavation is needed in order to fit the pool into the slope on one side, and where the frame around the pool serves as the deck, extending outward above the lower side of the slope.

However, such an installation requires engineering know-how, and a site that has not been properly leveled can increase water pressure on the liner in such a way as to cause punctures, especially when the vinyl becomes pinned against rocks.

If the pool is to be used for active water sports, you should figure on thirty-six square feet for each swimmer, and if there is to be a diving board, the depth under the board must be eight feet. The average rectangular built-in pool is eighteen by thirty-eight feet in size.

Usually the best spot for drainage is near the highest point in the yard rather than the lowest. But there are other considerations which must be weighed. The pool should be placed so as to relate to the areas of the house most used in the daytime, especially the patio and the kitchen. If children are to use it, the pool site should be clearly visible from the upstairs and downstairs windows of the house.

Southern exposure is best; the sun helps to heat the water, and you can use the pool over a longer season with or without a heater. Also, if there is a heater, it need not be turned on as frequently.

A windbreak, natural or especially constructed for the purpose, will help to keep the water warm and clearer. If the pool lies in the path of prevailing winds, these will not only chill the swimmers but deposit debris in the water. The house itself may serve as a windbreak; a hedge or a high wooden fence are other good windbreaks. Sometimes a cabana on the windward side helps to cut the force of the wind.

Thought must also be given to the location of the nearest bath or shower. Ideally it should be located so that dripping bathers will not be walking through carpeted rooms. If nothing better can be worked out, a cabana constructed to serve as a dressing room may fulfill this purpose. A simple overhead shower, or even a garden hose, will do, if there is drainage. Another solution might be to provide a shower-dressing room at one end of the garage.

Not least of the considerations in choosing the site must be the water source and drainage. This may in fact be determined by local construction codes.

Most of the time around a pool is spent out of the water rather than in it, and this means that the deck is almost as important as the pool itself. "Deck" means the area surrounding the pool, regardless of the material used for its construction. Concrete, slate, flagstone, or wooden decks are all popular and each has its advantages. The area should be spacious enough for entertaining guests, enjoying lunch or snacks, and for sunbathing.

Shade trees near but not directly above the pool are important for those hours when the poolside is the social gathering place. If trees are too near, leaves, sap, and insects from them will fall into the water and clog the drain. But if trees stand in the path of the late afternoon sun, especially in hot weather, the pool area will be a cooler and much more pleasant place in which to relax.

Beach umbrellas can make up partially for lack of natural shade, as can a gazebo or open cabana, but even when these amenities exist, the natural shade is desirable.

Above-ground pools

There are three advantages in purchasing above-ground pools. First, their initial price is lower; second, they can be put up in a single day, with two or three helpers; and finally, 80 percent of them can be and are installed by the homeowners.

When a dealer or contractor must be hired to do the installation, it is usually because there is a special problem involved, or because a large deck and special landscaping are desired and the homeowner does not have the time to do it himself.

However large it may be, an above-ground pool is regarded as portable and not subject to taxation. The initial cost and upkeep are considerably less than for an in-ground pool.

Not very long ago nearly all above-ground pools were round or oval in shape, but now they are also available in double-circle, figure eight, square, or rectangular shapes. Most are only four feet deep throughout, but some now have what is called a hopper at one end which allows for an eight-foot depth for diving.

The round pools usually range from fifteen to eighteen feet in diameter; the double-circle models average thirty feet; and some rectangular above-ground pools are twenty by forty feet.

The least expensive are those with a vinyl liner and walls of concrete block, steel, or plywood. Aluminum pools last longer but may require more upkeep.

The great advantage of the vinyl liner is that it can withstand extremes in temperature, is easy to patch even under water, and never needs painting. However, the average life of the vinyl above-ground pools is only seven to ten years. Most come with a guarantee of from five to ten years and may last as long as fifteen.

If properly cared for, vinyl pools need not be drained until the pool itself is replaced. The water is kept purified with chemicals and the filter system. Most manufacturers recommend that the liner rest on a bed two to four inches deep of clean fine sand or soft loam free of rocks or pebbles. These pools do not require any excavation at all—unless placed on an uneven or sloping site. Existing sewer and utility lines therefore need not be disturbed, nor is there any bill for blasting to add to the cost.

One family used the slab floor of an old, unused garage for the base of their pool. The slab happened to be twelve by twenty feet, the exact dimensions of the oval pool. The owner used a truck to pull the dilapidated frame structure of the garage from its base to a city dump, and afterward set up the steel walls to hold the pool liner according to instructions. The pool had been purchased at a department store sale for under $600. The owner built a wooden deck around the pool to a height that makes the pool seem to be recessed in the deck and sealed the wooden plank floor with a nonskid weather-resistant finish. The deck is surrounded by a cedar stockade fence for privacy. The cost of lumber and other materials for the deck and fencing was about $400.

Prices of above-ground pools

To give some idea of the wide price range for these above-ground pools, here are two examples. A round aluminum pool eighteen feet in diameter and four feet in depth, with a filter, vacuum cleaner, pool ladder, patch kit, and water-test kit, has a price tag of $485. This does not include the cost of installation nor materials for a deck or fence.

A larger pool, also aluminum but oval in shape, costs $2,000, including filter, skimmer, lock-up safety ladder, in-pool ladder, redwood deck ready to assemble, and aluminum fence. This price does not include installation costs, either. However, an in-ground pool of the same dimensions might cost $6,000, not including landscaping.

For those hesitant to do the installation themselves, it may be done by a contractor for from $150 to $300, not including decking or landscaping, and assuming there are no major problems connected with the site. But if drainage facilities must be added, or the water source is far away, this cost could triple. Piping in water runs to $50 every twenty feet.

One firm offers as part of a package deal a deck covered completely with nonskid vinyl surrounded by a solid fiber glass fence and "a steel superstructure like a suspension bridge." Steps leading up from ground level are part of the package, and the advertisement assures potential customers that all this will cost "surprisingly little." No figure is named.

Maintenance costs are much lower for any of the above-ground pools than for those built in the ground. One man asserted that his maintenance costs for the entire season were less than $50, but this is low. More typical is a figure of $15 a month. If you sign a service contract to have a man come regularly to clean the pool and check it out, maintenance charges will range from $30 to $75 per month, depending on how much of this work the family undertakes to do. Add to these costs higher utility bills, especially if the pool has a heater. In cool weather, a heater will add at least $25 a month to the electricity or gas bill.

Some very luxurious poolsides have been constructed around inexpensive vinyl or aluminum pools, with indoor-outdoor carpeting on the deck, built-in seats and shelters, and extensive landscaping, including shrubs, walks, and flower beds.

Although a luxurious in-ground pool costs many thousands of dollars to construct, the investment increases the property's value substantially.

In-ground pools

Nearly all the award-winning pools pictured in magazines have been built into the ground and range from a starting price of $7,000 for the pool alone to $25,000, or more. But, it is pointed out, that while other extras such as maintenance must be added, there are also allowable deductions from the federal income tax such as sales taxes, depreciation, and state property taxes.

Still more important, the investment will enhance the attraction of your property to prospective buyers. And in raising status, ownership of a pool is of incalculable value.

The cost of an in-ground pool varies according to its size and the materials used. For example, a sixteen-by-thirty-two-foot pool with vinyl lining might cost $5,300 while the same size pool with a sprayed concrete lining is likely to cost $8,000.

Vinyl liners in a twenty- to thirty-gauge thickness are now used in about half of all in-ground pools. These liners are unaffected by temperatures as low as forty degrees below zero, will not crack or chip, and never need painting. An additional advantage is that the pool water never has to be drained; not only is it kept clean by the filter system, skimming, vacuuming, and chemicals, but algae do not cling to vinyl as to concrete.

However, if not properly installed, the vinyl can be punctured or torn; its lifespan averages twelve years. To replace the lining costs from $300 to $1,000, depending on size.

Many people consider in-ground pools lined by the Gunite method, with sprayed concrete, to be the most satisfactory and durable. After the excavation is complete, the entire surface, bottom, and sides is covered with reinforced metal mesh, then the concrete mixture is sprayed through a nozzle over the mesh in an even layer. This results in a seamless surface. A Gunite pool has some disadvantages, however; it must be painted periodically, as must all concrete and metal pools, and for smoothness it should have several coats of waterproof enamel, or be finished with a Marbleite mixture. Also, algae will cling to the surface, which increases danger of infection and difficulty in cleaning. In very cold climates, there is a possibility that the concrete may crack.

One advantage of concrete pools is that they may have several different levels—a wading pool, a deep diving area, and a graduated bottom for swimmers. Some Gunite pools have what is called a "love seat," four feet wide, which doubles as a step and a place to sit partially underwater, so that ladders or other steps are not necessary.

Both the vinyl-lined and the sprayed concrete pools are available in a variety of forms, L- or T-shaped, kidney shaped, figure eight, or teardrop. The newest thing in vinyl is the "pebble-ground" effect; a black vinyl lining with silver sparkles is also in demand, though aqua remains the most popular color for underwater surfaces.

Steel, aluminum, or wood treated to prevent rot may serve as the structure for the vinyl-lined pools; do-it-yourselfers sometimes use concrete blocks. It is possible to place a heavy vinyl pool in an excavation without any other basic structure, but then the vinyl is more subject to tears or punctures from rocks or earth movement.

Essentials and extras

Every pool, large or small, above ground or in the ground, must have a filtration system. Usually filter, pump, and motor are included in the price—but do not take this for granted.

Every pool must have some kind of an in-pool ladder or steps. A safety ladder (usually an extra) which can be locked is recommended, especially when the pool is to be used by children. Most people consider two outside ladders or one ladder supplemented by steps as essential.

Every pool must have a water-test kit, to determine the degree of purity or pollution, and a chemical-dispensing kit. If the latter is not included in the purchase price, the cost ranges from $50 to $150.

A vacuum cleaner and a skimmer are other essentials; these often are included in the price. Purchased separately, a vacuum cleaner costs from $70 to $100; a skimmer runs from $10 to $30. Usually included in the price of in-ground pools are a three-foot-wide deck of concrete or other suitable material and "normal electrical work." The latter, however, does not include underwater lighting unless so specified. Fencing is required by law in nearly every state but the cost of fencing is never included.

If a pool is surrounded by trees, it should have a cover of some sort. These are available in a number of materials and range in price from $125 up. The least expensive are the plastic covers, but these are considered to afford only limited protection. The best are the aluminum or fiber glass covers, either of which could cost as much as $2,000, especially if they must be custom-made for a free-form pool. Canvas covers, if they fit tightly, are fine, and some of these can be pulled up to swing above the pool like awnings as protection from a blistering sun.

Whatever the material used, it is important that the cover fit tightly all the way around to prevent children or animals from tumbling in when the pool is not in use. Too many tragic drownings have occurred for lack of a cover. A good cover can also help to pay for itself by cutting down on the cost of chemicals, for when the pool is not covered, evaporation loss also reduces the strength of the chemical purifiers.

A diving board can be used only for a pool that has a depth of eight feet and enough area at this depth for plain and fancy diving. To add a diving board will cost from $100 to $150.

A heater is not an essential, but thousands of families have persuaded themselves that they cannot do without one, because it extends the pool season by several months. There are some filter-heater combinations that cost less than the prices of the two attachments when they are purchased separately. The most common type of heater is gas-fired; some operate on electricity; a few on solar-heat units. A heater can raise the water temperature to twenty degrees above the outside air temperature. However, the cost must be weighed; even in San Diego, it has been found that using a heated pool in winter can cost ten times as much as during the in-between seasons.

Other extras which some pool owners find to be irresistible include aquaslides ($150 to $300), underwater lights for night swimming, and various kinds of toys and games, floats, life jackets for nonswimming children, foot baths (not only to prevent the spread of infection but to keep the pool cleaner), bumper strips around the perimeter to protect the finish (for concrete pools), and an alarm system. If it is electrically operated, the alarm system costs from $85 to $125. The nonelectric types are somewhat cheaper. All these systems can be triggered to set off an alarm in the house if someone enters the pool. However, the alarm sometimes goes off when the only "intruders" are falling leaves or other debris deposited by the wind.

In addition to the above extras are fencing, decking, landscaping, and a poolside structure such as a cabana or shower-dressing room.

Maintenance and safety

The unavoidable maintenance costs for any pool are the chemical purifiers, which must be replenished regularly, and the utility costs in running the filtration system. Insurance is another must.

There is a great deal of work involved in keeping a pool clean and every member of the family able to do so should help. One family in Port Chester, New York, that had a very costly pool built and equipped with all the extras, abandoned it after the first year and never used it again. Instead they spent summer afternoons at the country club. When asked why they did not use the pool, the answer was that keeping it clean required too much work.

For those who can afford to have the pool serviced regularly, this particular headache can be avoided. But when members of a family insist that they must have a pool, an agreement should be reached at the outset that each person will do his share of the work.

During the summer season, the filter should be in operation for six to eight hours per day; in off-seasons, four to six hours. Once a day the system should be checked to make sure that the valves are working, to clean out any dirt or debris that may be clogging the line, and to see that the pump strainer is clean. The water should be cleaned with vacuum and skimmer daily during the season and the water tested regularly for chemical balance, both the PH and chlorine level. On hot days, algae will dissipate the chlorine rapidly and if the pool is used by a considerable number of people, the chemical content may have to be increased.

To keep the filter clean, it is suggested that a handful of diatomaceous earth (available from pool dealers or hardware stores) be added to it once a week.

Liability insurance costs only between ten and fifty dollars a year, and is important to have in case of injuries to visitors or guests at the pool.

Safety precautions begin when the pool is built or installed. Only a licensed electrician should be permitted to do the electrical work around a pool—this is not a do-it-yourself job. There must be a complete grounding of all metal objects inside or near a pool. Nor should there be any electrical outlets or grounding of metal fencing within ten feet. No electrical appliances of any kind should be in use near the pool unless protected by a ground fault interrupter. No one should be permitted to use any electrical appliances on long extension cords in the pool area.

If there is outdoor lighting, either underwater or overhead, or both, special equipment must be used to conform with the Underwriters Laboratory Code. Filter equipment for the pool must also be grounded.

The chemicals in the water should not be looked upon as protection against infections. There should be a firm rule against allowing anyone in the pool with a cold, ear infection, or any infectious skin conditions, including poison ivy. Everyone should shower before going into the pool, especially so if they have been using suntan oil (the oil will clog the filter).

Besides a first-aid kit, a lifesaving jacket or two should be at hand, and either a twelve-foot pole with blunt ends or a ring buoy attached to a throwing rope, in case anyone has a cramp in the water or a nonswimmer gets beyond his depth. Somewhere adjacent to the nearest phone there should be a list of numbers for reaching a doctor, the hospital, ambulance corps, police, or a rescue unit.

To avoid accidents, the pool deck should be treated with a nonskid heat-reducing paint or sealer—unless the surface is of concrete or is covered with outdoor carpeting. Only non-breakable (plastic or paper) dishes and glassware should be used for eating at poolside.

Not only must an eye be kept on children using the pool; any inebriated persons must be kept out of the water. There also should be a firm rule that no one is allowed to be in the pool alone at any time. Someone who can swim should always be at the poolside. And if a storm seems likely, everyone should vacate the pool when the first raindrops fall or the rumble of distant thunder is heard.

Even playtime equipment presents a potential hazard at a pool. Inflatable floats can deflate without warning. Those who go down the aquaslide head first may choke when they hit the water. Water polo is a great game, but not for nonswimmers.

A protective fence around the pool is now required by law nearly everywhere and should be at least four feet high. (Some localities stipulate five feet.) Not only must it be above the heads of toddlers, it is also important that it not have footholds of any kind enabling children to climb up and over. Gates should have a permanent lock.

In the past all pools were emptied at the end of the season, which is still recommended as a safety measure. But now many people assert that water can be left in the pool during the winter if the water level is beneath the coping on the side of the pool to prevent the formation of ice that could crack or warp the frame or edging. All water should be drained from pipes and filter, however, and the pool kept securely covered at all times—unless the cover is removed in freezing weather to use the pool as a skating rink. (But be sure that the ice is frozen deep enough for safety.)

If the pool has a heater, both heater and pilot light should be shut off whenever you are to be away, and naturally at the end of the season as well.

Painting concrete or metal pools

It will save both labor and money if the pool is repainted while its paint is still in good condition. If allowed to go too long, until the surface is cracked or peeling, the pool will probably have to be sandblasted to remove all old paint, then an acid wash must be applied to clean the pores of the sanding, and the acid in turn must be rinsed off before new paint can be applied. Any patching that needs to be done will have to be attended to before the acid wash is applied.

If the homeowner elects to paint a new pool as a way of cutting costs, the acid wash (a 10 percent solution of muriatic acid) must be applied to etch the surface. Before starting this job, put on rubber boots, rubber gloves, and goggles for protection.

Only special paints recommended for pools should be used, and the manufacturer's directions carefully followed. When more than one coat is needed, make sure that the first is completely dry before the second is added.

To repaint a pool that is still in good condition, a good scrubbing with a detergent may be all the surface preparation necessary. If there is any mildew or fungus present, this should be removed with a cleaner containing either sodium hypochlorite or trisodium phosphate. A thorough rinsing is necessary after this application.

Make sure that the coat of paint you apply is the same as that used originally—the same manufacturer, the same number or classification. If the paint of another manufacturer is used, it may peel or crack because of differences in chemical composition.

When a built-in pool is being constructed, the contractor should apply a waterproof coating on the outside of either concrete or metal walls before the backfill of earth is added. Otherwise, water seeping into the pool from the bottom or sides could cause blisters in the paint and corrosion in the metal.

Decking, landscaping, finishing touches

Pictures of handsome shimmering pools in sylvan settings make us all envious. This is the dream envisaged when the word pool is mentioned. But when all the costs are added up, to have such a landscaped pool at the outset often proves to be a financial impossibility. Then it is wise to make a plan for achieving this goal over a period of several years.

The first year, it is essential that the deck and fence be added. The second year the size of the deck might be increased and shrubs planted around the perimeter. The third or fourth year, a cabana or other outdoor shelter might be erected. Decorative overhead lighting to show off the pool to advantage also can be planned for a later time.

Fences can be decorative as well as protective. The least expensive kind, chain link fences, cost only three dollars a lineal foot but add little beauty to the scene. Such a fence might be put up as a start, to be replaced eventually, but making use of the same posts. Or, to hide its utilitarian appearance, vines or climbing roses could be planted at the base of the fence.

Wood fencing costs a little more but adds greatly to appearance. There are many styles to choose from. If complete privacy is wanted, basket-weave prefabricated sections, or a six-foot-high stockade fence, or board-on-board panels might be used. All these can be purchased in sections eight feet long and four, five, or six feet high.

For more air and almost as much privacy, picket fences or louvered fences are attractive. The pickets can be placed close together for privacy or separated slightly more if a see-through fence is wanted for overlooking the garden, as long as spaces between the pickets are not wide enough for children or pets to squeeze through.

For a louvered fence, boards are placed side by side at an

Types of Fencing

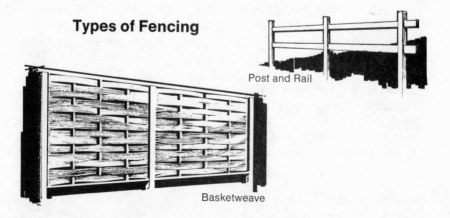

Post and Rail

Basketweave

angle, like a huge venetian blind on its side, allowing air to come through but preventing entry and effectively shutting off the pool area from the view of outsiders.

Redwood or red or white cedar are the most desirable woods for fencing, but these are now in short supply and quite costly. Pine or spruce cost much less and if chemically treated for insect and moisture resistance can be very satisfactory. For a board-on-board fence, two kinds of wood can be used in combination.

Most wood fencing is simply treated with a water-repellant finish and allowed to weather naturally to gray. If the color of new wood is preferred, the fencing should be stained and covered with a sealer. Or it could be bleached, then sealed. If painted, it will have to be repainted periodically. Never use shellac or varnish on exterior wood; the finish will deteriorate quickly and refinishing is difficult and expensive.

Other materials suitable for a pool fence include black iron pickets, vinyl-coated aluminum slats on wire mesh, fiber glass panels, brick, or masonry (or a combination of these last two).

Whatever the fencing material, it is important that the support posts be sunk at least two feet deep for a four- or five-foot fence, and two and a half feet for a six-foot fence. The posts can be braced with stones and tamped thoroughly with earth, but if the fence is higher than four feet, it may be advisable to sink the posts in concrete. Gate posts also might be sunk in concrete.

Be sure to select gate hinges and latches of good quality and of corrosion-resistant materials. For attaching pickets or

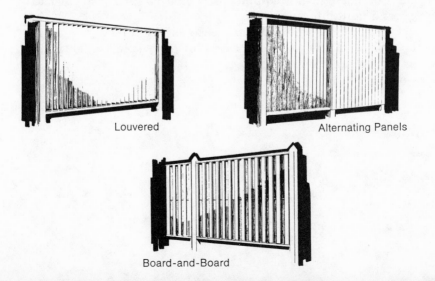

Louvered   Alternating Panels

Board-and-Board

prefabricated sections to posts and rails, use nails and bolts of either hot-dipped galvanized iron, or an aluminum alloy, or stainless steel. Regular nails will rust, which causes streaks on the wood that are difficult to remove. Also, the rusted nails will eventually work loose.

If the deck surrounding the pool is of wood, a wooden fence will look most attractive with it, but if the deck is of concrete, brick, or flagstone, a fence of iron or metal might be the best choice. Another possibility is to use decorative concrete blocks on one or two sides of the deck and metal on the other sides.

The do-it-yourselfer can send for patterns or kits which give details for building decks and also a shelter for storing pool equipment. A cabana can be a very simple homemade structure of metal or wooden supports with canvas stretched on top and sides, and furnished with a simple bench. On the other hand, elaborate ready-to-assemble cabanas have been known to cost several thousand dollars.

Poolside lighting adds immeasurably to the luxurious look of the landscape, but for underwater lights, the lines must be installed when the pool is built. Overhead floodlight illumination is not difficult to set up. Some lights can be placed high in tree branches, directed downward; others just behind shrubs or plants at the perimeter of the pool area—though all must be at least ten feet from the water. Some fixtures might be fitted with insect-repelling lamps. Any lights facing upward should be covered with wire mesh or tempered glass to avoid trapping leaves or other flammable debris. Only special outdoor lighting equipment should be used, attached to ground fault interrupters.

Outdoor lights not only increase safety in the pool area, but make sitting around the pool of an evening as enticing as during sunlit hours.

Making Yours an Outdoor-Indoor House

It has been said that a beautiful lawn can add $1,000 to the resale value of a house. Even more important is an attractively designed and landscaped patio, terrace, or other "outdoor room."

Exterior decoration can do as much to enhance the appearance and livability of your home as interior decoration. And a great deal of it can be do-it-yourself.

The front yard, entranceway, and the view of the house from the street are important for the impression they make on those who pass by and those who enter. The side and back yards are of primary importance for the hours of pleasure and relaxation they make possible for the family, especially during the warm months of the year.

It is a peculiarly American custom to put both name and house number in a conspicuous spot, either on or above the mail box, in the yard, or near the front entrance. This way of proclaiming to the world who lives in the house makes it easier for postmen, deliverymen, and friends coming to visit for the first time.

But the manner in which yard and entrance are beautified also proclaims to the world much about the people who live behind the front door.

The more conventional way of announcing name and house number is to insert the proper letters and numbers on the crest of a mailbox. But in California, where so many now well-established American customs originated, some families cut huge numbers—up to two feet high—from plywood, paint them in vivid colors or in colors to match the trim of the house, and mount them on the wall beside the front door. Others erect numbers of equal size over the entrance gate, or on a panel set between posts. There is a kind of competition over devising new and unusual ways to turn house numbers into decorative additions.

To plant flower beds so that flower patterns form the numbers is somewhat more difficult, but it has been done. Other families display signs that read, "The John Smiths live here," or put the names of every person in the household on a separate stake, with a series of stakes ascending the slope beside the entrance steps.

There is one disadvantage in advertising the family name for all to see: you are giving door-to-door salesmen and solicitors an easy opening wedge. But another new device will help to keep such strangers on the outer side of the front door: you can have a see-through, talk-through brass door knocker and when you do not wish to be bothered, simply refuse to open the door.

Amusingly decorative house numbers, gold-trimmed mailboxes, door chimes that ring a melody, and brass knockers that provide a secret look at visitors are all conceits that cost little and can be attractive.

But no other exterior detail is more important than the front door. This is where visitors stand as they wait for you to answer their ring or knock. If the front door is badly scuffed, you might try repainting it in a vivid color. Or, if it shows its age or its style annoys you, why not replace it with a new door? This is not a major renovation, but it can perk up the house wonderfully. Some of the new exterior doors have built-in insulation, making a storm door unnecessary.

Some are handsomely paneled; others are finished in rich veneers. Full-length door shutters on each side of the entrance can make it seem much wider than before. Twin carriage lamps at the sides are practical and attractive on a house built in traditional style. An old repainted door can be made to seem new by means of a larger door frame, easily constructed of decorative molding strips (made of wood for exterior use), nailed around the existing frame.

Foundation shrubs

Foundation shrubs are as important as the front door. The shrubs must be evergreen, to conceal the masonry foundation of the house, but azaleas and mountain laurel qualify in this category, adding blooms in their season and green leaves throughout the year. Annual or perennial flowers and spring bulbs can, of course, be planted in front of the shrubs, or in separate flower beds, or as a rock garden enhancing the entranceway.

The shrubs nearest the front porch or steps should be high enough to reach the floor level, but kept trimmed, to avoid shooting up to a height that obscures the front windows. Other shrubs should be in descending heights, or a combination of low and tall plants artfully arranged. A bed of white marble chips around the roots helps to set off the green of the foliage attractively. A mulch of peat moss or of redwood shavings could be used instead of chips.

If when you purchased the house its foundation shrubs had already reached the top of the front windows, it may be too late to prune them back to a more attractive and reasonable height. If this is so, consider having them transplanted, perhaps to screen a parking area at the side of the house, or in front of the children's play yard. Overgrown evergreens at the front of a house say so very clearly that the house is old, and suggest that it may be musty inside. Transplanting any bush or tree of this age must be done by a gardener or nurseryman who knows how to dig down far enough to avoid chopping off major roots, and how to ball the roots for transplanting, but even quite tall trees can be successfully transplanted by those who know how to do so.

In choosing new foundation shrubs from a nursery or garden supply house, be sure to get varieties that will thrive

where you plan to put them. Some do best in shade, others
need a good degree of sunlight, but even shade-loving shrubs
can have a hard time getting well started when there is no
direct sunlight at all. The earth around such plants should be
made extra rich with natural fertilizer, aerated with peat
moss, and kept moist with a heavy mulch. Also, it is necessary
to feed and water these plants, especially in the first year or
so, more frequently than if they were in a place that receives
sun at least an hour or so a day. It may seem surprising that
in an area where there is no sun at all, and therefore the
ground does not get baked dry, plants should need to be watered more often. But water contains nutrients the plants
need, and they need that much more if they do not receive
sunlight.

Making a walk

Walks leading up to the house and around to the back
should be neat, decorative, and practical. Concrete walks are
less interesting than those made with flagstones, slate, patio
blocks, or bricks. If a concrete walk already exists, it can be
made more attractive with a low hedge on each side. If you
are laying a new walk, try to curve it gently rather than keeping it absolutely straight.

To make a new walk, first mark out the path with string
and stakes, twenty-four to thirty inches wide, then between
the rows dig down on the sides to a depth of eight inches, and
in the center to six inches. The greater depth at the sides is to
hold framing boards, two by eights, of treated moisture-resistant timber, which not only mark the boundary of the
walk, but prevent or discourage the spread of underground
vines.

Cut out the bed as evenly as possible, removing any stones
that jut up into the path. Some that are sunk very deep and
are very large may be left in place as long as they will be
entirely beneath the surface you are about to lay. Tamp down
the earth (a tool for this purpose can be purchased at the
hardware store) until it is very firm and level. Then add a
layer of sand four to five inches deep: four inches if you plan
to use two-inch-thick stones or blocks, five inches for inch-
thick slate or flagstone. Place the stones over the sand, and
adjust them until they do not wobble when you step on them.

Concrete stepping stones, flagstones, slate, bricks, and paving blocks are all suitable. Fill in around the stones with more sand and with bluestone (tiny pebbles) or soil. Some people prefer to add top soil instead of bluestone and to seed the soil with grass, so that only the stepping stones are visible in the midst of grass. For ease in grass-cutting, the level of the walk should be slightly below that of the turf on either side, so that the mower can go over the top easily.

If a solid walk set in concrete is preferred, much the same process is followed, except that a mixture of sand and gravel is used for the bed, and over this mortar, concrete, or masonry mix is spread, and the stepping stones or bricks are laid in the mix while it is wet. Finally more mortar is caulked around and between the stones.

For steps on a slope, the design of walkway and steps should be coordinated. If you want it all in concrete, better hire a mason to do the job, for it takes professional know-how to set the mix so as to avoid cracking from ground-heave following the spring thaws. The amateur can do better with a combination of railroad ties and flagstones, though these steps, too, must be braced carefully to prevent them from sliding down the hill as the earth settles.

Railroad ties are now so much in demand for this kind of landscaping that timbers which have never been near a railroad bed can be purchased new, cut in the traditional shape (six by eight inches, six to eight feet long). The wood is treated with creosote to be moisture- and termite-resistant, and its durability is phenomenal. Considerably less expensive is "landscape timber." This, slightly less than four by five inches thick, comes in eight and one-half-foot lengths, also treated with creosote. In using either of these types of lumber, a pyramidical structure is set in place up the slope, each new layer above and slightly back from the one below, and each kept in place by stakes embedded twelve inches in the ground.

When steps four feet wide are wanted, each eight-foot railroad tie or length of timber can be cut in half. Or each may be left its full length with the steps formed in the center and rock garden plants, low shrubs, or spreading juniper planted at each end. As they take root these will help to hold the timber in place. The steps may be set in a bed of sand, or of black-top, the same mix used for constructing driveways. If black-top is used, white marble chips can be embedded in it, around the stones (flagstones, slate, or other).

Most American front lawns are open to the street and when there is any kind of fence or hedge in front, it is rarely more than three feet in height. But there are places viewable from the front that should be concealed. A parking area beside the house, for example, might be partially hidden with a tall hedge, large shrubs, evergreens, or a screen of quick-growing poplars planted close together. The place where containers for trash and garbage are kept should be as thoroughly shielded from view as possible. Decorative concrete blocks with a cutout pattern can be stacked in an L, one side adjoining the kitchen or side entrance; or L-shaped fencing in a basketweave pattern might serve to hide these unattractive necessities.

The universal patio

However small the yard may be, nearly every American family wants some kind of "outdoor room." Most often this is a patio with outdoor furniture and a barbecue grill.

There are many materials suitable for building a patio, and the choice may depend on the terrain as much as the cost. For level ground, a patio floor set in concrete is the most satisfactory in the long run, but when the ground is sloping, uneven, or rocky, a wood deck is easier to construct and offers several advantages.

For constructing a level patio, one may choose flagstones, black slate rectangles or irregular pieces of thin colored slate, concrete stepping stones, varicolored aggregate patio blocks, bricks (available in many different colors, shapes, and sizes) or wood circles cut in two-inch-thick slabs.

As suggested for laying walks, any of the above can first be set over a dry fill of sand, with bluestone pebbles or gravel for the borders and for the crevices between stones. Or they can, if preferred, be set in mortar from the beginning.

There are advantages in using a dry fill first. You can try out the patio for size, drainage, and traffic patterns, and if as you use it, you note the need for a larger area, or see that pools of water tend to collect at one end, you can easily make the necessary changes.

As in laying out walks, the first step in patio construction is to mark the boundaries with string and stakes, then dig down at least eight inches around the perimeter, removing all big stones and those that jut up from the ground enough to interfere with a level finished surface.

Next comes tamping the ground level with an iron weight. Use a carpenter's level for measuring. Then add sand, or a mixture of sand and gravel, to a depth of four or five inches, depending on the thickness of the surface stone. The larger in size the blocks or stones used for the surface, the easier the construction; not as many are needed, and fitting them together is therefore easier.

It may seem like double work to take up the stones and reset them in mortar, but you will meantime have been able to decide whether you like the dimensions, and to correct any faults.

Poured concrete can also be used for a level patio floor. Rather than one big slab, it will be more attractive, less subject to cracks, and easier to set if divided into sections. Use a frame of redwood strips to mark out the sections. When the concrete is poured within these frames, the redwood will form an interesting pattern, like a plaid. Some areas can be left free for plantings; steps in concrete could be laid at the side.

The larger the patio floor, the less lawn there is to be fed, watered, and cut. It is possible in a small lot to eliminate a lawn entirely.

A family in San Diego, after returning from a two-year tour of duty in Spain, decided to turn the rear yard of their town house into the type of patio they had enjoyed in Spain. With a stockade fence enclosing the yard on three sides, they filled in the garden area completely with flagstones, except for beds in which they planted rose bushes. In one corner, they built a small fountain of ceramic tiles with a motor to recycle the water, creating a serene, musical sound. Along the base of one fence they planted bougainvillea, which provides a cascade of purplish-red blossoms from July until September.

Although the flower beds are given over entirely to rose bushes, other plants grow in gaily-painted tubs, which can be moved as necessary to catch full sunlight. Because the yard is so small, they do not have space for shade trees, but they have an orange tree and a lemon tree to remind them of Spain, and use beach umbrellas for shade when they sit on the patio in their white wrought iron garden furniture. Because they have ground cover and shrubs at the front of the house—no grass there either—they do not even own a lawn mower.

Wooden decks for difficult terrain

Constructing a wooden deck is much easier in most circumstances than laying a patio with stone or slate. Such a deck is especially appropriate for hillsides or ground that is uneven or rocky. No earth need be dug up; you need only spread a heavy layer of gravel over the surface to inhibit weed growth.

To make the deck level, even when the slope is at a sharper angle on one side than on other sides, all that is necessary is to adjust the height of the support posts accordingly. These posts should be anchored by means of pins or collars in concrete bases installed below the frost level. Where the deck adjoins the house, supports can be fastened to the foundation wall, using special nails for masonry (do not attempt to do this with ordinary nails; they will not hold).

Redwood is the first choice for a deck, because it is naturally resistant to rot and attack by insects, and it fades gradually to a soft gray, requiring no further attention. But other suitable woods, which also can be allowed to weather naturally and need no other attention than application of a preservative sealer, are considerably less costly. Douglas fir and ponderosa pine are frequently recommended. When wood is to be placed close to the ground, it should be treated for termite-resistance if it was not so treated before purchase. For posts, use four-by-fours or six-by-sixes; for the decking, two-by-fours or two-by-sixes. A space of one-quarter inch between deck boards is recommended, to carry off rain so that no puddles remain on the surface.

Rails, roofing, and walls of the same wood can be added to make such decks more like outdoor rooms. When a deck is close to neighboring property, a wall on one side provides privacy. Many contemporary-style houses, especially in the West, have not just one but several decks, at different levels, creating a succession of outdoor rooms.

One such upper deck, for example, might be just outside

the master bedroom, offering a retreat away from other family activities, a place for reading, sunbathing, or napping. Another deck for the children might hold a sandbox (spilled sand disappears between the slats). Or the children's play area could be on a stretch of ground on a level lower than the family deck, so that parents could keep an eye on the children yet be able to enjoy grown-up talk. There can be decks on several levels, one leading to another with steps. By extending the decks over terrain that is difficult to cultivate, you can achieve a feeling of being out-of-doors with a minimum of garden maintenance. Each deck can be tailored to the landscape, sometimes built around trees that thrust up through it.

Patterns for building various types of decks can be obtained from the California Redwood Association, the American Wood Council, and the Southern Forest Products Association. These patterns come with exact specifications and instructions for treating the wood, setting posts, and measuring for correct alignment.

New wood will shrink somewhat, which must be kept in mind when spacing boards or strips. What seems barely noticeable space between boards in the beginning may with shrinkage widen to a larger gap than you wish. Some woods, the more porous pines especially, shrink more than others. This is one reason to be cautious in the purchase of cheaper grades; they could be quite green and shrink enough to create real problems. For deck posts and supports, select timber free from knots or splits.

Enclosing patios or decks

In the early part of the twentieth century, virtually every house had a sizable porch, usually facing the street so that it was possible to watch the world go by from a porch swing.

Front porches are now passé, but increasingly people are realizing that a screened-in porch at the rear or to the side of a house can be far more useful than an open patio, and in some cases what began as a patio or deck evolves into a year-round outdoor-indoor room.

A couple living in Greenwich, Connecticut, finding that mosquitoes made it impossible for them to remain on their patio after sundown, decided to screen it in, keeping the patio floor as it was.

Narrow width of 8-by-18-foot deck makes it ideal for a side yard location, outside a master bedroom or any other room. The fence provides privacy.

The contractor they consulted suggested that they might in addition wish to increase the area of the patio, because its size was that of only a small room. In the end, they doubled the size of the patio floor and had removable screens placed from floor to ceiling around the sides, beneath the slope of the new roof. In winter, the screens are replaced with windows. (Because the room was open on all sides, they decided this would be preferable to casement windows with screens, and also less expensive.) Eventually they put a shag rug over the patio floor, to cover it wall to wall. They have two electric radiators to use when the weather becomes chilly, and now enjoy the room throughout the year. It is the most-used room in the house, with a magnificent vista over a sloping lawn set with tall trees.

Roofing a patio or deck is often the first step towards enclosure. A roof increases the number of hours that this outdoor room is usable. It may be only a half roof, providing some shelter but leaving an open area for those who wish to sunbathe or sit beneath the stars at night. Once there is a roof, it is easy to add roll-up blinds, both for privacy and shade. Thin-slatted vinyl blinds, the best for this purpose, are now available in white, green, chocolate brown, and other colors besides the light tan of natural bamboo.

Many wooden decks have walls on one or two sides for privacy. Latticework has also been rediscovered as a lacy kind of wall for patio or deck. It provides a degree of privacy but also ample ventilation, and the thin wooden strips are quite inexpensive and easy to nail in place. Latticework can double as a trellis over which climbing vines or roses are trained, or as a roof over a part of a patio or deck, giving partial shade without cutting off light and air. It may also be used effectively to conceal an old-fashioned front porch from public view without interrupting air flow.

A screened porch, patio, or deck can be used much more frequently and for longer periods than one that is completely open. Even if windows are not put in place, it can be used in all but severe weather.

Another increasingly popular type of outdoor-indoor room is a combination of open patio adjoining a family room, with sliding glass doors the only separation. To make this seem one big room, the same outdoor carpeting can be used in the family room and on the patio. Even when it is too cold to make use of the patio, the view makes the family room seem larger.

In California, a large rear deck may have an enclosed room in the center, with windows on three sides. To create such a room, a three-year plan could be devised. Start with a large deck, next add a roof over the center part, perhaps with benches around the "room" beneath the roof. Next posts are put in place, so that screens can be attached. And finally an insulated floor, glass windows, carpeting, and possibly heating can be added, to make it a finished year-round room with a view.

Gazebos and other garden structures

A gazebo can be a fun addition to the yard, a wonderfully cool place for summertime dining because it is open on all sides and a place to spend after-dark hours protected from insects.

Not all gazebos are screened. Essentially this is a simple roofed structure, a garden house, which in other times was set in the middle of the lawn as a place to enjoy the view of flowers and grass. But with screening all around, its use is greatly increased. It is especially attractive to those who are so bothered by insect bites they are unable to stay out of doors for long even during the day.

Ready-made gazebos of aluminum and fiber glass which can be assembled in less than an hour are available for around $200 and up. At the season's end, the roof is removed and the sides folded for winter storage. For best protection from insects, such a ready-made gazebo should be placed above a patio or concrete floor rather than on grass or a wooden deck (unless the deck is covered with carpeting). After dark, candles in hurricane lamps or insect-repellant candles provide the coolest and softest light.

To build your own gazebo is not difficult and patterns for this, too, are available. The traditional gazebo is round with a built-in bench, but if it is to be used for outdoor dining and entertaining, a rectangular or square shape large enough to hold outdoor furniture is more practical and easier to construct. One pattern calls for six post holes, two of which support the end peaks in a sloped roof, a deck large enough to extend several feet beyond the exterior of the gazebo, and double sliding shoji type screens on the four sides. These, two of which are on movable tracks, can be removed when the mosquito season is over.

Many simple garden structures can be built without patterns: for example, a sandbox for toddlers, a tree house for children old enough to climb up to it, benches built in odd corners or around trees, or a permanent picnic table made of a round wooden slab nailed to a tree stump.

A more ambitious undertaking would be the construction of a playhouse which could double as a guest house for those young enough to bed down in sleeping bags.

Another Connecticut couple built an A-frame structure, like a wooden tent on a wide deck floor, for the use of their three sons. Having a large lot, mostly treed, they constructed the cabin in the woods, which enchanted the boys. The first year, the boys were satisfied to have nothing more than a roof overhead and open sides. The second year they helped their father to add built-in bunks at each side and both ends were screened in. It became a favorite meeting place for Cub Scouts, who volunteered in the third year to help construct built-in storage facilities and put wooden framing around the sides. A door on hinges was added for better weather protection.

Double play towers provide a variety of open and enclosed spaces to spur children's imaginations in devising new games on their home ground.

Metal storage sheds can be purchased ready to put up, but much more attractive and less costly would be a storage unit constructed so that it is attached to the outer wall of the garage, with compartmented sections, each with its own door. If anchored to the garage, no footings or support posts are needed, other than cinder blocks laid on the ground. It can be used to hold garden tools, sports gear, toys, and poolside equipment.

When any such structure is erected in the yard, it should conform to the style of the house. A little extra thought in planning its design will pay off in making it a distinct asset to the property.

A greenhouse is another structure that the home handyman can erect. It must be in a location which receives full sun, and for protection against wind damage, should be attached to an existing wall which will shield it from prevailing winds, if this is possible. If a greenhouse seems too formidable an undertaking (it must be heated throughout the winter to be really effective, and this could mean an enormous fuel bill), a cold frame for starting plants early is even easier to make. It requires only the simplest frame to hold glass windows at a slant. Inside, manure is used to create heat as well as serving as fertilizer.

Patterns for building cold frames and greenhouses are available from the U.S. Department of Agriculture.

Planning a low-maintenance garden

There are two principal methods of obtaining a low-maintenance yard and garden.

One is to have only shrubs, trees, and grass—no flower beds. If you must have a power mower anyway, cutting a large lawn takes only a little more time than a smaller one, and if you make up your mind to be content with a lawn that is green if not velvety, mowing whenever it needs it and watering during periods of drought may be all the attention it needs.

The other way is to plan so that no grass at all is necessary, only patio, walks, ground cover, large and small shrubs, and a limited number of perennial flowers and bulbs.

The second method requires much more work at the start, but once the plantings are well rooted, you can be away from home for weeks at a time without worry about your yard.

Foundation shrubs, as already noted, are essential. It is best to consult a local nursery as to which grow best in your area and with your sun (or shade) and soil conditions. But there are as well many flowering shrubs that provide a profusion of blooms, each in its own season.

The first year in establishing such a landscape is the hardest, when plants must recoup from the trauma of being uprooted and acclimated to a new home. They might not be happy at first with their surroundings. But if you can bring them through the first year and note signs of steady growth during the second year, you can relax. After that, they will almost take care of themselves. If they begin to droop, or do not flower as you had hoped, consult the nursery from which you purchased them or a good gardening book. Such a reference book is essential for any homeowner who wishes to have an attractive garden.

John and Sally Thomas did not set out to have a low-maintenance yard, but their lot was so heavily shaded, grass would not grow in the garden behind their house. Even certain of the shade-loving flowers, such as day lilies and impatiens, would not bloom. The Thomases marked out walks with bricks according to the contour of the terrain and encircling the trees with brick formations. Ivy and pachysandra fill in the areas around and between the circles of bricks. In the spring, tulips and jonquils shoot up from the green thickness of the ivy, each year spreading farther until they now fill most of the embankment. Lilies of the valley and wild flowers transplanted from woodland also provide bloom, as do the tall shrubs which form a hedge between their lot and the neighboring property in back.

There was no level space for a patio, so they decided on a wooden deck which John could build himself. This has steps leading from one level to another. Around the edge of the deck, cinder blocks laid on their sides hold ivy which, it is hoped, will eventually spread so as to conceal the cinder blocks completely.

Among the most popular flowering shrubs for home gardens are forsythia, azaleas, oleander, mimosa, flowering crab, flowering quince, mock orange, spirea, lilac, hydrangea, Japanese andromeda, mountain laurel, and rhododendron. Each requires certain climate, soil, and sun conditions, so inquire as to which are advised for your locality. To keep down weeds, surround the roots with a heavy mulch.

Ground cover

Ground cover takes time to get started and the only way to speed up the process is to put in more plants and to place them closer together. Of all the ground covers, pachysandra is the most satisfactory, if not the most beautiful. It multiplies rapidly after the first year and grows so close together, it crowds out all other growth. Spreading juniper can sometimes be used for ground cover on a bank, but requires special soil conditions, takes a long time to begin to spread, and the individual plants are costly.

English ivy does well in certain areas, usually with heavy shade, though it can also thrive in a sunny location. What many people do not realize about ivy is that its natural tendency is to climb up a surface rather than down, so that it should be planted at the base of the slope rather than at the top. Myrtle (sometimes called periwinkle) has very pretty blue flowers in the spring and glossy green leaves, but it takes a long time to spread and never has pachysandra's ability to squeeze out other plant growth, which means rather frequent weeding.

Planting bulbs

Bulbs, both for spring and summer blooming, require very little attention once they are planted but their disadvantages are, first, that they require a lot of space and, second, when their period of bloom is over, the foliage begins to wither and is unsightly until it has disintegrated. Only iris is exceptional; its green spikes continue to look respectable until frost.

Nevertheless, the spring bulbs offer the earliest flowering in the garden and they continue to pop up faithfully year after year. When a bulb garden is properly planned, something will be coming into bloom from early April until late September. Bulbs need attention only once every three or four years when clusters should be dug up and separated, then replanted. This need not be done if they have been planted among ground cover where they have ample space to "naturalize," that is, their roots spread naturally over a large area. However, when planted in a flower bed, if not dug up, the root clusters begin to decay in the center and finally die out.

The bulbs that can be planted successfully in the midst of ground cover include daffodils (some varieties are called jonquils), crocuses, narcissus, and most tulips. The larger hybrid tulips and hyacinths are better off in a cultivated flower bed. Annual flowers can be planted to grow around them as their leaves begin to wither.

Of the summer bulbs, the many varieties of day lilies and gladioli need considerable space. Day lilies will do well in either shade or sun under normal conditions. Gladioli need full sunlight. Most experts advise that gladioli bulbs be taken up each fall and replanted in the spring, but lazy gardeners have observed that if not taken up, most of them seem to be able to survive even quite severe winters. Tuberous-rooted begonias, however, are very sensitive to cold. It is best to pot them, so that they can be brought indoors in the winter. Dahlia roots, too, must have winter protection indoors.

Since all the above multiply, when they are dug up there will be an excess to share with neighbors. An enterprising gardener might well set up a neighborhood bulb exchange as an inexpensive way of acquiring different varieties in trade for his or her extras. In anticipation of such an exchange, when bulbs are separated at the end of the season, they should be bagged and identified as to variety and blooming period.

A perennial garden requires much more work than caring for either shrubs or bulbs, and no matter how carefully planned for a succession of bloom, some annual flowers are needed as a supplement. Roses, in a location where there is abundant sun, can be a particular joy, and by selecting a variety of colors and types, the blooming period will continue for most of the season. Roses require a great deal of attention, however. Chrysanthemums are less demanding and there are early as well as late varieties, some of which continue to bloom after light frost. It is possible to have a chrysanthemum display from August until late November.

Where the site suggests one, a rock garden can be a great asset and, once established, requires comparatively little attention except for weeding. However, building a rock garden is a time-consuming enterprise and before you begin, consult a book on how to lay the rocks, which plants are most satisfactory, and how best to achieve successive bloom. Some herbs should be included: thyme, parsley, and chives can be decorative as well as useful; the silvery-gray leaves of thyme, a perennial, are particularly attractive in a rock garden.

A vegetable garden plot

The high cost of vegetables and fruit, and a growing awareness of the greater nutritive value of natural foods, together have brought a great upsurge of interest in vegetable gardening.

This is a rewarding family activity, from the spading up in the spring to the gathering of the bounty in late summer and fall.

No matter how limited the area may be which is set aside for vegetable cultivation, the two vegetables always included are tomatoes and green beans. Both produce bountifully and both are universally liked. Sweet corn takes up too much space in proportion to its harvest; lima beans need poles or stakes for support and produce comparatively little in proportion to the area they require. Peas right from the garden have a flavor never to be found in those from either the vegetable counters in a supermarket or the frozen food bins, but they require quite a bit of space, must be trained on supports, and their productive season is of limited duration. Sweet bell peppers are worth planting because of their excessively high price even in season; summer squash and zucchini produce abundantly and have far more flavor when cooked right after picking. In the cabbage family, brussels sprouts and broccoli are worth planting because they continue to supply food for the table until late in the fall. Brussels sprouts are actually improved in flavor after the first "white frost," as farmers call it, and in some areas can be picked from their tall spindly stems as late as December.

Even though vegetables are annuals and therefore cannot be regarded as a home improvement in a reality sense, just to have garden under cultivation is an asset, and if well cared for, is an added attraction in the yard.

Growing fruit

Of the fruits worth growing yourself, strawberries are wonderful—if you have the space for them. However, they do not begin to bear seriously until the second year, they require a great deal of attention, and if the runners are not kept clipped, they multiply so fast that the plants become crowded and do not bear as well. On the other hand, if they are cared for, the everbearing plants provide fruit over a long season, and this is a perennial which comes up again year after year.

Berry bushes can be planted at the rear of the garden, or around it like a hedge, but must be kept pruned or they will begin to take over the rest of the yard, forming an impenetrable thicket of brambles and thorns. Red raspberries and the big cultivated blackberries are both easy to grow; gooseberries, an old-fashioned favorite, and currants, are worth adding if you like jam from these two fruits.

Melons require not only a great deal of space, but very special soil conditions. Unless you happen to have the sandy kind of soil in which they thrive, better leave their cultivation to commercial enterprise.

Creating and maintaining a lawn

The first essential for a good lawn is good soil. You can learn what your soil needs by taking a sample to the office of your U.S. Department of Agriculture county agent for analysis and advice on how to treat it.

Acidity is a common problem and liming is the usual method recommended for correcting this condition. But too much lime can hurt the grass, as can too little. Sometimes the soil can be improved by working organic matter into it, such as a mixture of dried manure and peat moss, or well-cured compost. But the grass itself can provide its own organic matter if properly cared for.

How the grass is mowed can be critical. More lawns have been ruined by improper mowing than any other single cause. The mower blade must be sharp so that it cuts cleanly without bruising the blades of grass, and the grass should not be cut too short. At no time should mowing remove more than one-third of the total grass blade surface. When more than this is removed, the grass suffers physiological shock and its alimentary system is injured. The green part of the grass produces food for the roots, gathering nutrients from air, sunlight, and rain.

How frequently the lawn is mowed must depend on weather conditions. Cut it only when needed—when its growth requires trimming—not regularly once a week, for example. If it grows too tall, do not try to cut it back to normal height with one operation. That would remove too much of the green. Instead, trim it a little one day, and a few days later give it a second trimming, thus reducing the level gradually.

High mowing in most cases is preferable to close clipping to prevent weed invasion, according to Dr. Elwyn E. Deal, turf specialist at the University of Maryland. Dr. Deal explains that most weed seeds will not germinate under the green light filtered through the chlorophyll of the grass blades.

The ideal height for a lawn depends on the type of grass. Bermuda grass, for example, should be one to one and one-quarter inches high; zoysia, one to one and one-half inches; Merion bluegrass, one to two inches; Kentucky blue, one to two and one-half inches; and fescue, two to three inches. When you buy grass seed, inquire at what height the grass from these seeds should be cut, and if the salesman does not know, check with the county agent.

A second common cause of lawn failure is overwatering. If watered too frequently and too heavily, the soil becomes soggy and causes the roots to decay. Even during very hot weather or periods of drought, the grass needs no more than a good soaking—an inch of rain or its equivalent—once a week.

Bare spots in the lawn may be caused by oil or gas spills, dogs, fertilizer burn, foot traffic, or rock salt used to de-ice driveways or pavements in winter.

Some lawns suffer from turf diseases. The best antidote is to seed them with disease-resistant varieties such as Fylking blue or Pennstar bluegrass. Spring is not the best season for seeding; late summer is better. This is because it takes three weeks for the seeds to germinate and frequently seed planted in the spring has not had time to become established before it must fight the double enemies of early hot spells and rapid weed growth.

If a lawn must take a good deal of punishment from children and dogs running across it, probably it is wiser not to worry about a velvety appearance and to just keep it mowed to the proper height. Unless such big-rooted weeds as dandelions and dock have spread widely, the smaller-leafed and smaller-rooted weeds are not all that apparent.

Trees for shade and beauty

Important as lawn and shrubs are to a property, nothing in the yard enhances a house so much as well-cared-for trees. The shade of trees also can be an important factor in reducing the energy load on air conditioners in hot weather.

However, on property with many large trees, excessive shade may also cause dampness, mildew, and rot inside the house, and when a tree begins to show signs of decay, the time may have come to have it cut down. This is nearly always an anguishing decision. It takes so many years for a tree to reach maturity, to cut it down seems a sacrilege. Only after it has been removed do the homeowners acknowledge that they now have more light and air and a feeling of greater space.

When dead branches and other signs of decay are noted, it is advisable to call in a tree expert. Ask him about clearing out the deadwood, and whether or not the tree has been struck with disease, or if some other factor is the cause of the apparent illness. He may help you to make the decision as to whether the property will be improved (or the opposite) by removal of this tree.

Trees can be classed in four general categories: evergreens, deciduous shade trees, fruit, and flowering or ornamental trees.

Evergreens, which include various types of spruce, fir, pine, and hemlock, are of value primarily for their year-round beauty. They give some shade when they have reached great heights, but when we speak of shade trees, we mean those that grow very tall, shed their leaves in the fall, and bud again with the running of sap in the spring. This group includes tall oaks, elms, sycamore, chestnut, beech, walnut, and the huge sugar maple whose leaves turn bright yellow or red in the fall. All these live to a great age under proper growing conditions. In the winter when their branches are bare, they permit sunlight to warm the house; in summer, their shade helps to cool it.

Fruit trees are both decorative and useful. Each is a thing of beauty when it blossoms in the spring. Some begin to bear fruit in their second or third year but finish when ten or eleven years old. Others begin bearing when more mature but continue to bear for twenty-five years or longer. Spraying is recommended to obtain worm-free fruit, though unless the homeowner does the spraying, the cost of having it done can amount to far more than the cost of buying the fruit from a store or stand. A growing number of ecology-minded persons believe that if trees are fed organically, spraying is not necessary.

Ornamental trees are of value strictly for their beauty, which should be enough. If you long to have a pink dogwood, or a cluster of white birch, or shaggy weeping willow on your property, and are not sure which is the most effective place to plant the tree or trees, ask at your local nursery whether they furnish the services of a landscape designer. Some of these designers will go to your home to help you work out a landscaping plan; others suggest you bring a blueprint or sketch of your yard area to them for advice.

Proper preparation of the ground is extremely important, and for large trees, it is advisable to have someone from the nursery do the planting. Then if the tree dies in its first year, the firm should replace it. But if you have done the planting, they may blame its demise on improper planting. (The same applies to shrubs.)

Decorative trees should be chosen for a balance of color and shape in the yard, and this worked out according to shrubs already planted or to be planted.

When it is necessary to remove a large tree, or several smaller ones, it may cost no more to purchase a chain saw than to rent one. Even if you have the tree cut down by professionals (which is always advisable for tall trees), you can save money by doing the cutting up yourself. If you have a fireplace, the wood will provide fuel for several winters.

Circles cut from the main trunk can be used for numerous decorative purposes: for steps, or a patio, and to make furniture (tops for tables and stools, as examples). Some of the branches can be used to make rustic furniture, a tree house, or even a miniature log cabin.

When using a chain saw, make sure that it is kept well-lubricated and sharpened. A saw with sharp-edged teeth speeds up the cutting.

Outdoor lighting

Increased electric rates are causing many a homeowner to dim the switches on outdoor lighting and replace high-wattage spotlights with fluorescents. But well-planned outdoor lighting is important both for safety and to enhance the appearance of your property after dark.

You need lights around the entrance for those approaching the front door, and if the approach is over steps, light fixtures should be placed so as to throw light directly on the steps and walk.

An inexpensive way to illuminate the walk is to place low-wattage Christmas bulbs inside old plastic bleach bottles, then lay these with their connecting wires in rows on each side of the walk. They will be more attractive if all are of one color, such as blue or green, and concealed under border plants or shrubs.

To light the driveway and garage entrance, lamps should be mounted at least twelve feet from the ground on poles or attached to the fascia above the garage door. Instead of glaring spotlights, fluorescent lights enclosed in boxes that diffuse light downward are more attractive and more effective and there is no danger of blinding those turning into the drive. Powerful PAR (for parabolic) quartzline lamps are made especially for outdoor use. These come in white, blue, green, yellow or red.

Lights in the garden area are important for safety whether or not there is a pool or gazebo used for evening diversion. Should any suspicious noise be heard in the yard, being able to floodlight the lawn and garden areas quickly will be reassuring if only to reveal that the noise was caused by a neighbor's dog or an invading raccoon.

The illumination will add considerably more glamour to your yard if fixtures are placed so as to accent its more attractive features. Some lights should be directed downward from trees, others should beam upward from behind clusters of shrubs or low walls or hedges. To emphasize three-dimensional effects and thus create an illusion of greater space, light should come from two or more directions.

When a room with wide glass doors overlooks the garden area, location of the lamps should be decided upon from inside the house, testing different spots to see how well each serves to illuminate the landscape most effectively as seen through that door frame, turning the garden into a theatrical setting.

Since incandescent lights consume so much more current, frames for fluorescent lights can be made inexpensively from simple box-like shapes, or from large tin cans punctured on the sides to form a snowflake pattern. Where you want light to be diffused only downward, the can should be cut lengthwise and shaped into a crescent, then positioned above the fluorescent tube.

Luminous paint may be used in place of electric lighting in some places. House numbers, for example, can be touched up with luminous paint; the risers on steps can be so painted; and so can the stepping stones of walkways that cross an otherwise poorly lighted area.

If electrical tools are used in the garden area, it would be helpful to have one or more properly grounded outlets, to plug in a hedge trimmer, power mower, chain saw, and so forth. These outlets would also be useful for poolside or lawn parties when extra lighting or an electrical small appliance for outdoor cooking is wanted, such as the rotisserie motor on a barbecue grill.

An underground cable is the safest method for carrying wiring into the garden area. The cable should be buried more than an inch beneath the soil but need not lie below the frost line. If underground, it is less likely to be damaged by storms, high winds, or falling trees. However, its path should be clearly marked to avoid someone cutting it inadvertently with the mower or some other heavy garden tool. For any overhead wires, a weatherproof aluminum cable should be used.

12

Improving
Apartment
Living

Home is an apartment to many thousands of Americans and, increasingly, apartment dwellers are owners rather than tenants as many more rental units are transformed into condominiums each year.

Those who continue to pay rent to a landlord can no longer expect the services that tenants received in a more competitive era. If you want improvements in a rented apartment, you might as well do it yourself.

In addition, a growing number of families have second-home or vacation condominiums which they use only a few weeks of the year, renting them out either on their own or through the condominium management the rest of the time.

Many of the home improvements discussed in previous chapters can be applied to apartments, though for the most part, even when one is the owner of an apartment, it is wise to make improvements that can be easily removed. For rental tenants, and sometimes for condominium owners as well, it is often forbidden to make structural changes or to change the color of the paint without special permission.

Creating more storage space

In the confined space of an apartment, inadequate storage room usually is a major complaint. Wall units, which can be put together in any combination you like, and in any or all rooms, offer the easiest answer to the storage problem.

In a living room wall unit there can be compartments for television set, stereo, bar, a dish and glassware closet, and a let-down desk. A shelf-and-drawer unit in the dinette can hold both dishes and linens. A bedroom unit can supply both drawer and shelf space in the center, with six-foot enclosed units at each end for hanging clothes. And in a one-room efficiency, several such units can be used, one for each "living" area (dining, sleeping, entertainment). Such units can be made to look built in, yet be easy to disassemble to take elsewhere when desired.

For a ready-made "portable closet," hunt around in second-hand furniture stores and antique shops for an old-fashioned wardrobe or armoire. These range from Gay Nineties styles in golden oak to box-like horrors in cheap veneers. But even the latter can be made surprisingly attractive with paint and imagination. First apply a base or primer coat, or cover it with enamel for the "wet look," then add a border. This could be a pasted-on wallpaper molding strip, stencils, or freehand floral decorations. Inside the panels marked off by these borders, make other stylized floral patterns, or stencils, or add decals, or a decoupage.

A curlicued golden oak wardrobe, or any that has an interesting paneled exterior, might be antiqued, carefully following the directions that come with the kit. You will of course first remove the hardware, and rather than replacing the old hardware when the antiquing is finished, attaching new hardware will serve to make the wardrobe even more attractive.

Before adding any kind of paint, however, it is wise first to clean the surface completely. If the wardrobe is made of solid wood or a very good veneer, consider stripping it. You may have picked up a "find," a piece old enough to be back in fashion. In many cases, old furniture brings a higher price

Shelves, cupboards, drawers, and desk hung on tension poles form a wall unit which can be easily disassembled when moving from an apartment.

than new pieces these days, because it is more sturdily built and its age is an attraction.

Portable storage cabinets on casters offer another possibility. For example, if you need additional cabinet space in the kitchen but there is no room for another built-in cabinet, make (or purchase, unpainted) such a cabinet, put it on casters, and keep it in the dinette or even in a corner of the living room, then wheel it into the kitchen when you need it there. It can be painted, antiqued, or covered with scrubbable adhesive-backed vinyl in simulated wood grain, or you can enamel the sides and install a laminate counter top in a marbleized pattern. If finished in a color scheme that complements dinette or living room rather than kitchen, its presence in another room will not seem inappropriate at all.

A bar-cart, holding glassware as well as ingredients for drinks, could also be finished in this way, rolled to the kitchen to pick up ice and hors d'oeuvres and rolled back to the living room for serving.

If your apartment has a hall or foyer, see if there is a place for a storage unit here. Hanging shelves on the wall, or a narrow bookcase with sliding doors over the lower shelves may fit somewhere between doors. If there is no coat closet, a hanging coat rack with shelf above can hold your coats as well as those of guests.

You might have a cabinet rather than a table in the foyer. Buy a secondhand bathroom vanity, antique it, put a slab of real marble on the top (if there is a firm that sells marble along with other building supplies in your area, you may be able to have a piece cut to fit), or simply glue together two shelving boards cut to the right lengths and cover with a marbleized pattern in adhesive-backed paper.

If you have no foyer, the front door opening directly into the living room, you could create a mini-foyer with pole room dividers forming an L. If these are sturdy enough, say made of wrought iron or with heavy "glass" (translucent plastic) panels, you might even install a hanging coat rack at the top of one panel.

Improving a kitchenette
In a new building, the apartment kitchenette may be a dream of luxury, but even then you probably will want to add

your personal touches. And the older the building, the more inadequate and cramped the kitchenette is likely to be.

First the question of storage. No matter how small the room, if you search for unoccupied space on the walls you are bound to find a place that could hold additional shelves.

Ronald, a young man sharing a two-bedroom apartment with his brother, cleverly transformed their tiny kitchenette. Noting that there was space on the side of the kitchenette's narrow broom closet, he put up six-inch-wide shelves from the baseboard upward, as a place for holding crystal stemware and tumblers. To make the new shelves look like a permanent fixture he covered the broom closet and the shelves with a dry-strippable adhesive-backed vinyl paper resembling natural wood grain. He also applied the same strippable paper to all the cabinets in the kitchen, after removing the old hardware, and installed new brass knobs in place of the old door and drawer pulls.

A different pattern of strippable paper, resembling grass cloth in dull gold, with a scrubbable, grease-resistant finish, was used to cover the walls. He then put hooks into studs in the walls to hold skillets and pots and their fitted covers, thus freeing cabinet shelf space for other uses. A hanging shelf on another wall space is covered with the same simulated wood-grain vinyl paper as used on the cabinets, and holds canisters and pitchers, while cup hooks beneath the lower two shelves hold cups.

Ronald tried "kitchen carpeting" on the floor, and it looked handsome, but when one day a jar of mayonnaise broke on the floor, he found that the carpeting was not as easy to clean as the advertisements claim. In disgust, he took up the carpeting and replaced it with press-on vinyl tiles. Before making this change, his total kitchen remodeling costs ran to less than $30, a sum that also included a new light fixture in the ceiling. Even replacing the carpeting with vinyl squares cost only $12.

Since the paper used was all strippable, the landlord was satisfied that Ronald had not made any permanent change, yet he had managed to transform an old, unimaginative, oft-painted apartment kitchenette into a charming room. Also, because of its monotone color scheme, the kitchenette seems wider than before.

Useful items

The rubberized vinyl-coated storage units available in hardware stores and housewares departments are ideal for apartment kitchens because they can be so easily removed. Among especially useful items is the shelf unit that can be placed on the back of the door hiding the under-sink drain. This unit can hold soap, detergent, cleaning pads, and so on. Other helpers include round turntables for upper shelves, pullout bins for base cabinets, drawer dividers, and spice shelves that can be used alone or in combination. Items sold as "plate racks" are equally useful for holding pot lids.

Another place to add storage is the wall space between the upper cabinets and the counter. Tilt shelves with sliding doors, made especially for this position, can be purchased ready to install with a screwdriver. These will hold spices, condiments, and small jars.

It may be possible even in a narrow kitchenette to fit in a "bookcase" thirty inches high, as suggested in chapter 8, to hold dishes and small appliances.

Cooking problems

The existing range in an old apartment kitchenette is often in dilapidated condition and even when in reasonably good working order, having to get down on the floor to broil a steak can be exasperating, especially so in cramped quarters.

If the range is an antiquated model, the oven may be way off its thermostatic control, or its insulation may be so poor that the kitchen gets as hot as the oven when it is turned on. But today few landlords are willing to replace any equipment that works at all.

The best way to solve the problem could be to purchase new supplementary small appliances. For broiling, there are a number of different counter-top appliances to choose from, all of which can be plugged into a regular outlet. The simplest is an electric frypan with a broiler attachment. Then there are broiler ovens which may or may not have rotisserie attachments, and some of these ovens are "continuous cleaning." A very effective broiler-rotisserie is the so-called open hearth type; this has no cover, but it does not smoke because the grease drops below the heating unit into a drip pan—and it is primarily burning fat that causes smoke in the kitchen.

As for counter-top ovens, for singles or working couples, a small toaster-oven may be adequate most of the time, especially for those who rely heavily on frozen food entrees. At the other extreme in price are the microwave ovens. Their high speed and cool exterior are a boon for small kitchenettes, especially those of working couples.

The "turbo" type of counter-top oven (sometimes called "jet fan") bakes, roasts, and broils more quickly than conventional ovens, at lower temperatures, and continuously cleans itself. The principle is a strong flow of heat on all sides, so that meat broils or roasts as if on a rotisserie spit. The thermostatic control can be set at temperatures as much as seventy-five degrees lower than standard recipes call for, and the "turbo" oven will bake, roast, or broil in much less time than is needed by a regular oven.

All the small appliances mentioned can be taken with you if you move. They can be plugged into any regular outlet, and will be just as useful in a house with a full-sized kitchen as in your apartment.

If the apartment does not have a dishwasher, you might buy a portable one—that is, if you have space for one and the landlord will grant permission. Or you may feel that a compact washer-dryer combination would be much more important than a dishwasher. Compact washer-dryers are much smaller than the fully automatic type and are ideal for apartment use. Since they can be plugged into any regular fifteen-ampere outlet and use a moderate amount of water (little more than for a tub bath), special permission is not always required for their use. Naturally, however, these appliances should not be in use on the same line used for such other high-energy appliances as a room airconditioner or a broiler oven.

Redoing an apartment bathroom

Most apartment bathrooms are unimaginative in design, occupying as little space as will hold essential equipment. In older buildings, the white ceramic tile on walls and floors has stood the test of time amazingly well and, if in good condition, can form a useful backdrop for attractive additions.

Bath carpeting is one of the easiest of these additions. The loose carpeting, as observed previously, looks plushy and soft but, except for the fact that it can be removed to be machine washed, it is not as satisfactory in other respects as the adhesive-backed carpet tiles for bathroom use.

If the paint above the ceramic tile level is peeling (a quite common fault in apartment baths), strippable vinyl-coated paper or vinyl-backed fabric covering can cover up the damage to ceiling and walls more effectively than any other treatment. The old paint must be removed with a scraper and any rough edges sanded down. For best results, after this preparation, a sealer-primer should be applied to the surface before the new wallcovering goes up, to seal out the accumulated moisture in the plaster.

However, for a rental unit where you may not remain for more than another year, you may decide to take a chance on doing it the easier way, simply removing the flaking paint with a paint scraper, then putting up prepasted wallcovering without the protection of a sealer.

This is all the more reason to make sure that the bathroom is kept well-ventilated to prevent wallcovering from coming loose because of moisture. Remember to open windows, or turn on the exhaust fan, whenever the mirror in the room becomes clouded.

If the grouting has come loose around the edges of the bathtub, and the landlord drags his heels about repairing it, caulking the edges is not difficult or costly (see chapter 8). Or you may decide to invest in ceramic molding strips to install around the edges, to match or contrast with the color of your new carpeting and wallpaper.

If this is your own condominium, but in an older converted building, you may decide that investment in a new laminate bath cove over the existing tile is worthwhile for a fresh, new look. You may also want to improve the lighting.

Storage in an apartment bathroom is rarely adequate, but a visit to a well-stocked bath shop should change all that. As in the kitchen, examine every free bit of wall space to see if it might not serve for shelves, narrow cabinets, or a pole cabinet.

A telephone in the bathroom can be an especial convenience for anyone living alone or for a woman whose husband is away frequently. Make sure that the telephone has an extra-long cord so that you can enjoy soaking in the tub while chatting.

Climate controls

In newer apartment buildings, the costs of central heat and central airconditioning are included in the rent, so most tenants do not consider these items their concern. But indirectly they should be concerned, because excess energy consumption causes brownouts and rising utility rates provide landlords or condominium managers with a justification for raising maintenance charges or rents, and also for revising thermostats (downward in winter, upward in summer).

In the interests of everyone, those who live in apartments should be conscious of conserving energy and water. During the winter, if thermostats are lowered throughout the building as a fuel conservation measure, those who find the lowered temperatures hard to bear might invest in portable humidifiers (some look like furniture and can double as end tables). A humidifier can make a sixty-eight-degree setting seem as comfortable as a seventy-two-degree setting. Also, dry heat, especially over hot-air ducts, is hard on the respiratory tract, skin, hair, complexion, and furniture.

If an apartment has airconditioning, either from a central source or a room unit, this extracts moisture from the air while lowering indoor temperatures and so a dehumidifier would not be necessary. But in a very humid climate, in an apartment which has no airconditioner, a dehumidifier could be of great benefit, especially if used in combination with one or two fans.

Two fans, each with reversible controls, can be more than twice as effective as a single reversible fan in cooling an apartment. One fan is turned to "in," bringing air from the cooler side of the building, while the other is turned to "out," pulling the cooler air toward it while also removing hot air. If the temperature is so high out of doors that there is no "cooler" side of the building, both fans turned to exhaust help to pull out hot air with double force.

It is best in the hottest weather not to open windows more than four inches until after sundown. During the day, especially when the occupants are away, all windows should be closed and heavily shaded.

Soundproofing

Soundproofing is often a crucial problem in an apartment,

as it is in so many town houses. Most of the factors that help to insulate against heat and cold also help to deaden or absorb sound. Perhaps the easiest is to add carpeting. Room-size rugs may fill most of the floor space, and if you watch for special sales, these often are available at very low prices. If laid over a styrofoam base, rugs are even more effective in absorbing sound.

Sometimes two smaller shag rugs can be sewn together to make a single big rug. The shag pile hides the seams. Or you may find it more satisfactory to put down shag carpet tiles (each twelve inches square) with foam backing—especially in a smaller room such as a dinette or small bedroom.

If you own the apartment, and its original wall-to-wall carpeting needs replacing, you may want to install foam-backed parquet oak tiles over the subflooring instead of new carpeting, to create the most elegant of floors. Over the parquet, place colorful area rugs.

Walls can also serve as sound absorbers, if paneled, and paneling will also help to keep the apartment cool in summer. Panels can be screwed to studs in the walls, or to furring strips attached to the studs. The latter method is better for easier removal later.

Cork tiles provide excellent soundproofing and insulation. The chocolate brown color of compressed cork is best confined to one wall, probably the wall adjoining a particularly noisy neighbor, leaving the other three walls in a lighter finish. Use the cork wall for hanging pictures, decoupage plaques, or a large mirror. Hangings on the wall also help to absorb sound.

Fabric wallcovering provides more sound absorption than paper, though not as much as paneling or cork. The strippable vinyl-coated fabrics and papers that can be easily peeled off later may be used even when there is a rule forbidding a change in paint color on the walls.

Draperies at the windows also help to soundproof, especially those backed with acrylic foam. Fabric so lined is now available in all sorts of textures and patterns, from rough weave with a hand-loomed look, to woven stripes, pebbled "silk," satin, or damask, and are thus suitable for almost any decor. Cafe curtains as well as floor-to-ceiling draperies come so lined.

The acrylic foam lining is an excellent insulator when used

over the windows on winter nights and during the day in summer.

To keep out street noises, any window treatment that is recommended for insulation will also be of some help in noise abatement, including the addition of storm windows.

Another area that can be treated with soundproofing material is the ceiling, by adding acoustical tiles. These, too, have insulating properties, which could make a difference in a top-floor apartment. Some can be applied direct to the existing ceiling, but most are attached to grids or furring strips, and therefore would require special permission from the landlord.

"Enlarging" apartment rooms

The same general rules apply in creating an illusion of space in apartment rooms as were previously discussed with regard to houses. The lighter in color and simpler in design the materials used on walls and floors, the more spacious the room seems to be. Mirrors can do wonders in expanding apartment living rooms. The choice of furniture and its placement also drastically changes the room's apparent size.

The best test of this is to visit several apartments in the same building, each with the same room layout. The living room in one may seem smaller than that in the apartment immediately below or above, even though the room dimensions are exactly the same.

In buying furniture for an apartment with small rooms, select pieces that do not take up a great deal of space. For example, instead of an upholstered armchair, you might select one or two rattan tub chairs that are lightweight and inexpensive and can be easily moved from one part of the room to another. These cost about $20 each. Wicker chairs, often found in secondhand furniture stores, can be lacquered and fitted with colorful pillows. Even occasional chairs with upholstered seats and backs take up much less room than the big overstuffed armchairs.

Double-duty furniture also helps conserve space: a coffee table with a storage compartment, a low cabinet used as an end table, a hassock that opens out into a bed. In a narrow room, a daybed covered with many pillows can look luxurious, while occupying much less space than an upholstered sofa.

Another way to create the illusion of more space in an

apartment living room is to add a large panel on which you have mounted a distant scene. This could be a blowup of a photograph, or a scenic wallpaper, or a montage of exotic scenes, or your own freehand mural. Some art studios carry enormous posters which can be so mounted.

Also take a look at the way your furniture is arranged in the living room. Can it be rearranged so as to provide more open space in the center of the room, or to allow more light through the windows, or a better view of the outdoors?

Lighting, too, can make a big difference. Since permanent fixtures will have been installed by the landlord, you will have to depend on portable lamps to distribute light effectively and pleasantly. Three light fixtures, each against a different wall, will diffuse the light and provide a more relaxing atmosphere than one lamp with a strong bulb. For example, you may have one lamp fitted with a 60- or 75-watt bulb for reading, two others with 40-watt bulbs, instead of one big lamp with a 100-150-watt bulb.

Pinup lamps are quite useful in an apartment, especially above beds or in the dinette area. "Swag" lamps with long chains suspended from hooks in the ceiling can often be used effectively to brighten a dark corner.

For a party, spotlights can be used to throw indirect light on walls. If these are hidden behind plants in tubs or large ceramic pots, they will form lacy shadow patterns over the wall, making the setting quite exotic, and the room will seem far larger. Or build a cove just above the baseboard on one wall to throw indirect light upward on that wall.

A lighted fish tank or terrarium also can supply a pleasantly soft area of light to help expand the room's size.

Even though the permanent light fixtures are already in place, you may want to replace one or two of them with fixtures of your own choice. To make the room seem larger, choose fixtures which direct light against the ceiling in a wide arc.

One difficulty frequently encountered in apartments is a shortage of wall outlets. Having several extension cords plugged into one outlet by means of double or triple sockets can be hazardous, and hiring an electrician to install new outlets is costly. When only one extension cord is involved, it can be fastened to the baseboard with insulated staples (but not plain metal staples). However, a better solution is to buy what are called "plug-in strips," available at any electrical supply store and UL approved. These can be attached to wall outlets, the lines run along the baseboard and the extension outlets screwed to the floor boards. Fixtures can be plugged into these as into any wall outlet.

Room dividers

Efficiency apartments are usually efficient only in the way they limit space and necessitate using a single room to serve several purposes.

The worst type of efficiency is one in which the kitchenette has been stuck on one wall of the living room, without even the pretense of separation. One good way to deal with this problem is to put up pole room dividers, extending out into the room for two feet. (These are the same type as already suggested for creating a mini-foyer.)

But for the most part, the best type of apartment room divider is a movable screen, so that the room can easily be divided or opened up as necessary.

Screens can be useful for hiding a view across an ugly courtyard, for cutting off the dining area of the living room while the table is being readied, or for providing some privacy for an overnight guest who has slept on the living room sofa.

The best apartment screens are those of translucent material or see-through patterns, such as shutter doors or wrought iron. Bamboo slates (or vinyl in imitation of bamboo), the same material used for roll-up shades, can be effectively mounted to shoji-type screen frames on casters, to be moved from one part of the room to another as needed. These can also double for window shades. Insulation shading, the material mentioned for window treatment in chapter 2, can be fitted onto homemade folding or shoji screens, to diffuse the light softly but not exclude it.

Besides louvered shutter doors hinged together to make screens, a type of shutter which can be used effectively has panes or panels of opaque "stained glass." Still another type of amusing room divider could be made by using full-length mirrors mounted on adjustable poles. The mirrors swivel in any direction, and three of them could be combined in a unit, each slanted at the same angle. These would create an illusion of more space and also partially screen one area of the room.

Imaginative screens can be made with wallpaper, shiny aluminum patterned paper, patterned mirror tiles, decoupage designs, or freehand murals. Or make a nonobjective mural by dropping splashes of acrylic paint in four or five vivid colors on a plain white vinyl panel, and between the big splotches of color, create delicate spatterings by dipping just the tips of the bristles in paint, then shaking the brush over the surface. For a modern decor, this can be quite striking.

Double-duty furniture

As already noted, any article of furniture that serves more than one purpose is a space saver. The most obvious are daybeds or sofa beds. Even in a one-bedroom apartment, extra sleeping space is often needed for overnight guests. There are, of course, chairs that can be transformed into a bed, and some studio couches now open into one queen-size bed instead of two smaller ones.

If there is no dining table, and most of the time all you need is a coffee table, you might make a table that can be easily adjusted to serve both purposes. As a coffee table, it has four short legs which, on occasion, can be folded under the top. It has four other longer legs which can be pulled down, to transform it into a dining table. You can transform any dining table into a permanent coffee table by removing its legs and replacing them with shorter legs, which can be purchased at building supply houses in one of several styles, ready to screw in place. Or, conversely, turn a long coffee table into a dining table by changing the legs.

For an inexpensive dinette table, either buy a secondhand round table, or have a round top cut from framing plywood and attach legs to it. Over this, place one of the fashionable round cloths that reach almost to the floor. The table top is not going to show, so its appearance will not matter.

One advantage of the permanent dining table is that it can serve so many other purposes: as a place to study, cut out dress patterns, write letters, make out accounts, create your own Christmas cards, paste up a photo album, or make sketches of your next home-improvement project.

For anyone who likes to sew, a sewing machine table may

be an irresistible investment. Let it double as an end or lamp table and it has more than an occasional function.

Many people, whether or not they have a dinette or dining table, want a place to eat in the kitchen. One solution, even when the kitchen is tiny, is to add a hinged drop leaf that can be folded against the wall when not in use, and pulled up to horizontal position for use as either eating or work space.

For the younger generation, sitting on the floor is more fun than on chairs, and for them, plenty of big pillows solves the chair problem. The pillows can be stacked high when not in use. A little more comfortable for their elders are low stools. These can be adapted from modular cubes, to be stacked one inside another when not in use.

Coffee and end tables with glass tops are ideal for an apartment, easy to make, and they add to that airy feeling. A simple frame of four straight legs and four connecting pieces, enameled in a bright color, can be topped with heavy glass cut to size. Another method is to make the legs and frame of plastic pipe (rigid vinyl), which can be cut with common tools to any size desired, bent into curves at the corners, easily glued together, then enameled in color.

Gardens for apartment dwellers

Lucky are those who have a bit of balcony or patio from which to escape the four walls of an apartment. Even a small balcony can have its own "garden" of potted plants, an umbrella for shade against the sun (and to provide some degree of privacy for sunbathing), and even a spot for a barbecue grill.

Many different plants can be grown successfully in pots, including some vegetables. Beautiful tomato plants on stakes have provided a bounteous harvest for some apartment gardeners; lettuce, radishes, and herbs can be grown in flower boxes. If there is not enough room on the floor of the balcony or patio, some pots can be hung from the ceiling.

Sunlight is needed, of course. Even shade-loving plants need some sun occasionally. And on a balcony that seems to be flooded with sunlight, plants receive less full sun than those in an outdoor garden. On the shaded side of the building, only shade-loving plants will thrive, but there are many of these. Consult a gardening book on the subject.

Window boxes can sometimes be hung outside the windows. In this location, if an adjoining building is not too close, the plants will receive much more sun than on a balcony. The window box must be placed so that there is easy access to it, for planting, weeding, watering, and harvesting. There are also large terrariums made to fit into windows: the window itself is removed and replaced with this big garden "tank."

Still easier is to have a planter on wheels: it can be rolled from window to window, as the sunlight moves.

So popular has apartment gardening become, some garden supply houses even maintain a special department for such customers, selling seeds, plants, equipment, and special books on the subject. Indoor plants can do much to make an apartment more of a home.

13

Investing in a Vacation Home

A trend that is growing rapidly and promises to accelerate in the future is the acquisition of "second homes" for vacation living. But there are almost as many kinds of vacation homes as there are kinds of people.

Some prefer to purchase resort condominiums with recreational facilities. Frequently these are rented or exchanged (the management acts as a broker) during those weeks of the year when the owners do not use the quarters. Others have purchased lots in a leisure-time development where roads, recreational facilities, and sometimes water lines and electricity have been installed by the promoters. And some like to be far away from any commercially-operated resort facilities and so look for old farmhouses or abandoned log cabins.

"Shells" of cabins or chalets, offered for sale by a number of manufacturers, consist of the exterior only; inside is a big unfinished room. Other manufacturers offer package kits of all the materials needed to put up a simple cottage in the

How Land Values Have Increased

The table shows increases in value for various types of property on Puget Sound. Similar increases have taken place throughout the United States in desert, high mountain, wooded back country, and waterfront property.

	1960	1964	1969	1976
Minimum quality salt-water frontage, per foot	$ 60	$ 74	$ 100	$ 125
Maximum quality salt-water frontage, per foot	239	296	400	600
1/3-acre lot, salt-water access	1,761	2,185	2,950	5,000 -10,000
Lake frontage, per foot	60-119	74-148	100-200	100-600
1/3-acre lot, access to community beach on lake	1,463	1,815	2,450	5,000 and up
Riverfront of fine quality, per foot	30	37	50	175-250
1/3-acre lot, river access	1,164	1,444	1,950	5,500 and up

Sources: American Plywood Association, American Federal Savings and Loan Association

woods or near the beach, including precut lumber, walls, and roofing.

Some vacation homes are luxurious, containing all the amenities found in an expensive urban or suburban home. Others have no conveniences at all and the owners choose to rough it in sleeping bags and use portable drinking water and kerosene lanterns while they gradually fix up the place.

Paying for a second home

If you are still in the process of looking for a vacation home and wonder which type you should purchase, a major consideration must be how much you can afford to invest in the initial payment and the upkeep. In this period of abnormally high mortgage rates, it is wise to put as much cash in the investment as possible.

Many families when they consider buying vacation property persuade themselves that they will be able to rent it out when they are not using it and that this income will help the property to pay for itself. But finding reliable tenants usually proves to be more difficult than anticipated and one bad experience will make most families decide that what little income they receive from rental is not worth the cost. The owners are often too far away to check on the tenants, and if the matter is handled by a rental agent, he or she may be too busy to keep tabs on the tenants and their care of the property.

Higher rents can be realized if the property is located in a prime tourist area—good skiing and waterfront accommodations are always in demand, but then the purchase price will be higher, too. A house or cabin in an out-of-the-way place is harder to rent because there are fewer people who want to spend their vacation in a backwoods location.

If you hope to rent the property in cold weather, heat must be supplied, and either you must charge a large enough rental to cover this added cost or arrange for the tenants to pay for what they use. Even when they agree to do this, it is sometimes hard to collect for fuel and utility bills after the tenants have vacated.

For a vacation property, the landlord must furnish everything, bedding, bath and table linens, dishes, cooking utensils. This, too, must be weighed in making the decision as to whether to rent or not.

There is a tax advantage if your vacation home is rented out to others for a considerable portion of the year, but if you use it for one month and receive rent for only two months, the IRS ruling considers such rental under the same classification as if used by "friends and relatives," not a business income. For more about this, see the discussion of tax advantages for homeowners in the next chapter or IRS publication 530.

The time-sharing concept

The most satisfactory method of renting is when the management of a resort development takes responsibility for finding tenants, collecting rent, and looking after your property when you are not there. If this agreement is spelled out in the initial contract, you receive some tax advantage as a landlord with a minimum of headaches.

Carrying this idea still farther is the new time-sharing arrangement in which a condominium, cabin hideaway, or beach house in a resort development is purchased for only a specific period each year. The rest of the year the property belongs to others who also are part-time owners. All of you contribute to maintenance and property taxes; all of you receive prorated tax advantages.

Further, some of these resort properties are part of a huge conglomerate which maintains a clearinghouse of owners in various resort areas who are interested in exchanging or swapping homes. This service makes it possible for the part-time owner of a Florida condominium, for example, to swap it for three weeks with someone who has a mountain chalet in Colorado or a beach house in Hawaii.

The tax advantage of ownership is much smaller in the time-sharing arrangement, but the purchase price may be no more than that for a camping trailer. Also, part-time owner-ship opens the way to carefree vacations with prime recrea-tional facilities at the doorstep. For many families, this is the only way that they can hope to realize such a dream.

It is an intriguing arrangement for those who enjoy typical resort facilities, and an expansion of such time-sharing and exchange plans is anticipated for the future. But part-time ownership makes it impossible to alter or decorate the prop-erty in an individual fashion. It is more like hotel living, and also means becoming part of a huge leisure-time community, which is not to everyone's taste.

Do-it-yourself vacation homes

Those who want a vacation home that can be more truly their own are likely to be attracted by advertisements offer-ing "shells" that can be purchased for as little as $4,600, or easy-to-construct cabins which may be delivered by rail or helicopter in a giant kit with complete instructions for assem-bling.

If payment for your vacation home can be managed with-out having to rent it, you can fix it up as you please and when you leave, simply lock up, leaving clothing, sports gear, and other personal possessions ready for use when you return.

But there are catches in all these seemingly easy solutions. It is far wiser to shop around for an existing cottage or cabin, even for one that needs a great deal of renovation to make it livable. At least you know from the start what you are get-ting, and it is easier to estimate the overall cost.

The shells that cost under $5,000, not including land, are in reality nothing more than nice-looking wooden tents. Inside

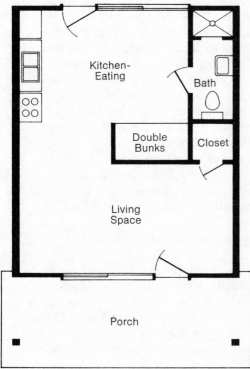

Kitchen-Eating

Bath

Double Bunks

Closet

Living Space

Porch

The suggested floor plan for this rigid frame cabin can be varied because there are no load-bearing walls. The basic plan provides 480 square feet of interior space plus a 176-square-foot porch. Inside or outside living space can be increased simply by adding more frames. The cost of installing utilities is a factor to be considered when purchasing a cabin of this type.

there is nothing; no bathroom or kitchen facilities, no water, septic, or electrical systems, no walls, not even finished flooring. You must bring in your own drinking water and use kerosene lanterns for light, buy a chemical toilet (or dig a pit for an outhouse), rough it just as much as if on a camping trip. Sooner or later most people want more than this.

The same problems must be faced by those who buy package cabins to be put up with a rigid metal frame, precut lumber for floors, walls, beams, and joists, and precut and finished panels for both exterior siding and interior walls. These kits, too, cost about $5,000 for the simpler styles. But when these cabins are erected, though they have floors and walls, they still lack plumbing, electricity, and water. Electricity is particularly important; without it you cannot have your own water, because the pump for the well operates by electricity.

There are some leisure-time development tracts where utility lines have already been laid and roads built. It is an advantage to buy a lot where you can hook into nearby electric lines, get a phone installed in a reasonable time, and know there are people nearby to turn to in an emergency. There may even be a source of cold running water, as at campsites.

But if you must install your own well and septic system, be prepared for considerable expense. No one is ever sure in advance how far down it will be necessary to dig before striking water, and each foot downward raises the cost. A New Yorker, after purchasing a seaside lot in Maine for a vacation home, instructed a man in the nearby village to dig a well on his property. He telephoned from his office two weeks later to find out how things were going—and learned that the man had already run up a $7,000 bill, but had not yet reached water.

"We think we may hit it soon, though," the man said reassuringly.

To the purchaser of a lot in a development, it might seem that the promoters would already have obtained necessary clearance for installing private wells and septic fields in each lot for sale, but this is not always so. Each lot must measure up to local codes and pass a soil test for absorbency. If the terrain is rocky or hilly, more distance will be required between the septic fields and private well on one lot than another. The buyer might learn, after purchasing a lot with a magnificent view, that he cannot build on it. While a chemical toilet can be used, and garbage and trash transported to a public dump, if local authorities approve such arrangements, many vacationers doing this could result in an unsightly, odoriferous, and unhealthy environment.

Check these points

In buying any country property, there are eight matters to check into:

1. What utilities and services are nearby and available? Check on water, electricity, sewerage, telephone service, and heating oil or bottled gas delivery.

2. What are the zoning and building codes or restrictions? Can you take possession of your "second home" before electric lines, pump, and septic fields have been installed? These facilities will cost a minimum of $4,000.

3. Is title to the land free and clear?

4. What about access to the property? Are there good roads leading to it? Will you have to cross someone else's land to reach yours? If so, this involves getting a right-of-way agreement, which in turn means lawyers' fees and court costs.

5. How near are shopping facilities, medical help, and fire protection? Are there neighbors within easy reach to contact in an emergency?

6. How close and available are recreation facilities, such as beaches, ski slopes, golf course, and mountain trails (or whatever your favorite leisure-time activities happen to be)? Are these free to the public or are there restrictions on their use?

7. What are the facilities for garbage and trash disposal? If you have to take care of this yourself, how will you handle it?

8. How much time will it take to reach this place and how much will transportation cost? The farther away from your regular residence, the more costly it will be to make use of your vacation home, no matter what form of transportation you plan to use.

And a final question—in some ways the most important consideration of all: how much of your vacation time are you willing to devote to what may turn out to be back-breaking work?

It would be wise to vacation in one or more places where you think you would like to buy property. Talk with other people who live there year-round and other vacationers. Find out what advantages and disadvantages each place offers. If you are interested in any land development offer, check with the local banks, the Better Business Bureau, and any others who are likely to know the reputation of the promoters of the development. Full-page advertisements in quite respectable publications, offering vacation lots or shell homes, upon inquiry have turned out to be promoting wildcat ventures. The promoters may build an impressive club lounge and inn, and may construct a golf course and a swimming pool, but the lots they have for sale are virtually worthless.

The step-by-step vacation home

There are many building plans available which show in blueprints how it is possible to start with a simple one-room cabin and add to it year by year until eventually you have a three- or four-bedroom house.

The same sort of plan can be applied to an existing cottage. If you have purchased a simple one- or two-room cottage and wish to expand it, you can work out a plan for turning a deck into an enclosed living room, and later add an upper story or construct a wing at the back or side. Instead of a regular staircase leading to a second story, a metal spiral staircase can be installed quickly. If the cottage already has plumbing, electricity, and other such essentials, you are off to a good start.

Most building plans for inexpensive vacation homes show them resting on posts or stilts. The practical reason for this is that it avoids having to excavate for the foundation. However, if the cottage is to be used in cold weather, the floor should be well insulated from beneath and a vapor barrier laid over the earth. Batt-type insulation can be attached directly to roof or ceiling beams. If a rustic look is desired, place ceiling tiles over the insulation in such a way that the edges of the beams will show. Insulated walls also will help to keep heating and cooling costs down and provide greater comfort. Few vacation home plans call for insulation because it is assumed they will be used only for short periods of time, but insulation is an improvement which will save fuel costs while

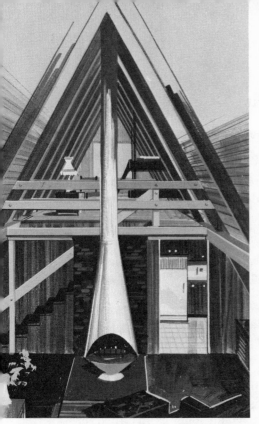

This A-frame cabin is designed to provide maximum living space on a minimum building budget. The living area is centered around a prefab fireplace, and the kitchen is nearby. A sleeping loft supplements the bedroom.

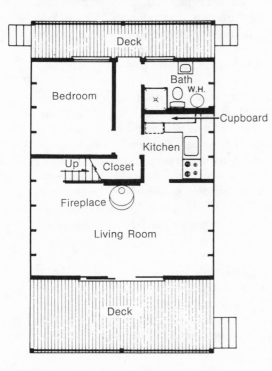

Deck

Bedroom

Bath

W.H.

Cupboard

Kitchen

Up

Closet

Fireplace

Living Room

Deck

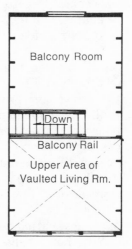

Balcony Room

Down

Balcony Rail

Upper Area of
Vaulted Living Rm.

you own the property and also will add greatly to its intrinsic value.

When the basic cottage already exists and you wish to add on to it, the metal frames, precut lumber parts, and exterior siding sold for "package" cabins can be used for erecting a wing.

Most vacation homes, if they have any heat source at all, rely on prefab fireplaces or Franklin stoves. These are ideal for the informality of vacation living and, as discussed in chapter 9, are inexpensive and can be installed in a few hours. But for a cottage to be used in winter months, if the prefab fireplace is showing signs of old age, it might be wise to replace it with a prebuilt fireplace with ducts to circulate heat through the entire cabin.

For owners of cabins or cottages in a year-round warm climate, the problem often is how to keep cool. Insulation, especially roof insulation, will help in this respect. But the manner in which the cottage is constructed can make a difference in comfort. Unless an air conditioner is installed, cross ventilation is imperative, with screened windows on all sides. A flat roof is less desirable than one with enough of a peak to allow hot air to rise, with a fan-ventilator to pull out the excess heat. Clerestory windows, if they can be opened by means of chains, will help to cool the interior and provide more natural light inside as well.

In the first-stage plan, many vacation homes have just one big living-sleeping area with a kitchen and bath at one side of the room. Folding vinyl doors or roll-down blinds are used to form rooms for sleeping. If the room is large enough, eventually permanent partitions may be erected to make regular bedrooms. Another way is to erect a second building especially for sleeping, the two buildings joined by a common deck with a peaked roof. This has its advantages when some members of the household wish to go to bed much earlier than others.

Making vacation homes more livable

Whether a vacation home is an apartment or a cottage, a basic problem in nearly every instance is lack of storage space. For the apartment, the same storage ideas suggested in chapter 12 can be applied to second-home condominiums.

A folding door allows the division of one large bedroom into two reasonably private spaces in a vacation cottage.

The vacation cottage is even less likely than a condominium to have adequate storage space, especially if it was originally erected as a one-room structure. Furniture for this second home can also fill the need for storage facilities. For this dual purpose, make built-in benches with lift-up seats which conceal storage compartments. Construct bunk beds with pull-out drawers beneath the bed. Make box-like chests which can double as end tables. A coffee table can have open shelves beneath to hold magazines and books. Simple unpainted chests of drawers can become room dividers by lining up two or three together and holding them in a unit with a backing all across of plywood or particleboard, which can be painted, papered, or decorated with decoupage. Above the chests, open shelves can hold dishes.

Wall units can be used wherever there is space for them. A bar opening off the kitchen can have open shelves beneath the counter for dishes, while narrow shelves on the adjoining wall hold glassware. For more closet space, a portable wardrobe may be the easiest solution.

One fault in many vacation homes is lack of privacy. For the first year or two it may seem like a lark for everyone to be bedded down in one big room, but eventually privacy becomes an urgent need. Room dividers are fine for separating a large room into various living areas, but when guests are still asleep and the host or hostess wishes to clean up around them, it can be awkward.

Walls put up with adjustable modules can make a big difference. Suppose, for example, the balcony area in an A-frame house is partially walled, for six to eight feet of the height of the area. Those still asleep up in the balcony can be left undisturbed while the rest of the house is tidied.

Folding vinyl doors are useful in making two bedrooms out of one where it is difficult to install a permanent wall, and they have the advantage of versatility. They can be pushed back when those using the temporary bedrooms are up and about, and the beds can be covered over to serve as couches.

The Japanese idea of shoji screens which can be rolled wherever they are needed is another excellent way to divide large rooms into two or three smaller ones on occasion. The screens can be made of four-by-eight-foot panels mounted on casters.

For a cottage in a southern climate, vinyl flooring is the most suitable and easiest to keep clean, especially if bathers are going to be walking in and out. For a colder climate, washable shag carpets add warmth to the floors. All fabrics as well as wall and floor finishes should, of course, be chosen for ease of maintenance. Indoor-outdoor carpeting may help to give a living room a feeling of comfort, especially when everything else is stark and functional.

Shades, draperies, or blinds at the window can serve a dual purpose: keeping out sunlight on hot days and protecting the room from drafts on cold nights. These need not be expensive. Vinyl roll-up blinds are appropriate and can be fitted over windows of almost any size. Draw draperies with acrylic lining on traverse rods are easier to manipulate and can add elegance to a country cabin, if that is what you want. Another reason to cover large window expanses at night is the feeling of protection it gives when a crackling of the underbrush might be caused by either strange animals or humans and you are not sure which.

Not only should the interior furnishings be as carefree as possible, but the landscaping also should require little attention. Try to avoid a lawn that must be cut. Shrubs around the deck add a certain neatness. Tall weeds can be cut down with a sickle, only enough to make it easier to pass through them. If the site is heavily wooded, it is quite possible that grass will not grow anyway.

Vacation cottage into retirement home

When shopping for a vacation home, many couples look for one that they might use for their year-round residence when they retire.

Since year-round occupancy calls for more comforts and conveniences than a place where you intend to stay for only a few weeks at a time, the choice for a second home in these circumstances must be one that is substantially constructed and in a locality with congenial permanent residents.

If it is in a southern area (the choice of most couples looking toward retirement), a slab foundation is adequate, but even this requires some excavation. A house on stilts certainly would not do for year-round living.

If the house selected does not have the recommended insulation when it is purchased, this can be added bit by bit. There should be a long-range plan for insulating the roof or attic and also windows and doors to reduce airconditioning costs.

When the purpose is eventual year-round use, there is more reason to increase storage space, to remodel kitchen and bath more attractively, and to make well-designed repairs to walls, floors, and basic structure.

For the same reason, interior decoration should be approached differently, with a selection of furnishings to give the house an air of permanence as well as charm.

Protection during your absence

A family with a large vacation home in the Northeast contrived a clever way to prevent vandals or burglars from breaking in during their absence. Each of the large sliding windows and doors has a fitted plywood panel which slides on a track to cover the glass area and is locked onto the frame for security. This not only prevents forced entry, but protects the glass against storm damage. Further, they have pull-up steps leading to the entrance deck and a pulley arrangement for hoisting up the deck floor to cover the sliding doors leading to the living room area.

This may seem an extreme way of protecting a house, but a dwelling in an isolated location seems to attract vandals, who can do far more harm than burglars. Malicious mischief costs homeowners many thousands of dollars each year.

This is one good reason for covering windows and installing strong locks on all windows, doors, and outdoor storage facilities. If a house has shutters, it would be well to pull them across the windows and fasten them with padlocks.

Upon departure, you should notify the local police that you are leaving so that if they notice anyone on the premises, they will investigate. Similarly, if you rent out your property, the police should be notified that someone will be occupying it for a specified time.

However, the police can do nothing about keeping out squirrels or birds in your absence, and squirrels especially can do a great deal of damage to furniture. Board over any place through which these little visitors might squeeze. Also, make sure that the damper on the fireplace is closed to prevent birds from entering the house.

It is important to have insurance protection for your second as well as your first home, covering storm damage, vandalism, malicious mischief, theft, and fire, and this should cover personal and household effects as well as the building itself. You need liability insurance, too, especially if either or both your properties are rented or exchanged at any time, to protect against any claims of bodily damage.

If yours is a condominium or part of any resort community, the management should be responsible for guarding the property when it is not occupied. However, this does not negate the need for insurance and for locking up when you leave.

If others will be occupying your premises in your absence, you need to lock up those things which you do not wish them to use. It may pay to have a separate set of dishes and linens for the use of tenants if you value your own tableware and linens highly.

Improvements that count the most

In making improvements on a vacation home, it is important to weigh the cost of the improvement against its ultimate value in equity or potential resale.

People will always be looking for comfortable vacation homes and little things that add to comfort and ease of maintenance increase a house's attractiveness. Built-in storage that also serves as furniture is in this category if it has been carefully constructed and finished. Attractive flooring that needs little attention is an asset. Blinds or draperies at the windows may be considered a luxury in a vacation home, but they add greatly to its attractiveness, and as an insulator, they also help to conserve energy.

Insulation is a decided asset, especially when it will mean a reduction in energy costs. Receipts showing what kind of insulation has been added should be kept on file for this reason, for it may not be apparent. A vacation home that can be occupied at any time of the year is more attractive to most buyers than one limited to summertime use, so anything done to make it snugger or sturdier is a worthwhile improvement.

Because storage facilities are so often inadequate in a vacation cottage, they are that much more important to add to yours. This includes closet space, storage chests, and built-in storage units. If some chests and cabinets can be locked, so much the better. In this way you are providing protection for items that could be easily carried off by an intruder, and a place to put away more valuable household effects when you are renting. Any outside storage units should have padlocks and be so constructed that breaking into them would be almost impossible. Not only human but animal intruders must be guarded against in construction of such outdoor lockers. Raccoons are notoriously clever about breaking into trash cans.

Attractive kitchens and baths matter almost as much in a country property as in a year-round residence, though no one expects them to be luxurious. But such conveniences as a dishwasher and a garbage disposer are every bit as important during vacation as at home, and a washing machine will save many trips to the town laundromat. (A dryer is not so necessary; clothes can be hung outdoors on a line.) An extra shower, in addition to one in the bathroom, can be important in a beach property; the best location for it would be outdoors, attached to the back of the house, which also makes the shower easier to construct (only three sides being necessary, one with a door).

Privacy is another precious commodity. The addition of bedrooms whose doors can be closed will make any country property more attractive to future buyers. Separate buildings, such as a gazebo or guest house, are also attractive additions. The guest house need not have plumbing or even electricity; a chemical toilet would help lighten the regular bathroom traffic, a washbasin and pitcher of water could be provided in each guest room, and candles or kerosene lanterns used for illumination.

Finally, if your country house is in a choice location, it pays to make it attractive and comfortable because you can then ask a higher rental, besides being able to command a better price if and when you decide to put it on the market.

It might even be possible to expand what began as a small guest house into a rental unit with electricity and plumbing. Then you could rent the guest house while you occupy the main house. This is the sort of future plan that owners of vacation homes can work toward, even in the first years when they are still roughing it in a one-room cabin.

CHAPTER 14

Financial Realities:

Contracts, Loans, Taxes, Insurance

When you have decided to go ahead with any improvement, the next step should be to get cost estimates from several sources. You could do this on your own, making a list of all materials needed and then getting prices for them from one or more supply houses. Or you may approach several contractors and ask them for bids. As pointed out earlier, contractors' estimates for a large job can differ by several thousand dollars and the lowest bid is not necessarily the one you should take.

It is always prudent, when you are getting bids from contractors, to double-check prices on your own and also read consumer reports to determine which materials you wish to be used in the construction. In addition, you should consider very carefully before engaging a contractor, or applying for a loan, how much this particular project will add to the intrinsic value of your home.

Certain improvements add almost as much to the resale

potential of your property as the amount invested. At the top of the list, according to those in the real estate field, is expansion of living space. This might be adding a wing, expanding an attic with dormers to provide more bedroom space, enclosing a porch, or converting a garage into a family room. Such an improvement can sometimes bring a return of nearly 100 percent of the investment—depending, of course, on the quality of the work and how it fits in with the overall appearance of the house.

Modernization of kitchens and bathrooms also increases property value to as much as 75 percent of the money invested in such a renovation, though again this depends on how the modernization is carried out and how it relates to the rest of the house.

An attractively landscaped patio or swimming pool will make your home definitely more salable, and you are likely to get back more than 50 percent of the investment in terms of an increased sales price.

A factor always to be considered is how your property compares to others in the neighborhood. If yours is already in a higher price bracket than other surrounding houses, more improvements will not increase its sales value appreciably. On the other hand, if yours is a modest home in a very desirable neighborhood, the chances of your getting back most if not all of your investment are that much better.

To add a one-story wing will cost approximately $25 to $30 a square foot, depending on the locality and local labor and material costs.

To convert an attic into additional bedrooms, if you are adding dormers, may run anywhere from $20 to $30 per square foot.

The cost of basement renovation varies still more since it depends on what improvements have previously been made, how extensive are the changes you now plan, and how much of the work you will do yourself. The total cost might be as low as $2,000 or up to $8,000.

To add a new five-by-eight-foot bathroom, assuming a nearby drain is available, could cost from $2,000 to $3,000. A kitchen renovation costs between $3,000 and $6,000.

However, inflation is on your side in one respect, because property values continue to rise year after year, and the longer the period of time the property remains in your hands, the more likely you are to get back all of your investment in it.

The extra value of good workmanship

If changes are to be made, the work should be done well. It is easy to be penny-wise and dollar-foolish, to economize by using cheaper materials, for example, which may cut the overall costs by perhaps $50 when the total expenditures will run to more than $2,500.

Similarly, getting half-trained or moonlighting workmen to do some of the work may save on labor costs but result in a botched job, perhaps even create hazards. An apprentice plumber extending a gas line, for example, might lay the lines improperly or make poor fittings, leading to a possible gas leak and explosion later.

You cannot be too careful in your choice of workmen, whether it is a handyman, plumber, electrician, carpenter, or mason hired as subcontractors, or a contractor hired to supervise the entire project.

Much has been said earlier about how to select a contractor. A caution should be added about resisting high-pressure salesmen, unrealistically low prices or bids, and extravagant guarantees.

Recently it has been reported that certain weatherproofing "experts" are telling gullible homeowners that they can correct basement dampness by injecting chemicals in the soil of the fill around the foundation, and they guarantee results for forty years. Anyone making such a claim probably will not even be in the vicinity by next spring.

Scare tactics are another gimmick. If an unknown salesman points out a condition and tells you it is urgently in need of repair, check with others with whom you have dealt before to see if they agree. Also be wary of any contractor who offers to give you a bargain price if you permit your home to be shown as a model, or because he wants you to tell your friends about his work.

A good contractor who does careful work will help to make your house more salable and he may be able to point out economies that are sound or suggest ways in which for just a little extra you can greatly improve the overall effect or usefulness of the renovation.

The contract

Any piece of paper you sign is a contract. Even if it is nothing more than a sales receipt thrust into your hands by a delivery man, you should read it carefully before adding your signature. The slip may contain a printed notice stating that you have received the merchandise in good condition, and your signature testifies to this. But after the truck has pulled away, you may examine the delivered item and find that it is far from being in good condition.

Read everything carefully before signing, and note whether you are agreeing to any liability clauses.

Similarly, anything a contractor has signed is also binding. When asking for bids from several contractors or subcontractors, you should request that they give you their estimates in writing. Later, when you have decided on a contractor, and the two of you work out a complete and detailed contract, his written estimate becomes the basis of the contract figure and you can hold him to this.

The contract is a legal document, binding on both of you. It is also a means of clarifying your joint agreement, spelling out exactly what work is to be done and how, and what materials are to be used, specifying brand name, style, and color.

Attached to the contract, and initialed by both of you, should be blueprints, specification sheets, and possibly pictures and/or sketches.

There should also be a clause in the contract stipulating when the work is to begin and when to be completed. Some homeowners insist on having a penalty clause in the contract, that is, that the contractor will pay a penalty for each day of delay after his promised date of completion. Most contractors object to such a clause and with reason, because it is not always their fault when the work is delayed. Strikes may hold up delivery of essential materials; illness on the part of workmen may cause long delays; weather conditions may also interfere. It is in fact rare for a job to be completely finished on the promised date. The penalty clause should in fairness contain provisos for the contractor's benefit, taking unavoidable factors into account. But he should have to prove that any delays are beyond his control. Otherwise, there are sometimes delays of from six to eight months before the job even gets under way.

Home Repair and Modernization Loans
(In Millions of Dollars)

	Outstanding Year-end 1974	Extensions 1975	Liquidation 1975	Outstanding Year-end 1975
Commercial banks	$4,694	$2,515	$2,400	$4,813
Other financial lenders*	3,704	1,818	2,034	3,488
Total	8,398	4,333	4,434	8,301

* Mutual savings banks, savings and loan associations, and finance companies.

Sources: Federal Reserve Board, National Consumer Finance Association

All guarantees should be clearly spelled out, and you should note exactly what they include, whether only essential working parts, or all workmanship and service, and for what period each guarantee will be in effect.

Do not sign a contract that contains any blank spaces. A good safeguard would be to have your copy of the contract photocopied immediately after signing it.

This provides you with an extra copy, which you can give your lawyer. Should any changes be made in the contract— changes your lawyer suggests or that you, upon studying it carefully, feel you want to make—each change, no matter how minute, must be initialed by you and your contractor. Before signing, have your lawyer make sure that the changes are clearly stated. He will study it from a legalistic viewpoint, looking for ambiguous phraseology or dangerous loopholes. Only you, however, can determine whether the contract fulfills earlier verbal agreements and includes everything you want included. Do not sign until all details and questions have been thoroughly discussed and resolved.

Do not permit a contractor to attach a lien to your property for any reason. A bank or other lending institution may demand this if advancing money as a second trust, but before obtaining this type of loan, discuss with your lawyer whether or not it is advisable.

During the period that work is in progress, keep a notebook handy and jot down dates and notes when any problem arises, when changes are to be made, or mistakes occur on the part of the contractor. Also copy down any promises or suggestions that the contractor might make, with the dates on which he makes them. If in discussing a change he should give you an estimate of its cost, be sure to write down these figures, and date them. If any damage is done to your property by the contractor, his workmen, or their equipment, you should make a note of this, too, with the date on which it occurred and a description of the damage.

Finally, do not sign the completion contract or make final payment until the work is finished to your satisfaction. Also make sure before turning over the final payment that the contractor has paid off all his subcontractors and suppliers. Otherwise, they could demand payment from you, and even attach a lien to your property.

Your signature on the completion contract relieves the contractor of further obligation, except for the written guarantees of workmanship or materials. If the loan was made through a bank, he can take the signed completion contract to the bank for payment. If you took out a personal loan, and will be paying him direct yourself, postpone signing the completion contract and making final payment for a week or so, to check out any defects which might not at first have been apparent.

Where to turn for financing

Even when you plan to do all or most of the work yourself, you can apply for a home-improvement loan to cover the cost of materials and/or appliances. The smaller the loan, and the shorter the time span in which you plan to repay it, the easier it will be to obtain the money, sometimes by the very next day. But do not be in a hurry. It pays to shop around carefully for the best interest rates and to know specifically how much extra it will cost you to obtain a loan.

Before you apply to a bank for financial assistance, one of the best sources for a loan is the company with whom you

Homeowner's Equity Increases Slowly

For each $1,000 of the original loan, the table shows what you would still owe on an 8.5 percent mortgage at various maturities. Naturally, payoff rates at other interest rates would vary from this, but the table illustrates how equity builds up faster with shorter-term loans.

At End of—	20-Year Loan	*You Would Still Owe—* 25-Year Loan	30-Year Loan
1 year	$980	$988	$992
2 years	958	975	984
3 years	935	960	975
4 years	909	945	966
5 years	881	928	955
6 years	851	909	943
7 years	818	889	931
8 years	782	867	917
9 years	743	844	902
10 years	700	828	886
11 years	654	790	868
12 years	603	759	849
13 years	548	725	828
14 years	488	689	806
15 years	423	649	781
16 years	352	606	754
17 years	275	559	725
18 years	191	508	693
19 years	99	453	658
20 years		392	620
24 years		92	432
29 years			88

Source: U.S. League of Savings Associations

have a life insurance policy. You can borrow up to the full amount of your policy, in its accrued valuation or equity, at a rate of interest ranging from as low as 4 percent up to $6\frac{1}{2}$ percent. The money is available for any purpose you choose. However, should death occur before the loan is repaid, the amount of money borrowed will be deducted from the proceeds of the policy to be paid to the beneficiary.

Another bargain in loans is one secured by your savings account, either passbook or certificate savings. The amount borrowed may be up to 95 percent of your savings, which are held by the bank as collateral. According to federal law, neither banks nor savings companies may charge more than 3 percent more interest than you receive on your deposit. This means that if your passbook account pays $5\frac{1}{4}$ percent interest, the interest on the loan cannot be more than $8\frac{1}{4}$ percent. Because your savings continue to pay interest, the loan will run about 1 to 3 percent net cost to you. This is preferable to cashing in your savings because, once cashed, it always seems twice as hard to build up the savings again. This way you can protect your nest egg while making periodic repayments on the balance of the loan at your convenience. In addition, the interest you pay may be applied as an income-tax deduction.

Personal loans may also be made through your bank using securities, bonds, or any other marketable property as collateral without the need of a cosigner, but interest rates will run considerably higher, anywhere from 10 percent to 14 percent, 16 percent, or more on an annual basis. Interest on such loans is figured on the initial sum borrowed, which means that the true annual percentage rate (APR) may total 18 percent to 22 percent. The total interest charges are added to the loan in the beginning and this amount is divided by the number of months over which the loan is to be made. Even if you are able to liquidate the loan before the due date, the original interest rate must still be paid. This is frequently referred to as "add-on interest."

Money for home improvements can also be obtained in the form of a second trust or second mortgage, sometimes called an "equity loan." The loan is secured by a lien on the property, which means that if the borrower defaults, the property can be foreclosed even though first trust (mortgage) payments have all been made on time. Such second-trust loans are now offered by commercial banks, savings institutions, finance companies, and credit unions, usually on a short-term basis of five to seven years, and invariably with "add-on interest." Thanks to the truth-in-lending law, the true APR must appear on the documents; if you are told, for example, that you are paying 12 percent interest, and the "add-on interest" brings the APR up to 18 percent, this must be spelled out somewhere on the papers you sign.

Still another type of loan is described as a "discount loan," a deceptive term because it is anything but a bargain for the borrower. For example, you may be applying for a $10,000 loan, yet receive only $8,000 in cash and be forced to pay interest on the full $10,000 throughout the agreed period of time for repayment. This is because the interest is deducted or "discounted" in advance from the capital sum. Other loopholes to be on guard against are special service fees or points. Fortunately, the truth-in-lending law now forces the lender to spell out to the borrower just how much interest the borrower is paying on an annual basis; the borrower's obligation is to take the time to read the fine print.

Another type of bank loan is what is called a Title I FHA-insured loan. These are now available for up to $10,000 for a Class 1 (a) loan, that is, one to finance repairs, alterations, or improvements in a one-family residence. Repayment can be spread over a period up to twelve years, at an annual interest rate of 12 percent. If the loan is for $7,500 or less, no other security is needed than your signature on the note; no co-signers are required. The only requirements are that you own the property, have a good credit rating, and your total income is enough to repay the loan within the agreed period. However, if the loan is for more than $7,500, a lien may be attached to the property, as for a second mortgage. Also, there are two disadvantages: many banks will not make FHA loans, and when you find a bank that will, delays up to five or six months may occur.

Inner-city homeowners may qualify for rehabilitation loans based on Community Development grants with interest in some cases as low as 3.75 percent. Regulations vary from city to city; most carry income restrictions, but not all. San Diego, for one, requires only owner-occupancy in targeted areas. Check local housing agencies for details.

Home Loan Payment Calculator
(Monthly Principal-and-Interest Payments per $1,000 of Mortgage)

Interest Rate	Length of Mortgage 20 Years	25 Years	30 Years
7½ %	$8.06	$7.39	$7.00
7¾ %	8.21	7.56	7.17
8 %	8.37	7.72	7.34
8¼ %	8.52	7.89	7.51
8½ %	8.68	8.06	7.68
8¾ %	8.84	8.23	7.87
9 %	9.00	8.40	8.05
9¼ %	9.16	8.57	8.23
9½ %	9.33	8.74	8.41

To use: multiply monthly payment-per-thousand in table by number of thousands to be borrowed. Result will be monthly principal-and-interest payment during the life of the mortgage.

Refinancing your mortgage

To obtain money you may also refinance your present mortgage or arrange for an open-end mortgage. Both depend on what equity you have built up and the interest rate you are paying. Suppose you took out a $20,000 mortgage ten years ago at 6 percent interest and have paid off $8,000. The bank or savings institution holding the mortgage will probably be happy to refinance it, allowing you as much as you want up to the original amount, but at a much higher rate of interest. Formerly, open-end mortgages could be extended at the original interest rate, but in today's market, that is no longer possible.

If your original mortgage carries only a 6 or 7 percent interest rate (a few are still around with 5 percent interest), the lenders will be eager to refinance, since interest rates as low as this mean an income loss to them today.

Still another way in which a home-improvement project may be financed is through the contractor as part of a package deal. Contractors often present this as a very simple arrangement, citing a seemingly moderate monthly payment.

However, such financing usually costs more than a bank loan, for the contractor is permitted to add a fee to cover his carrying costs. But if the homeowner is unable to obtain financing by any other means and has determined, after careful investigation, that the contractor is reputable and reliable, this method may be satisfactory—providing payments are made in stages as the work progresses, according to the schedule spelled out in the contract.

Contractors sometimes obtain financing for the homeowner from a private individual rather than a lending institution in the form of a second trust. This practice is increasing because so many people have discovered that it is a good form of investment, pays well, and is protected, since the property can be foreclosed if payments are not met. But the borrower must be doubly careful: to demand an explanation of the total interest being paid, plus fees, and to be sure in advance that these payments, on top of monthly mortgage payments, will not prove to be an undue hardship.

For those living in small towns (under 10,000 inhabitants) or rural areas, loans may be obtained through the Farmers Home Administration to "buy, build, improve or relocate" homes, or to make repairs which will improve health and safety standards. For further information about this type of loan, inquire at the Farmers Home Administration office in your locality, or through your county agent's office. It might be possible to obtain such a loan for a house in a rural setting to be used as a vacation home, though the loans are intended primarily for families of low to moderate income.

The Veterans Administration insures first mortgages at lower than prevailing interest rates for eligible veterans who can meet established credit requirements. Any veteran who has been holding such a mortgage for some time, and has paid off a large portion of it, may be able to refinance the mortgage to make improvements on the same property, as in an open-end mortgage. However, only 85 percent of the appraised value or accrued equity will be made available.

Both home-improvement loans and first mortgages are available for repairs or improvements on vacation property through all the sources named above. If you plan to add a swimming pool to your vacation home, specifications for this could be made a part of the mortgage application.

The high cost of borrowing

The interest rate charged by a bank or other lending institution may be only part of the cost to the borrower. Carrying charges and other hidden costs are often added. It is the right of the borrower, under the truth-in-lending law, to demand an explanation of all such charges. To learn whether the charges conform with existing laws, check with the nearest FHA insuring office.

Naive borrowers are often taken in by what sound like easy monthly payments, unaware of how much extra they are paying for the privilege of obtaining a loan. It is most important to be aware of the ultimate cost.

For example, take the advertised loan rates of two finance companies. One firm advertised an available loan of $7,500, to be extended over a ten-year period, requiring a monthly payment of only $106.25. Another company's advertisement listed a $5,000 loan to be extended over a five-year period, for which monthly payments of $108.34, $2.09 more, would be required.

To receive an extra $2,500 and pay $2 less per month might seem like a bonanza. But let us take a look at what each of these loans would actually cost the borrower. The $7,500 loan was offered at 11.86 percent, and total payment over the ten-year period would amount to $12,750, or $5,250 more than the initial sum. For the $5,000 loan, the rate was 10.75 percent for five years, at the end of which time the borrower would have paid out $6,500, or only $1,500 extra, proportionately much less than for the other loan.

For a $15,000 loan over a ten-year period with an interest rate at 12.03 percent and monthly payments of $212.50, according to figures published by the firm, the borrower would finally have paid the finance company $25,500, or $10,500 extra, two-thirds as much as the initial cost of the renovation.

Instead of borrowing at such high rates, the homeowner might well consider other ways of raising money, such as cashing in stocks or other securities that are paying poorly, or selling possessions such as a second car which is not used enough to warrant keeping it in the garage and paying for its insurance.

The figures cited also make clear why it pays the homeowner to do as much of the work himself as possible, cutting the labor costs, which may amount to at least half of the total.

Information for the lender

Before approaching any lending institution for a home-improvement loan or a mortgage, you must have blueprints or detailed sketches of the work to be done, along with cost estimates. If you have decided on a contractor whom you wish to do all or part of the work, you also should be able to provide information about him, his firm's location, and how long he has been in business.

In addition, the lender will want the following information:
- Present combined income of you and your spouse.
- Employment history of both of you for the preceding five years.
- Total cash in saving and checking accounts.
- All additional sources of income, including securities and rentals.
- Information related to your present home and any other real estate in your name: mortgage monthly payments, equity earned, and current market value.
- Current market value of automobiles you own.
- Amount of life insurance.
- Debts outstanding, including all monthly payments for which you are currently obligated.
- Credit references.

The credit references are particularly important, because this is a record of whether or not you pay your bills on time. Character references may also be requested, and do not be surprised when a representative of the bank or finance company comes to your home to check out information.

In some cases, it may help to get a loan if you first have a real estate appraiser estimate how much this projected renovation will improve the value of your property. When a very old house is being restored, and a sizable construction loan is being requested, someone knowedgeable about restoration of properties should do the appraising.

It will do no harm if you can also produce figures showing what other improvements have previously been made to the property, including installation of up-to-date heating, plumbing, or other basic facilities, to demonstrate to the lenders that the property is distinctly more valuable than when you purchased it.

Suppose that five years ago you purchased a $30,000 home,

taking out a $25,000 mortgage at 8.5 percent for twenty years. You still owe $22,025 (since the ratio of interest to equity is much higher in the first years of the mortgage loan), but meantime you have made a number of improvements. The basement has been remodeled into a recreation room; the kitchen has a new range, garbage disposer, and new flooring; you have relandscaped the yard, adding ornamental trees and shrubs; and you have installed central airconditioning and new carpeting in several rooms. The house for which you paid $30,000 could now easily bring $45,000, perhaps more. You might be able to cite selling prices of other houses in your neighborhood which do not have as many improvements as yours to indicate your home's value and sales potential.

Bankers are hardheaded individuals. If they feel sure that they can get their money back, they will be more ready to approve your request, and any homeowner who has taken excellent care of his property, keeping it in good condition and making repairs and improvements regularly, is automatically regarded as a better credit risk.

In applying for either a first mortgage or a second trust, the borrower should avoid if possible any prepayment penalty in the mortgage contract. When homeowners are able and willing to pay off the full amount of the mortgage sooner than the full term, they are sometimes shocked to discover that they will have to pay a stiff penalty fee. This could mean that when a homeowner wishes to sell his house and the buyer refuses to assume the existing mortgage, the seller must pay a penalty fee in addition to all the other closing costs, seriously reducing his profit margin.

Tax advantages for homeowners

Interest paid on debts is deductible from federal income tax returns. This includes interest on your principal mortgage and also interest on any kind of second trust or homeowner's loan.

Property taxes and state and local taxes are also deductible from the federal return. As stated in the first chapter of this book, you should therefore keep receipts of all materials purchased for home improvements and make notes from the receipts of the amount paid in state, city, or county taxes.

If a contractor is hired to do the entire job and also to purchase the materials, he is the one permitted to deduct the sales taxes for the materials he bought. However, if you purchase all the materials and pay him only for his labor and supervision of the job, you may claim the sales taxes.

Deductions based on rentals, or on using part of your house for business purposes, must be prorated, as explained previously. If you can prove that certain services or repairs applied only to the rental unit or to the room or rooms used for business, that entire amount can be deducted.

If you have separate meters for utilities, the tenant will probably pay his own; if you pay for the tenant's utilities, but keep receipts of these bills, the amounts are entirely deductible. If the tenant does not have separate meters, you can deduct the prorated portion of the total you pay for utilities. (Taxes on utilities, however, cannot be deducted.)

Depreciation can be figured for furniture, kitchen equipment, flooring, light fixtures, and even for that part of the house used for rental income. Estimate the total life of each item and divide the original cost by that figure to arrive at annual depreciation.

Repairs made on rental property are tax-deductible but improvements are not. A repair is defined as anything necessary to "keep buildings, equipment or other rental property in ordinary efficient operating condition," while improvements are those things which add to the intrinsic value of the rental unit, or are merely cosmetic.

If a house you own is entirely rented out to others, either as a single or multiple-family dwelling, all repairs, maintenance, service costs, utilities, and depreciation can be deducted. It is even possible to show a loss on a rental property that brings in cash income of $400 a month.

Vacation home tax deductions

An entirely different set of regulations applies to rental of vacation homes, whether houses or condominiums. Your tax advantages as a landlord are extremely limited, if you use the property at all for yourself or nonpaying guests or relatives. Even the rentals received from strangers are put in the same classification by the Internal Revenue Service as "rent to friends or relatives."

You may deduct mortgage interest and taxes whether you

rent out the property or not. But any rental income you receive must exceed the interest-and-taxes deduction, and even so you can claim only a prorated portion of maintenance, repairs, utilities, and depreciation for the balance, figured according to the ratio of how much time your family has spent in the unit and how much time it has been rented. Unless the property has been rented for, say, half a year, the allowable deductions may turn out to be so small that they are hardly worth claiming.

This may come as a shock to those who have purchased resort condominiums with the expectation, as promised in promotional literature and the salesman's pitch, that they would enjoy benefits as landlords which would help to pay for the condominium. They will reap substantial benefits only if the condominium is in a locality where apartments are in demand over a considerable part of the year.

When larger rental income is realized, so that making deductions becomes worthwhile, there are other costs, such as long-distance telephone charges in connection with tenant problems, that may be deducted on the income tax return.

A country property in an area that attracts tourists during winter and summer might bring in sufficient rental income to put it into a more rewarding situation, and for a house, there are likely to be more repair, service, and maintenance costs than for a condominium. Repairs to furnishings (kitchen equipment, chairs, washing machine), recreational equipment, and structure, such as windows or roof, could be deducted on a proportional basis, as can insurance and depreciation.

For tax purposes, and for records needed when you sell the property, be sure to keep on file all receipts and correspondence related to improvements for all real estate in your name. Such improvements are considered part of your total investment, and keeping records of them could make it unnecessary for you to pay any capital gains tax when you sell the property, even if you realize a substantial cash benefit. Any improvements involving structural changes, heating, air conditioning, making your house sounder, construction of walks, a patio, or outbuildings are allowable. However, what are called fix-up improvements do not qualify, that is, painting, papering, carpeting, or other strictly cosmetic changes.

Suppose, for example, you can show proof of having spent $12,000 in permanent improvements to a house for which you originally paid $30,000. If you should sell it for $45,000, you might not have to pay a penny in capital gains tax, because by adding $12,000 to the original $30,000 your investment becomes $42,000, and if it is sold through a broker at the normal 6 percent brokerage fee, in this case, $2,700, your net on the sale would be $42,300, only $300 more than your total investment, and this sum would undoubtedly be absorbed by other closing costs. You have, of course, put that much money into the property, and so technically have not made a profit, but you have meantime enjoyed the benefits of the improvements and the amount of money invested plus your accrued equity is like putting cash in a savings account.

Another possible tax deduction for homeowners is loss caused by theft, storm damage, or other casualties, not fully covered by insurance. This applies to vacation homes as well as year-round residences.

For still further information on tax benefits, see the Internal Revenue Service publication 530, *Tax Information for Deductions for Homeowners*, available from your nearest IRS office.

Determining insurance needs

Insurance on your house is essential to cover your investment against loss, but personal and household effects also should be covered, and liability insurance is necessary as well.

To determine the amount of coverage needed, figure out a realistic replacement cost, anticipating inflationary prices for everything.

To estimate the replacement cost of the house itself, separate its value from that of the land. You may be able to determine these figures by checking your annual property tax, because the assessor's office in appraising property for tax purposes makes one appraisal of the land value and another of "improvements," meaning the structures on it.

In estimating how much it would cost to replace the house should damage be total, do not use the original construction costs, because even if the house was built only ten years ago, construction costs today for a house of the same size and quality would be at least 50 percent higher. A builder or real estate agent could give you an estimate of how much it would cost to have a house comparable to yours built now. Your insurance agent may also be qualified to provide this information.

The most costly types of damage are from fire, burglary, vandalism (malicious mischief), storm, and flood. If you live in an area where there have been violent storms, hurricanes, or flooding conditions in the past, a recurrence of such natural disasters could cause extensive damage to your property, including trees and outbuildings as well as the main house.

For personal possessions and household effects, the best way to figure replacement estimates is to make (and keep) an inventory of everything you have of any value with a notation of its original cost. When looking around in shops, note the current prices of these items. You can be covered for loss or damage to personal effects wherever you may be, at home or away.

Liability coverage is important in case anyone should suffer bodily injury while on your premises, due to your pets or to some such accident as walking into a glass door or falling downstairs.

Insurance for personal possessions and household effects is strongly advised for those living in rental units as well as for homeowners.

Protection against fire

Insurance against damage or loss is important, but equally important is to take steps to prevent such loss if possible, because you may not receive 100 percent of the replacement cost, and there are always things that money cannot replace.

More than half a million American homes are destroyed by fire each year and more than 20 percent of all accidental deaths result from fire.

Two of the most common causes of home fires are short circuits and smoldering cigarettes. Have your wiring checked throughout the house to be sure that there are no faulty connections or exposed wires. Avoid a battery of appliances plugged into double sockets or long extension cords. This could lead to an overloaded circuit, which in turn could spark a fire. It pays to have plenty of wall outlets, so that it is never necessary to use an extension cord more than six feet long.

Make sure each high-wattage appliance, in any part of the house, is on a separate circuit from other high-energy appliances, and when purchasing any appliance, note in the printed instructions what voltage outlet it may be plugged into. If the appliance is marked 15V, it may be used with any ordinary outlet. It may say 20V or 30V, which means it should be plugged into only a circuit or fuse of that strength.

Circuit breakers can guard temporarily against overloading, but when there is continuous overload, wires may overheat and ignite nearby wood or other flammable material.

A considerable number of fires have started in color television sets. Never leave a color TV set on when no one is in that part of the house. When you leave on vacation or for a long weekend, unplug all color and black and white sets.

To avoid fires from cigarettes, have plenty of large ashtrays around, even if no one in your family smokes. At some time guests or workmen will be smoking in the house and their carelessness can be a hazard to you. Do not buy furniture made of material that is highly flammable or that causes toxic fumes if ignited. By law, there should be labels on such materials. Particularly dangerous are upholstered chairs and sofas and mattresses with stuffing that ignites easily and spreads quickly.

In any home where there are small children, whether or not their parents are smokers, it is important to avoid having highly flammable objects or materials in the house because of the propensity of very young children to play with matches. Naturally, all matches should be kept out of their reach, including book matches which often are left near ashtrays.

Fire-retardant paints should be selected for all interior painting. Also do not hang curtains or draperies near any source of excess heat, such as a kitchen range or fireplace. Many fires originate in the kitchen from ignited grease or fat, so the kitchen should be as free from flammable materials as possible. This is one good reason for having a metal hood above the range. A kitchen exhaust fan should be cleaned periodically to remove accumulated grease, and fat drippings should be stored in the refrigerator or disposed of, not left on the stove.

In chapter 9, the various hazards presented by a fireplace

were mentioned. A screen in front of the fireplace will contain flying sparks but even so, care should be taken to see that the fire is completely out before going to bed or leaving the house.

Christmas trees and evergreen branches used for decoration are other fire hazards. Lights should not be left burning on a tree when no one is at home or when the family has gone to bed. The drier the tree becomes, when kept in the house throughout the holiday season, the greater the hazard from hot lights.

Still another fire hazard is an accumulation of old newspapers and other flammable materials in the basement or workroom. A good housecleaning periodically is the best cure for this.

Emergency escape planning

Even when all such precautions are taken, it is wise to have an emergency plan for escape from upstairs bedrooms or from the basement in case of fire. Many tragic deaths have occurred when members of the family were trapped on the second floor, unable to get down a blazing stairwell—this space tends to become a natural air tunnel, sucking up flames. Bedroom windows, including storm windows, should be easy to use as exits or entrances in case of emergency. (One tragic case involved six-year-old twins asleep in a converted attic room whose windows were too small for firemen to enter to rescue them; both little girls died in the blaze.)

Examine the exterior structure of your house to see if there is an adjoining roof, such as that of a garage or porch, which could be used as an escape route by anyone caught on an upper floor.

The basement is usually not as hard as upstairs rooms to escape from, if it has windows that can be opened easily, but the danger of suffocation from smoke could be greater in the basement if anyone asleep there were not alerted in time.

Knowing the telephone number of the fire department and that of the police is another important way to be prepared for emergencies.

In July, 1974, the Federal Housing Administration issued Minimum Property Standards regulations which call for installation of smoke-detection alarm systems in all new buildings insured by FHA. Either one or two detectors, depending on the design of the house, must be permanently connected to the building's electrical system; they cannot be the plug-in variety. A number of localities are following suit by passing similar legislation related to all new houses, both single and multiple-family units. The smoke-detection alarms have been found through tests to be far more effective than those set off by the heat of the fire.

To install such a fire-detection system in an existing house is considerably more costly than in a new home, but it is a form of insurance in a sense, since it warns of fire early, before damage becomes extensive and while escape is easy.

Keeping a fire extinguisher on the main floor, where it can be reached easily in an emergency, may also prevent a small fire from becoming a disastrous one.

There are some all-in-one systems which warn against both fire and forced entry. The best of these cost around $1,000 but are less expensive than installing two or three separate systems.

Security protection

Those who live in cities or urbanized suburbs have reason to install extra protection against intruders; home burglaries have increased by 286 percent since 1960. The incidence of break-ins is far greater in some communities than others, but the spread of this type of crime from inner-city to suburban areas has been occurring at an alarming rate and many who previously were careless about leaving doors unlocked in their absence have learned the hard way that it no longer pays to be so trusting.

A couple visiting San Francisco one weekend were wandering through a local appropriately-named "thieves market," on the lookout for antiques, when they spotted furniture that looked extraordinarily like their own. Upon closer examination they found it was their own. Thieves had broken into their house shortly after they had left it and with a hired drive-it-yourself moving van, emptied the house of virtually everything. Fortunately for the couple, the furniture had been unloaded on the dealer in the open-air market within the hour, and after the couple quickly called the police, the thieves were caught.

Good locks on all doors and windows are the first and most

obvious form of protection and an inexpensive one. A double-cylinder interlocking bolt lock costing about $15 is one of the most foolproof for exterior doors. It is designed to prevent jimmying even by safecracking experts and can be locked with a key both inside and out. A chain lock for inside use that permits the door to be opened slightly yet prevents anyone on the outside from pushing it wide open is good to have when only one person is at home, both during the day and at night, since daytime burglaries are greatly on the increase. A viewer, through which one can peek to see who is on the other side of the door, belongs above such a chain lock.

Many patio doors have inadequate locks, but now there is a lock called a Charley Bar which can be swung into place across the expanse of glass in such a way that the door cannot be forced open from outside. Those who live in areas where there is a high incidence of crime might be advised instead to have metal security doors which can be pulled across sliding glass doors and also large window areas at night or during absence, at least for doors and windows on the ground floor.

All windows should be kept locked when everyone in the family is out of the house or on vacation. In most cases, a simple window lock is sufficient, especially if the house is in full view of neighboring homes. But for extra protection during extended absence, or in an area where there have been many burglaries, window locks that operate with a key and only from inside are advisable. These cost about $4 each.

As mentioned earlier, lamps that turn on and off automatically at different times and in different rooms are recommended as a means of fooling would-be intruders into thinking someone is at home when in fact the house is empty. However, professional burglars know all about these preset lights and are shrewd enough to study homes which they plan to break into. Should they observe that the same lights come on in the same rooms at the same time each night, they recognize them as preset, and for this reason, relying entirely on this system for protection could offer a false sense of security.

There are two basic types of residential security alarm systems. One, called perimeter protection, monitors the normal opening of doors and windows in a residence and warns those inside the house of an intruder before he actually enters. The other type, called area protection, uses photo-optical devices or microwave detectors within the house. This alerts those inside after an intruder has entered, giving them little opportunity to warn the police or to prepare their defense. Another disadvantage of this system is that a sleepwalker in the family, a restless dog, or someone getting up in the dark to search for something could set off the alarm and cause panic, which might even lead to a tragic use of a gun against the supposed intruder.

Acquiring adequate security equipment is of course a home improvement—one that will not only raise your house's market value but also increase the peace of mind of its occupants, enabling them to derive even greater pleasure from home-ownership.

Glossary

amperes—the standard unit for measuring the amount of electric current used by an appliance, fixture, or wiring system. A *volt* (indicated by the letter V) is the unit used to measure electric pressure generated by each appliance or the total pressure created by all electrically-generated fixtures and wiring on one circuit. Amperes plus volts equal *watts*. A *kilowatt* is 1,000 watts; a *kilowatt hour* (KWH) is the amount of electricity (combined current and pressure) used hourly, the means by which electric bills are tabulated. See also *fuse* and *circuit breaker*.

anodized aluminum—aluminum treated with an oxide film by hydrolysis to make it resistant to rust.

asphalt paper—heavy paper treated with tar and petroleum, used for roofing or as a vapor barrier.

asphalt shingles—composition shingles, a petroleum product, covered with colored granite particles.

atrium—in contemporary usage, a central or inner courtyard which often has a glass roof or a large skylight.

backfill—replacement of soil dug up around a foundation, or new soil brought in to fill the space created by excavation.

batten—small width of board nailed over joints between wider boards. *Board and batten* is a style frequently used in siding, including aluminum sidings simulating wood finishes, and in fencing.

batting or blanket insulation—fiber glass insulation in thicknesses ranging from two and a half to six inches enclosed in heavy paper, usually sixteen inches wide to fit between studs. The best type has foil on one side or both sides to serve as a vapor barrier.

below grade level—any part of the house structure, particularly the basement, that lies below, or partially below, the surface of the ground.

blueprints—designs and specifications detailing structural details and materials to be used in building construction. Originally published as negatives on blue paper with markings and printing in white, today they are more commonly black and white photocopies of the original.

caulk—to fill in and seal a crack or seam with a compound that becomes hard as it dries.

cesspool—a deep pit for disposal of sewage. See also *septic system*.

cinder blocks—another name for concrete blocks, used in forming foundation walls, retaining walls, and exterior walls of houses or sheds. When used for house walls, they are usually covered with stucco.

circuit box—the center from which all electric circuits are wired into the rest of the house, each circuit having its own fuse or switch. In larger houses, there may be as many as half a dozen circuits, including main circuits and special circuits for heavy-duty appliances.

circuit breaker—a safety device for electric systems which automatically cuts off current by thermostatic control in case of overload. Much safer than fuses, which it is now rapidly replacing. To reset a circuit breaker, disconnect all lamps and appliances on that circuit, return switch to "on" and then reconnect all fixtures. If there is a break or an overload in the circuit, this may help to determine where the trouble lies.

condominium—individually-owned apartment or town house in a building or complex. Each apartment or town house owner also owns a percentage of the grounds and facilities. See also *cooperative apartment*.

contractor—individual or firm in the building trade who works under contract to build, remodel or repair private homes, apartments, and other structures. A *subcontractor* is any individual, such as a plumber, carpenter, or electrician, who performs a specific function but is not responsible for other work. When a homeowner becomes "his own contractor," he takes over ultimate responsibility, supervising those he hires as subcontractors to do such work as plumbing, wiring, or masonry.

cooperative apartment—a living unit in a building or complex for which shares are sold by a corporation which owns the buildings, grounds, and all facilities. A shareholder owns a percentage of the entire complex but does not own a particular apartment. See also *condominium*.

crawl space—area beneath structure which has not been excavated or has only a shallow excavation. Normally, framing is not more than eighteen inches above ground, sometimes less.

custom house—a house built to individual design, rather than one in a development or a house built before a buyer has been found.

decoupage—a decorative appliqué in which pictures are pasted onto a surface such as a cabinet or wall, then brushed over with a clear sealer, varnish, or shellac.

dehumidifier—appliance which draws excess moisture or humidity from the air, condensing it into water. Portable room dehumidifiers are equipped with a tray for collecting the water, though some types have an outlet to which a hose can be connected, carrying the water to a central drain. Dehumidifiers installed in forced-air furnaces absorb excess moisture throughout the house, and automatically drain off the water. See also *humidifier*.

downspout—vertical section attached to roof gutters, carrying water to run-off or dry well.

drainage tiles—piping with perforation over the top, laid underground to carry water away from house into dry well.

dressed lumber—wood which has been cut into standard sizes and trimmed at the sawmill.

dry rot—a decay of wood caused by fungi.

dry wall—another name for plasterboard, sheetrock, or gypsum board. Now almost universally used rather than plaster for interior walls in new residences.

dry well—the drainage area into which water run-off is directed from gutters and the area around the house's foundation. It is not a well but an area where soil conditions are such that water can be absorbed without flooding.

duplex—an apartment on two floors, or a two-family dwelling unit.

electric service entrance—wires and equipment through which electric power enters a building.

equity—the owner's share of the property (not including unpaid balance of the mortgage), or the total cash or value accumulation accruing to the owner.

escrow—contract, cash, or bond deposited with a third person until fulfillment of contractual agreement.

exterior plywood, hardboard—panels especially treated for exterior use in construction. If not so labeled, these products can be used only for interior construction.

fascia—a board front over an empty space or one concealing pipes or ducts, or for recessed light fixtures.

flashing—sheet metal used to cover and protect certain joints and angles from rain and snow, on a roof around chimneys or vents, or above window and door frames.

fir—lumber from any species of evergreen firs; harder and more durable than soft pine. Used where extra strength or endurance is needed.

foamed plastic or **plastic foam**—rigid insulation board used over slab foundations and outside perimeter walls, and sometimes behind paneling.

footings—concrete pilings sunk at least three feet below foundation to carry weight of building.

furring strips—thin narrow wood strips used over joints in wall construction.

fuse—electric plug or container with a protective device consisting of a thin metal strip with such a low melting point that when circuit is overloaded, the strip dissolves or breaks, cutting off current.

galvanized pipe, gutters—iron plated with zinc to resist rust; now largely replaced by vinyl or copper products. Some galvanized gutters have a baked-on vinyl coating for greater durability.

glazing—filling of cracks or seams with a pliable compound which becomes hard as it dries.

ground fault interrupter—a safety device more sensitive than a circuit breaker for protection against leakage of electric current that is difficult to locate but serious enough to cause damage. Called "ground fault" because uninterrupted current flows to the ground through any path open to it. Styles are available for both outdoor and indoor use.

grounded outlet—an electric outlet which runs into moist earth to prevent shock due to overloading, damaged equipment, or faulty wiring.

gypsum board—composition board or panel used for interior walls or for subflooring. The terms sheetrock, gypsum board, and plasterboard are used interchangeably.

hardboard—composition board or panels of sawdust and other wood scraps and by-products compressed with resins to form a smooth surface. May be textured or grooved. Comes in several grades.

humidifier—appliance that supplies moisture to the air.

hydronic heating system—one making use of hot water run through copper pipes inside finned convectors.

insulated or double-glass windows—double panes of glass with air space between. Best type has sealed-on vinyl edging to prevent intake of moisture which can cause condensation or fogging. Available with either wood or metal frames.

joists—boards used as support under floors or ceiling structure. Always installed at right angles to framing.

knee walls—part of wall in attic room closing off low headroom area adjoining roof.

laminated plastic or **laminates**—synthetic materials used for counter tops, cabinet fronts, and bath coves, characterized by glass-smooth surface which is resistant to moisture and heat, and easy to clean with a damp cloth or sponge.

masonry—any finish using cement, concrete, stucco, or brick.

parget—thin layer of cement troweled over surface of cinderblock or other masonry foundation walls before waterproofing is applied.

particleboard—similar to hardboard but thicker and containing larger wood scraps or particles.

pegboard—hardboard with regularly spaced holes in which special hangers can be inserted.

perimeter—the outer edges of a room or exterior of a building, measured in linear feet.

piggyback storm windows—the type that clamps onto the outside of casement or sliding glass windows. See *storm sash*.

polyethylene—a synthetic which comes in large, thin, very pliable sheets, used primarily as a vapor barrier in construction.

polystyrene foam—used in making plastic foam for insulation board; also sometimes bonded to aluminum siding for added insulation.

polyurethane glaze—a clear synthetic product like a varnish which dries to a hard, smooth, gleaming surface, resistant to dents and scratches; can be wiped clean with moist cloth. Used to seal floors, cabinets, counter tops, even furniture.

resilient flooring—composition flooring which gives slightly when walked on, as different from completely rigid surface of ceramic tile, marble, slate, and wood. All types of vinyl and linoleum are in this category.

second mortgage or **second trust**—loan made with a lien on the property as security. If borrower defaults on payments, lender can force foreclosure, even when payments on first mortgage are up to date.

self-adhesive—adhesive backing on vinyl or paper, protected with thin paper covering which pulls off easily. Can be applied to any clean, smooth surface. Sometimes referred to as "adhesive backed."

septic system—home sewage disposal system in which sewage is first drained into a large concrete tank and then into a series of underground drainage pipes which snake over a wide area so that the sewage cannot concentrate unduly in one section. Septic "fields" range upward in size from 5,000 square feet, depending on the number of bedrooms or bathrooms in the house. Trees often must be removed to enable sun to dry out excess moisture received by soil.

sheetrock—laminated plastic between reinforced paper in four-by-eight-foot panels. See *dry wall.*

siding—any material used to cover the exterior walls of a structure. Includes wood, wood by-products, vinyl, aluminum, masonry, and brick.

slab floor—poured concrete floor of basement or garage.

slab foundation—slab floor that rests on deep footings under a house or other structure without a basement.

sleepers—floor joists installed directly on concrete slab to raise or level floor; plywood cannot be placed directly on concrete.

soffit—dropped ceiling, generally below the fascia board, often concealing recessed lights. Used above sinks and vanity mirrors. May also conceal ducts or pipes. Term is also used to mean the bottom board under rafters or roof overhang.

spackling—a soft compound used to fill holes in plaster or plasterboard.

storm sash—framed storm windows that fit over regular windows, especially those with movable sash. See also *piggyback storm windows.*

strippable or **dry-strippable wallcoverings**—those that can be easily pulled off walls without using a steamer.

stucco—plaster applied over exterior walls of a house.

studs—vertical supports, usually two-by-twos, installed in the wall between framing, most often spaced sixteen inches apart, though in old houses they may be eight inches apart, and in some situations, as much as thirty inches apart.

subflooring—inexpensive plywood or particleboard used beneath finished resilient or hardwood flooring.

thermal resistance—self-insulating qualities of any material used in construction. Those materials with "low thermal resistance" are less effective in preventing energy leaks.

town house—in some areas of the country, this term is synonymous with "row house." Elsewhere it may mean any urban residence on a narrow lot, whether or not detached.

UL approved—electric fixtures judged safe according to Underwriters Laboratory code.

vapor barrier—any material that keeps moisture out and helps to prevent heat loss or gain.

voltage—see *amperes.*

waterproof sealer—clear synthetic which can be brushed over a porous exterior surface to prevent absorption of moisture.

watts or wattage—see *amperes.*

Supplementary Sources

Many of the books and brochures listed contain patterns, diagrams, and sketches detailing how to make your own home improvements. Others contain descriptions of additional patterns available and tips on do-it-yourself construction.

U.S. Government Printing Office

For any of the following, send check or coins (not stamps) to Superintendent of Documents, Government Printing Office, Washington, D.C. 20402.

Title	Order. No.	Price
Construction Guides for Exposed Wood Decks	0100-02577	$1.25
Exterior Painting	0100-00815	.25
Fireplaces and Chimneys	0100-01520	.40
House Construction, How to Reduce Costs	0100-02788	.25
Interior Wiring	0820-00401	1.45
Peripheral Circulation for Low-Cost Central Heating in Old Houses	0100-01079	.30
Planning Bathrooms for Today's Homes	0100-00876	.35
Planning Your Home Lighting	0100-00800	.35
Plumbing for the Home and Farmstead	0100-01487	.30
Power Hand Tools	2203-00902	.45

Protecting Shade Trees During Home Construction	0100-01308	.25
Selection and Use of Wood Products	0100-02501	1.00
Septic Tank Care	1702-00068	.25
Simple Home Repairs (Interior)	0100-02815	.25
Simple Plumbing Repairs	0100-02684	.25
Wood Siding, Installing, Finishing, Maintaining	0100-02680	.25
Designs for 11 Low-Cost Wood Homes		.50

Summary sheet describes the eleven homes, showing floor plans, interior and exterior sketches. Detailed plans can be ordered by number. All the houses can be constructed at considerably less than usual cost for homes of similar size and convenience because of design simplicity, use of economical wood materials, and new construction systems. Developed by the Forest Service, U.S. Department of Agriculture, each includes complete working plans for construction.

American Plywood Association

The following may be obtained from American Plywood Association, 1119 A Street, Tacoma, Washington 98401. Specify order number and enclose check or money order.

Catalog of Handy Plans (Sketches and descriptions of patterns available for many build-your-own units including, among others, entertainment center, laundry center, shelf-door wardrobe, wall desk, garage wall storage, tool cabinet, gazebo, child's storage wall, and trash can bin.)	Form Y630	$.50

The following are available three for $1.00 or $.50 each:

Some Solutions for Clutter	Form Y415
The Art of Adding On	Form Y416
Easy Changes, Large and Small	Form Y417

California Redwood Association

For the following, send to California Redwood Association, 617 Montgomery Street, San Francisco, California 94111.

Redwood Garden Structures You Can Build	$.25
Redwood Decks	.50
Redwood Fences	.35
Redwood Interiors	.35
Redwood Exterior Finishes	.20

Miscellaneous

The following may be obtained from Western Wood Products Association, Yeon Building, Portland, Oregon 97204.

The Outdoor Room	$.15
The Second Home (18 home designs; how to order construction plans)	1.00

Index

PICTURE CREDITS